STOLEN VO

ZLATA FILIPOVIĆ became renowned internationally when her teenage diary, published in 1993 and chronicling life in war-torn Sarajevo, was an instant best seller. Published in editions by Viking and Puffin Books, it has since been translated into thirty-six languages. She holds a BA in human sciences from Oxford University (2001) and MPh in international peace studies from Trinity College, Dublin (2003–4). She has spoken extensively at schools and universities around the world about her experiences and has worked on many occasions with different organizations such as the Anne Frank House, the UN, and UNICEF, as well as being a three-time member of the UNESCO Jury for Children's and Young People's Literature Prize for Tolerance. Her written work includes contributions to several books and newspapers, including a foreword for *The Freedom Writers Diary* (Doubleday, 1997), and the English translation of *Milosevic: The People's Tyrant* (Tauris, 2004), for which she has also written a foreword, and more recently a contribution to *Prentice Hall Literature, the Penguin Edition: Grade 6* (Prentice Hall, 2007). She has recently worked within the UN Children in Armed Conflict Division in New York under Olara Otunnu and completed an international symposium in conflict resolution.

MELANIE CHALLENGER is an award-winning writer of both poetry and prose. In 2005, she won the Society of Authors' Eric Gregory Award for poetry, and has since published her first collection, *Galatea*. As a librettist, she adapted the Anne Frank diaries for British composer James Whitbourn's *Annelies*, which formed the main musical contribution for the sixtieth-anniversary Holocaust Memorial Day at Westminster Palace in London. After graduating from Oxford University in 2000 with a degree in English literature and language, she devised the Mostar Foundation, working with organizations such as the Anne Frank House, UNICEF, the Royal Philharmonic Orchestra, and the British Council on projects that use music and literature to promote moral awareness in young people. She is currently collaborating with British Composer Award winner Tarik O'Regan on an oratorio to mark the UN International Day of Peace in New York.

Stolen Voices

YOUNG PEOPLE'S WAR DIARIES,
FROM WORLD WAR I TO IRAQ

Edited with commentaries by
ZLATA FILIPOVIĆ AND MELANIE CHALLENGER

Foreword by
OLARA A. OTUNNU

PENGUIN BOOKS

PENGUIN BOOKS

Published by the Penguin Group
Penguin Group (USA) Inc., 375 Hudson Street, New York,
New York 10014, U.S.A.
Penguin Group (Canada), 90 Eglinton Avenue East, Suite 700, Toronto,
Ontario, Canada M4P 2Y3 (a division of Pearson Penguin Canada Inc.)
Penguin Books Ltd, 80 Strand, London WC2R 0RL, England
Penguin Ireland, 25 St Stephen's Green, Dublin 2, Ireland
(a division of Penguin Books Ltd)
Penguin Group (Australia), 250 Camberwell Road,
Camberwell, Victoria 3124, Australia (a division of Pearson Australia Group Pty Ltd)
Penguin Books India Pvt Ltd, 11 Community Centre,
Panchsheel Park, New Delhi – 110 017, India
Penguin Group (NZ), cnr Airborne and Rosedale Roads, Albany,
Auckland 1310, New Zealand (a division of Pearson New Zealand Ltd)
Penguin Books (South Africa) (Pty) Ltd, 24 Sturdee Avenue,
Rosebank, Johannesburg 2196, South Africa

Penguin Books Ltd, Registered Offices:
80 Strand, London WC2R 0RL, England

First published in Great Britain by Frances Lincoln Limited 2006
Published in Penguin Books 2006

1 3 5 7 9 10 8 6 4 2

Copyright © Zlata Filipović and Melanie Challenger, 2006
All rights reserved

Page 293 constitutes an extension of this copyright page.

ISBN 978-0-14-303871-9
CIP data available

Printed in the United States of America
Set in Minion
Designed by Elke Sigal

Foreword

THE VOICES OF THESE CHILDREN GIVE US INSIGHT into the ways in which the horrors of war destroy the innocence of childhood and corrupt the most precious resource we have, our children. In the last decade 2 million children have been killed in situations of armed conflict, while 6 million children have been disabled or injured. Over a quarter of a million child soldiers are being used today in situations of armed conflict around the globe. Since 2003, over 11.5 million children have been displaced within their own countries, and 2.4 million children forced to flee conflict and take refuge outside their home countries. The scourge of land mines results in the killing or maiming of between 8,000 to 10,000 children every year. The future peace and prosperity of many countries will depend upon how well we are able to care for the children affected by today's conflicts and their future rehabilitation and development.

I assumed my mandate as special representative of the United Nations Secretary-General for Children and Armed Conflict in September 1997, after the groundbreaking report by Ms. Graca Maçhel on the impact of armed conflict on children. Over the last several years, through the efforts of my office and the international community, significant advances have been achieved, creating a strong momentum for the protection of children. These efforts have resulted in an increased global awareness of and advocacy for children affected by armed conflict, as well as the development of an impressive and comprehensive body of protection instruments and norms. Also, the protection of war-affected children is now firmly placed on the international peace-and-security agenda, and the protection and well-being of children is increasingly reflected in the mandates of United Nations peacekeeping missions, including the deployment of child protection advisers in such missions. Children's concerns are also now being incorporated in peace negotiations, peace accords, and postconflict programs for rehabilitation and rebuilding.

In spite of these advances, the situation for children remains grave and unacceptable. The international community is now faced with a cruel dichotomy. On one side, there are clear and strong standards for the protection of children affected by armed conflict, and important concrete initiatives, particularly at the international level. On the other side, atrocities against children continue largely unabated in real life. The key to overcoming this gulf lies in a concerted global campaig for the enforcement of international standards and norms, that is, a redirection of energies from the elaboration of standards to the mission of application and enforcement on the ground.

Since 2001, the annual report of the UN Secretary-General for Children and Armed Conflict has included specific information on grave violations against children and annexed monitoring "lists" that explicitly name parties to conflict who recruit and use children in situations of armed conflict. The Security Council has also expressed its intention to take concrete and targeted measures against those parties to conflict listed in the report that do not undertake the necessary actions to end the violations for which they have been named. These efforts, together with the advocacy and action of civil society at international and national levels, can create the "critical mass" necessary to end abuses against children.

Today, as never before, we have the necessary means to ensure the protection of all children exposed to armed conflict. In today's world, parties in conflict do not operate as islands unto themselves. The viability and success of their political and military projects depend crucially on networks of cooperation and goodwill that link them to the outside world—to their immediate neighborhood as well as to the wider international community. In this context, the force of international and national public opinion represents powerful means to influence the conduct of parties in conflict. Books like *Stolen Voices* are written to contribute to that critical mass.

Olara A. Otunnu, UN Under-Secretary-General,
Special Representative of the Secretary-General for Children
and Armed Conflict, 1997–2005, New York, July 2005

Acknowledgments

THE EDITORS would like to thank:

Barry van Driel, for introducing us to one another in 2003, from whence "thought leaps out to wed with thought"!

The Anne Frank-Fonds (Switzerland), the Scarman Trust, the Big Lottery Fund, and the Bridge House Estates Trust (UK) for funding the development of this book.

Jack Boas; Paul Salmons, and the education and archives departments at the Imperial War Museum, London; Georgina Fitzpatrick, Karen Murphy of Facing History and Ourselves; Kay Schaffer, Janet Symes, and Katy Radford of Save the Children UK; Jehan Helou of the Tamer Institute; Basima Takrori, Suzanne Bunkers, John Pinkerton, Helen Basini, and Kanan Abid of War Child; Alex Ross, Toine van Teeffelen, Marlies Hagers of NRC Handelsblad; Marie Masumoto of the Japanese American National Museum; Rivka Schiller of YIVO Institute for Jewish Research; Diane Gordon and the staff at the Auckland War Museum; Karen Coe and the staff at the United States Holocaust Memorial Museum; Musab Hayatli, Mohammed Thamir, Linda and Andrew Hutchinson, Lucrecia and Bill Coomber, Libby and Laurie Weisman, George Landau, Mark Davies, Fran Sterling, Alexandra Zapruder, Stephen Glantz, DeeDee and Gary Whitman, Olara Otunnu, Lisa Nicoletti, Tina and David Micklethwait, Antoine Audouard, Susanna Lea and her staff—particularly Katrin Hodapp—Tobias and the rest of the Munthe family, Jonathan Tepper, Iason Athanasiadis, Martina Lajtner, Aoife Daly, Henry Raymont, our editors at Penguin Books, and of course our dear parents, friends, and family.

Contents

(Note: An asterisk [*] indicates diaries that have been published but are now out of print; a dagger [†] indicates diaries that were previously unpublished.)

———————

Introduction

BY ZLATA FILIPOVIĆ

I THOUGHT THAT WARS HAPPENED TO OTHER PEOPLE. Until I was eleven, living in Bosnia, all I ever heard about wars was that they happened far away in history, like World Wars I and II; or they were happening in Lebanon, Africa—somewhere far away geographically. Even as the war was slowly creeping toward my native city of Sarajevo, crawling into towns and villages around me, I thought that it could never happen to me. Wars are like terrible diseases, like poverty, like all bad things we know to happen in the world, but think will never happen to us. As a natural way of protecting ourselves, hoping and ensuring that we never live them, we prefer not to think about wars, and we designate them to other people, far away from us.

In the beginning of 1992, I was eleven, living a happy and carefree life in my native Sarajevo, looking forward to each day, to going to school, to holidays, to growing up in my city, to working and building a family there. It never crossed my mind that a war would happen to me, turn everything upside down, split my life into two periods: the one *before* the war and the one *since* the war began. A year or two before the start of "my" war, I read the diary of Anne Frank. It horrified me that such suffering and injustice could happen to someone whose words had encouraged me to know and like her, and whose private writings provided the material for my own self-identification. Anne Frank's diary, as well as that of the fictional Adrian Mole (Sue Townsend's hilarious invention), inspired me to start writing my own diary. I thought that it would be my personal treasure, something to turn back to in the years to come and laugh at my innocence and the happy daily events of my childhood and adolescence. Unfortunately, brutally, and suddenly, war entered my life, and my diary became a war diary, a record of terrible events happening to my family, my neighbors, my city, and my country. A series of events precipitated the publication of my diary—an individual story that became a testament to the siege of Sarajevo and a child's life under gunfire.

In 2003, I was contacted by a young British woman who was thinking of putting a collection of war diaries together, and she asked whether I would be interested in creating it with her—this is how my collaboration with Melanie Challenger and the story of *Stolen Voices* began for me. My own personal experience and my interest in studies of peace and conflict combined gave me a chance to be a part of an unprecedented collection. Until now, war diaries have either been presented to the public singularly, with one individual's diary representing their own life in the midst of conflict, or if they are collections, they concentrate on a specific event—such as World War I, the Holocaust, or the Vietnam War. This collection is the first of its kind to expose the shared experience of conflict by young people, wherever and whenever the violence may have occurred. As editors, Melanie and I chose to interpret the concept of war more broadly to include not only things that have been known and designated as wars but various world conflicts and instances of collective violence. We also decided not only to have diaries of young people who were experiencing conflict in towns, cities, camps, hiding places, and ghettos but also to include those whose hands sometimes took or were assigned a gun. The young soldier is as much a reality of conflict as is the noncombatant, and we felt it was important and honest to show both sides of this coin. The finished collection holds thirteen previously published and unpublished, forgotten, and archived diaries that bring us close to each young person whose life was touched by the violence of the twentieth and now the twenty-first century.

Through researching this book, I have been struck by parallels between different people's lives and writings, because by living through a conflict, young people both experience and write about very similar things. Of course, it is always problematic to talk of universality, to amalgamate various individual's experiences into one joint experience—but it is also impossible, when looking at various young people's war diaries, not to notice themes and similarities. In all of them, I recognize the moments of desperation, of confusion, of injustice and pain; the aware-ness of loss of childhood, youth, and innocence that I personally wrote, felt, or thought about. I also recognize the less expected instances of mundane everyday events, as well as the continuations of life and the process of growing up, of hope, of desire for nature, music, humor, of plans, ambitions, and playfulness—despite there being a war, this terri-ble dark thing that is meant to "swallow" life. Sometimes it feels as if these various voices are talking to each other, complementing each other and singing together in one single voice of stolen childhood and irre-placeable youth.

Perhaps the question is: Why have a collection of diaries, as op-posed to any other form of expression? Diaries provide an immediate experience of events, before the benefits of hindsight or tricks of mem-ory can distort or influence an account. Diaries contain the words of the time, but they are also very private and usually not intended for publication; therefore, they convey the nature of conflict in a real and very immediate manner. While they are not written to be historical records, the diaries end up being exactly that, in a powerful, personal, and human way.

It is interesting for a moment to consider how the diaries pre-sented here came to exist. Most young people who write diaries are generally interested in reading and writing, and harbor ambitions of becoming novelists, poets, or journalists once the "dreadful" wars are over. Besides the opportunity they afford to record daily events, di-aries also provide for their authors a refuge from the madness that surrounds them and become spaces for communication and self-expression. The diaries are both records and confessionals, while the process of writing is a method of transformation, allowing authors to assimilate and personalize events around them that are beyond their control. During conflict, the outside world is strong and uncontrol-lable; death lurks behind every corner and every moment, and so the creation of this personal, private space that an individual can master and utilize to make sense of his or her life becomes incredibly impor-tant. Through observing and writing, the diarist also experiences a form of distancing from the terrible situation, even if it is only for the duration of the writing. While the outside misery and deprivation manifests itself in each sentence, the process of writing itself belongs only to the diarist and helps preserve his individuality and sanity. At times, this desire to write is so strong that it overcomes threats of punishment (as is the case in some war camps) or the constraints of time and space in which to write (as with most battlefield diaries). This is a strong desire to communicate, to believe that someone, even if it is a blank piece of paper, is listening, that someone can hear and understand.

There are many diaries that have not been included in this collection—some were too short, some were too long, some inaccessible to a wider audience by the virtue of their style of writing, and some were simply not (yet) discovered. It is also important to remember that those who write diaries are those who are literate, who have the time, the space, the paper and ink to write and whose cultures have a tradition of diary writing. This is not the case all over the world, which is why it has been extremely difficult to uncover diaries from Africa and South America, as well as from groups such as Native Americans, Aborigines, or Maoris, although violence and persecutions have played a strong part in the histories of these peoples. Given this, Melanie and I have not been able to represent those voices within this collection. However, throughout our research, we have come across incredible oral or written testimonies, short stories, drawings, and poems written by young people who lived through conflicts, and they provide powerful insight into their experiences.

I hope that the diaries that have been included will provide some insight into what it means to be a young person growing up in the middle of war. We see war as an enormous and alien concept that is impossible to grasp. By getting to know the people who live through it, grow up in it, and share with us their daily fragments of war, we can break up the concept of war into smaller pieces and begin to understand what it means. For me, living in war meant not having water, for example. It meant not being able to go out. It meant not having cotton wool. It meant that everyone knew at least one person close to them who was killed. It meant inventing new ways of cooking food, it meant inventing new recipes. It meant people still making babies. It meant people still dying from natural causes. It meant people still getting married. It meant still hoping, planning for the future. It also meant the presence of death in every moment. It meant so many details of life—and if you begin to collect those pieces, you get a bigger, more coherent picture of what life in conflict looks like. You also learn the weight of the simple practicalities of life, and the effect of their absence.

Perhaps *Stolen Voices'* diaries will help refine the historical and current-affairs thinking we currently employ. Wars *do* happen to people like us—people with hopes, desires, and problems, wherever and whenever they live—they happen to us all. Developing an intimate relationship with individuals who have lived through conflict forces us to go beyond the dizzying body counts and images of faceless refugees and survivors and actually imagine these people, one by one—imagine their lives and stories and draw on our capacity for empathy and compassion to actually feel the closeness of these victims and survivors with whom we are connected in this world. Maybe then we can also see that the young people whose writings and whose lives we get to know here share a common humanity that transcends culture, faith, and geography. It is also a humanity we all share with them.

My great desire is that the reader will be able to connect to each and any diarist, follow their "war story," and learn a bit more about the otherwise cold and abstract historical (or current-affairs) facts of their conflict. These diaries may allow the concept of war to become less mysterious and more accessible, so that we know what we are dealing with, what it is and how it works. We can look conflict straight in the eyes, through the eyes of the young diarists. By understanding what conflict is, we might be in a better position to deal with it. Our deep desire for peace and the actual existence of peace may sadly always be at odds, but it does not mean that we should give up on the laborious work of knowing peace, maintaining it, and finding it when it is gone. Throughout history, countries have turned to dictatorships and marginalized and prosecuted groups for political and economical reasons, but biased education and focused propaganda were hugely influential in the manipulative processes of inventing enemies, creating fear, and distancing the "other." If we take this view of education working negatively, against peace and coexistence of different peoples, then there is nothing to stop us from saying that it can also work positively—for peace.

Some months ago, I received an e-mail from a ten-year-old American girl who had read my diary and who had such a pertinent point that I have to relate it here. She was finding it strange that my story was the only one that she had read about the war in Bosnia, or that the most famous story from the Holocaust is that of Anne Frank. But after thinking for a little while, she realized that in order to understand, you follow one story and subsequently accept that Anne Frank is, in a way, the face of the Holocaust, and that I am also, in a way, the face of the Bosnian war. She couldn't help wondering, however: "Who will be the face of peace?"

Zlata Filipović
Dublin, 2006

Introduction

BY MELANIE CHALLENGER

WHEN ANNE FRANK, THE MOST FAMOUS DIARIST OF the twentieth century, died in the Bergen-Belsen concentration camp in March 1945, she died in complete anonymity, stripped by the Nazi government of individuality and rendered as nothing more than one of 6 million Jewish men, women, and children put to death during the Holocaust. But somewhere her diary lay in darkness, refusing and countering this sentence. The diary exclaims from every page that Anne Frank was not just a Jew. She was, like all human beings, a broidery of emotions, desires, failings, and gifts, the complex details of a life. She aspired to be a writer, had a crush on a boy called Peter, a best friend called Hannah, and she loved and was infuriated by her mother in equal measure. In the pages of her diary, she states her dream that one day she and her family will be "people again and not just Jews."

I first met Zlata in Amsterdam at Prinsengracht, in the house where Anne Frank wrote her diary. It was a beautiful, sunny day in the spring of 2003, and together we walked through the rooms that the Frank family inhabited for several years and looked out at the chestnut tree that Anne describes, blossoming again for another season nearly sixty years after the death of the Dutch teenager. The site at which she hid and wrote her diary has now been turned into a museum visited by millions of individuals who learn about the further atrocities that have occurred since 1945: the conflict in Vietnam, the Khmer Rouge in Cambodia, the collapse of Yugoslavia and the massacre at Srebrenica, the 1988 gassing of the Kurds, the genocide in Rwanda, and now the conflicts in Afghanistan, Iraq, and Sudan.

Both of us had read *Anne Frank: The Diary of a Young Girl* and had written diaries from a young age ourselves. My diaries remained private, the musings and self-examinations of a teenage girl in peacetime. Zlata's diaries underwent a sinister metamorphosis into a war diary, an eyewitness account of a grievous period in history, a record of suffering and endurance. It was a record that bestowed upon her the solemn title of the Anne Frank of Sarajevo.

Together, we conceived of a book that would trace the path of war throughout the century as it entered the life of child after child after child, each shell and bullet sending ripples, hypnotically, violently, across the internal life of the child, out into the lives of their friends and family, and outward into the future of their country and the world at large.

I came out of university with the naive belief that I would be a creative writer. But as I put pen to page to produce a novel of entertainment and distraction, I found myself wrestling with the words on the page. It was the year 2000, the five-year anniversary of the end of the conflict in Bosnia-Herzegovina. The detail I possessed about this conflict had come to me by way of visual images and news footage via the mediums of television and the Internet, channels of passive reception, the armchair consciousness. Born in the late 1970s, I belonged to the generation of experience as distraction, and the writing I had supposed for myself seemed to possess the symptoms of this malaise. Through a series of conversations and coincidences, I learned of a number of ways—through music, film, and literature—that writing was being used *actively* in postconflict Bosnia. In this recovering country, film scripts, diaries, poems, novels, and libretti belonged to what Walter Benjamin called the dying social function of art, the function of communicating something powerful to the apathetic and the numbed, catalyzing our minds for active thought. While I was encumbered by the difficulties and guilt experienced by an artist dealing with such subject matters as genocide and conflict, and struggled to rise above the dangers of exploitation and commercialization, I felt the risks outweighed the importance of reclaiming this social function of the writer.

Writing is used to understand things better, to organize thoughts and ideas, particularly difficult ones, to memorialize and persuade, to manipulate and overlord. The nation-states that lead people into war rely upon writing to make their violent intent concrete, writing laws that are then imposed upon others, hampering their lives. Masses of documents were written during the Nazi years, and the Nazis, once aware of the likelihood of losing the war, engaged in the destruction of the damning articles as systematically as they attempted to erase the lives of those they did not envision in the perfect German state. Imagine the Jewish people of Europe reading, for the first time, the restrictions that the Nazi government forced upon them. Or the young women of Afghanistan reading the laws, as set down by the Taliban in the 1990s, that strictly curtail their lives and rights to education. Stalin personally signed thousands of death warrants during the Communist purges. One wave of the pen, and he terminated the life of a person whose face he did not look upon, whose voice he did not hear.

Against this abuse of writing arises a countermeasure. On scraps of paper in the dimness of cells, on old exercise books in candlelit cellars, in notebooks on a battlefield, young men and women gaze inwardly to observe the effects of their horrific circumstances upon their personalities and outwardly to record the transformations of the world around them under the burden of wartime. As a poet, I was particularly affected by the survival of a poetry magazine founded secretly by several young boys in the midst of the horrors of the Nazi concentration camp Terezin. Through *Vedem*, which translates as *In the Lead*, the teenage boys expressed their anger, bewilderment, and hope in a series of startling poems. These poems stand as testament to the extraordinary value of writing as an instrument for human expression in the most prohibitive and dire of circumstances. By the defiance of their writing, the voices of those young individuals survived long after the Nazis sent the authors to an early and anonymous grave.

Conflict and genocide echoed through the twentieth century, an unbroken sequence of death knells begun during the Great War, the first world war in human history, desolately resounding in the twenty-first century. Tens of millions of individuals were estimated to have lost limbs during these military campaigns, a hand that yearned to touch a child's hair or a lover's brow, a hand that once held a pen, forfeited to the ambitions of a nation-state.

The frail flesh of man succumbs to amputation by shrapnel, bullet, grenade; the body of a human being is transformed to a new and cruel design by the scalpel of war. So, too, the fragile borders of a country undergo transformations, a spur sliced here, an edge severed there, an outline brutally shaped beyond recognition. Maps are redrawn, and new names are inked upon the page; just as Kurdistan was written into invisibility by the pens of cartographers, so Yugoslavia's boundaries dissolved from existence, and dozens of other countries came and went. These countries, erased from the maps, linger in the minds of their countrymen, for whom the homeland, surgeoned into invisibility, remains alive.

Learning to adapt to the new form of their bodies and of their country, men and women carry into the future years a profound sense of loss and a potentially poisonous seed of nostalgia, a seed that may remain inactivated or become the roots of the kind of nationalism that makes an enemy of neighbors in wartime.

Yet a greater threat exists than the amputation of bodily flesh or of homeland: *the amputation of imagination.* The freedom to think to our best ability is significantly thwarted by the daily traumas of conflict and in the general climate of censorship created by the aggressive nation-states that inaugurate war. The will to survive in times of crisis overmasters all other acts of thought that, by their nature, call for an extension into the lives of others: compassion, empathy, sympathy. Shored off from the lives of others, individuals in wartime forfeit the faculties of commonality; they become isolated from all but themselves and their kin, sealed off from any sense of shared humanity.

The South African novelist Nadine Gordimer upholds that writing is *always and at once an exploration of self and of the world, of individual and collective being.* The diarist that holds a pen in wartime begins to counteract the amputation of imagination that threatens our capacities for empathy and compassion. Through diaries, both writer and reader recognize that people, beyond their individual idiosyncrasies, respond in many parallel ways, and that people share profound similarities through time and through cultural difference. It is therefore an absurdity to uphold views that accredit lesser and greater qualities to different races and nations.

In 2002, I had begun adapting the Anne Frank diaries for a choral work to commemorate the sixtieth anniversary of the end of the Holocaust. I recognized that what was so extraordinary about her diaries was that, after she had been incarcerated for a long time, her consciousness split into two halves—the individual social entity and the "purer, finer" part of herself, the human consciousness we all share. I asked myself what is the most important function of our consciousness—and the imagination, with its skill for reaching into ourselves *and* outward to the lives of others, seemed to be that by which we advance our minds and the moral quality of our actions most profoundly.

Every diary of power presents both a distinct sense of individuality and the universality of our experiences as human beings, uncloaking the truth that humans are inherently similar across nations and cultures, and thereby denying the deadly belief system that imagines some humans as the other, an alien and inferior race, something to be erased and forgotten. The forgetting of the individual beneath the obscuring veil of war is countered by the defenses of writing, whereby the diarist's exploration of self and country carves the intimate and profound details of life indelibly upon the tombs of the unknown, details of life that are at once personal and collective in their scope. Though they hold their pens in times of war, when the air rattles with the threat to remove the traces of their bodies, their lives, and their countries, writers contemplate and observe in the full glory of life.

In the research for *Stolen Voices,* I have been most moved by the snuffing-out of three beautiful and universal qualities—love, compassion, brilliance of thought—all sacrificed so unfairly, so quietly, without trial or resistance. Through these writings, we are witness to the ardor of Nina Kosterina's love, and its brutal curtailment on the freezing Moscow Front; Stanley Hayami's tenderness, wrought into a futile act of bravery and compassion for another, resulting in the forfeit of his life for the very government that had made him into an enemy; and Yitskhok Rudashevski, clearly so bright, so capable, crushed in a moment. Without their words, Nina, Stanley, and Yitskhok would be three of what the young World War I poet Charles Sorley called the "millions of the mouthless dead," silenced and forgotten.

Briefly, I am going to write of three places in the world where young individuals, their lives sacrificed to war, have remained in anonymity without the artifact of a diary to exclaim on their behalf, *I once lived!* In 2002, developers of an industrial estate at Boezinge, near the Belgian town of Ypres, unknowingly excavated the no-man's-land between the opposing trenches of the British and German troops. Coming across the preserved carapace of a British-made steel helmet, the developers uncovered the bodies of two fallen and forgotten soldiers, delicately preserved in attitudes of war. In the United States, there is the Arlington National Cemetery's Tomb of the Unknowns, in whose marble stronghold lie the unnamed, the unidentified. At the west end of the nave of Britain's Westminster Abbey, the Unknown Warrior is interred, another unidentified young man from World War I covered initially in the soil and subsequently in the black marble of the country in which he fell. The colossal loss of life experienced by dozens of countries during the wars of the twentieth century has been abstracted in the minds of those that have inherited an earth in whose soil somewhere close to 200 million now rest, forfeited to a century of violence. The number is so much beyond what can be imagined that to begin to think of those that died is to partake in an act of forgetting.

There is a famous anecdote about the Jewish historian Simon Dubnov, whose last words before being shot by the Nazis in Riga were the battle cry, "*Schreibt und farschreibt!*" Write and record! As we enter the twenty-first century, we close our eyes to the thousands of forgotten conflicts, neglected by history books. While in diaries, letters, documents, and retrospectives the unknown soldiers of the United States and Europe have a few voices that rise above the obscurity of soil, there are dozens of the world's countries whose people have suffered atrocities in all but complete silence. How many of our children in the

West know of the thousands of men, women, and children killed in Laos during the "Secret War" on the Laotian front during the Vietnam War, their villages razed to the ground? Or the devastating air attack on the Spanish Moroccan town of Chechaouen? Or the acts of violence in Yemen during the route to independence?

Writing remains one of the most powerful antidotes to this century of violence, writing whose primary function is to activate our minds for positive, generous, and serious acts of thought, to remember, to empathize, and to begin the process of comprehension. By the threads of the diarists' writing, the concertinaed numbers of anonymous dead and living that succumb in times of war can be teased apart, one by one, and recognized. It is my desire as a young writer to confront my readership with the voices of other young writers whose details of individuality, threatened by the annihilating grains of war, cry out from the page, *Listen*. I attend to the reveille of Nadine Gordimer, who in the 1992 UNESCO symposium in Harare called for "the fingerprint of flesh on history." These diaries are the fingerprints of flesh, the traces of those hands that dared to hold a pen in wartime.

Melanie Challenger
New York, 2006

Stolen Voices

WORLD WAR I

1914–18

Voices

Piete Kuhr

*I shall soon finish my war diary. It will be the last war
diary that I write in my life, for never again must there be
a war, never again . . .*

Piete Kuhr was born in 1902. Her mother ran a small singing school in
Berlin, which dominated her time, and so the young Piete spent her childhood with her grandmother in nearby Schneidemühl. She was encouraged to start writing a diary by her mother to document the events of
World War I.

War entered Piete's life in the summer of 1914, when the Austrian
archduke Franz Ferdinand took part in a state visit to the city of Sarajevo. There, a young Bosnian, Gavrilo Princip, shot and killed the archduke and his wife, Sophie, setting into motion World War I. Princip was
captured and put on trial. The exact date of his birth could not be established, but it is certain that he was either nineteen or just turned twenty
at the time he committed the murders. His youth saved him from the
death penalty, although he died in prison of ongoing tuberculosis in
April 1918.

The provinces of Bosnia and Herzegovina had been under Austro-
Hungarian government since 1878. Austria took full control of the
provinces in 1908, which outraged Serbian nationals, who wanted to in-
corporate the region into a Serbian state. Consequently, the Serbian terrorist group the Black Hand, to which Princip belonged, resolved to
assassinate Franz Ferdinand. Since the turn of the century the whole of

Europe had suffered from numerous political tensions which divided Europe into two blocks. The crisis that followed the assassination forced Germany to decide whether it should or should not stand by Austria-Hungary in any military response towards Serbia. Germany, Austria-Hungary and Italy were a part of the Triple Alliance formed in 1882. By authorizing Austria to retaliate against Serbia, Germany had effectively declared war. Germany feared the military response of both France and Russia (that were part of the Triple Entente together with the United Kingdom), and so planned for a brief conflict with France and, possibly, a further six-month conflict with Russia. It was the march by German troops through Belgium toward France that led Great Britain to join the fight and declare war against Germany.

Much of what Piete's diary details are the hardships endured by Germany as a result of its military policy, and the changes in sympathy among people as the war showed no sign of ending. In 1915, when it became increasingly apparent that the war would not end as swiftly as expected, Germany passed further economic policies to deal with the burgeoning costs of prolonged battle. There was a general atmosphere of instability in Germany, with many senior officials being fired and replaced by new candidates as military defeat continued. By the winter of 1916–17, food was scarce, and many Germans grew war-weary. Left-wing feeling increased, but German workers ultimately refused or were afraid to strike or rebel, despite encouragement from Russia.

The decisive battle was fought by Germany against France and Britain in 1918. Initially Germany seemed to be gaining victories, but the opposing forces retaliated with devastating consequences. On October 3, 1918, it was officially declared that Germany had lost the war. The consequences of this defeat were enormous for Germany, which was encumbered by a peace treaty forged by the Allies. The terms of this treaty left Germany with vast debts, which had to be picked up by tax-paying Germans. It was amid the colossal postwar insecurity caused by this debt (both financial and psychological) that Hitler's extremist policies found root, paving the way for the horrors of World War II.

The initial years of World War I, up until 1916, consisted of conventional warfare; however, the second phase degenerated into never-before-seen methods of fighting, as both sides became more desperate to secure their survival. For the first time, chemical weapons were used, such as mustard gas, which resulted in horrific injuries. Long miles of trenches were carved out of the French-Belgian borders, and conditions for soldiers, many of whom were younger than twenty-one, were appalling. In early 1918, the involvement of the United States signalled the beginning of the end of the conflict. The armistice treaty was signed on November 11, 1918, which ended the war and created the German republic.

1914

I AM called Piete.

I won't say what my real name is, it is so stupid. Yes I will, though; it is Elfriede, Frieda. (Frieda is the utter limit!) My brother's name is Willi-Gunther, he is fifteen years old. I am twelve. We live with my grandmother in Schneidemühl in the province of Posen. My mother has a music school in Berlin, the "Leading School of Music and Drama." She often visits us. Those are great times.

Today is the first of August, 1914. It is very hot. They started to harvest the rye on July 25, it is almost white. When I came past a field this evening I plucked three ears and fixed them over my bed with a drawing pin.

From today Germany is at war. My mother has advised me to write a diary about the war; she thinks it will be of interest to me when I am older. This is true. When I am fifty or sixty, what I have written as a child will seem strange. But it will be true, because you must not tell lies in a diary.

The Serbs began it. On June 28, they hosted the Austrian crown prince Franz Ferdinand and his wife Sophie. The royal couple were traveling by car through the town of Sarajevo, and as they were driving along in fine state and waving, shots were fired from an ambush. No one knows who did it. It says in the newspaper that the whole of Austro-Hungary is in indescribable uproar. In Vienna an ultimatum was drawn up and sent to Serbia, but the Serbs have rejected it. Everyone says the Serbs want war in order to maintain their independence and Russia will support them. I once got to know a Russian student in Kolberg, Nikolai Kedrin; my brother Willi-Gunther was very fond of him. Now he too will be involved in the shooting. I asked Willi whether he could imagine this. Willi thought for a moment and said, No.

Austro-Hungary, Germany, Serbia, Russia, and France have mobilized. We have no idea what war will be like. There are flags on all the houses in the town, just as if we were engaged in a festival. They are black, white, and red.

AUGUST 2, 1914

I MUST now describe the town of Schneidemühl. It has 25,000 inhabitants, three Evangelical churches, one Lutheran, one Catholic, and one Jewish church, and several bridges. There are also a large number of squares with old trees in them. The biggest square is the Neue Markt, a smaller one is called Wilhelmsplatz, another is Alte Markt. Our river is the Kuddow; where it is at its narrowest it is called the Zgordalina. That is a Polish name. So you see indeed that Poles live here too—many Poles, in fact. The seasonal workers, who come to work on the land, are nearly all Poles.

The Kuddow is a little river with many whirlpools and rapids, shallow and covered in vegetation that looks like blue-green hair. It is not navigable. It is most beautiful when the sun goes down, and also in moonlight. I am definitely going to write poems about it—at any rate I will try to.

My mother is visiting us at present. She had wanted to spend her holiday in Sweden, but as the situation was critical she came here. My mother is quite tall and slim, she has bronze-colored hair and wears unusual clothes. She has high-heeled shoes. She is the most beautiful lady that my brother and I know. We glow with pride when we walk the streets with her.

It is Sunday today. There is no school. When I woke up I heard Mama and Grandpa talking excitedly together on the veranda. I wanted to understand what they were saying, but Marie, our maid, was making so much noise that I couldn't hear. She was scrubbing the floor hard because she had spilt some milk. I ran on to the veranda in my nightie and called out "What has happened?" Mama, who was drinking coffee and eating a ham roll, said, "In Berlin two Russians have fired on our crown prince. He is said to be seriously wounded." I was flabbergasted. Grandma said, "People talk so much, you can't believe all they say." Why shouldn't you believe it? If the Russians declare war on us, they'll fire on the crown prince. It's obvious.

When Grandma and I were on our way to church, we stopped by the window of the newspaper office where many people were crowding around. There was a paper hanging behind the glass with a statement written in blue pencil—

> The report of the attempt on the life of the German crown prince is not true. The crown prince is in the best of health.

"You see!" said Grandma.

Countless people sat and stood in church. The air was hot and stuffy. The minister preached a very fervent sermon, speaking of Germany's exaltation and the fight for justice. I was very cross because I was only twelve years old and was not a man. What's the use of being a child when there is a war? A child is of no use at all in wartime. You have to be a soldier. Most men enroll of their own free will.

We sang "A Mighty Fortress Is Our God." Grandma sang in her thin voice, which sometimes quavers a bit. I am terribly fond of Grandma. The minister said the Lord's Prayer and ended with "God give victory to our brave troops."

"I have lived through this twice before," said Grandma on the way home. "It was just the same when the Danish war broke out, and again in 1870. Why can't people live in peace!"

AUGUST 3, 1914

AT SCHOOL the teachers say it is our patriotic duty to stop using foreign words. I didn't know what they meant by this at first, but now I see it—you must no longer say "adieu" because that is French. It is in order to say "lebwohl" or "auf wiedersehen," or "Gruss Gott" if you like. I must now call Mama "Mother," but "Mother" isn't tender enough. I'll say "Mommy." We have bought a little tin box in which we'll put five pfennigs every time we slip up. The contents of the war savings box will go toward buying knitting wool. We must now knit woolen things for the soldiers.

I said to our Nature Study teacher today, "Am I to write the history of the buzzard in my journal?" Herr Schiffman answered, "We have decided to speak in our lovely German language. The word for 'journal' is 'kladde.'"

I thought Herr Schiffman was joking, and began to laugh. Then he got cross. I can't help it, it seems comic to me when any one says "kladde."

AUGUST 4, 1914

... NIGHTTIME. In bed, I must write some more.

The 149th Regiment of infantry is stationed in Schneidemühl. It is going to be sent to the Western Front. This evening we heard the faint sound of drums, bass drums and kettledrums. "A military band!" I shouted. We strained our ears to listen to it. The music kept getting louder and clearer. Now it was the Hohenfriedberger March that was being played. We couldn't bear to stay any longer in the room and ran out into the street. "To the station!" cried Willi. We ran through Grandpa's subway (which he had built) and pushed our way through the crowd of people on to the Droshkenplatz. The arc lamps were alight, and the foliage of the chestnut trees in the white light looked just like paper. I climbed on the iron fence; from there I could see everything: on the left the yellow station building on whose four turrets stood sentries with shouldered rifles, in front of me the railway platforms, and behind me the square with crowds standing shoulder to shoulder. At Platform 3 there stood a goods train, full of reservists. They leaned against the open doors of the wagons, waving and laughing.

I heard Willi exclaim "They're coming! The Hundred and Forty-ninth!" Our regiment marched down the street to the station. The soldiers wore the new gray field uniform and gray spiked helmets. Their boots of peacetime! Their packs were so full that the soldiers half disappeared beneath them. In front came the regimental band in full blast. I strained my eyes to see whether the big white poodle that always carried a kettledrum was with them, but he was not there. The drummer was beating time with the staff with the red and silver tassel. The band called "There's a call like a clap of thunder." Then we heard the soldiers singing, ". . . firm and true stands the watch on the Rhine," and everyone joined in the singing with shouts of "Hip, hip, hurray!"

So came the 149th shoulder to shoulder, flowing over the platform like a surge of gray water. All the soldiers had long garlands of summer flowers round their necks and on their chests. Bunches of asters, as if they would shoot down the enemy with flowers. The soldiers' faces were serious. I had expected that they would be laughing and rejoicing. But there was only one lieutenant rejoicing. I knew him, he was the son of Frau Schön, a member of Grandma's sisterhood. Lieutenant Schön was cheerfully bidding good-bye to all his relatives and friends and was kissed, hugged, and patted all the way through the crowd. I wanted to shout "Hello, Lieutenant Schön!" but no words would come out.

Now the band was playing "The Laurels of Victory Be Yours." The people remaining in the square waved their hats and handkerchiefs. The reservists in the rear wagon mimicked the instrumentalists with their hands and mouths and caused a good deal of laughter. Some of our 149th rushed to the pump and made water spurt all over themselves and down their necks. It was very oppressive with the August heat and the crowd of people packed close together. One of the reservists at Platform 3 now climbed on to the roof of his goods wagon and shouted to our soldiers: "You, fine sirs, are already in full battle array but we have yet to get dressed," and on the words "have yet" he plucked so comically at his civilian gear that all around broke into laughter and clapping. Then the reservists' train began to move off, the reservists sang and cheered, and we waved for as long as we could see anything of them. The crush in the station square had meanwhile become so great that I jumped down from the fence; I was half suffocated. An old lady wailed loudly: "Paul! Where is my darling Paul? Let me at least see you, son!" She was pushed forward to the railings, but I couldn't make out whether she found her Paul in the crowd of soldiers. She had little red eyes, probably inflamed with crying. I made a quick prayer to God: "Dear God, protect this Paul! Give him back to her! Please, please, please, I beseech you!" I was suddenly as much taken up with this Paul as if the heavens were falling.

"Good-bye, soldier!" suddenly called out a tiny boy and stretched his hand through the railings.

"Good-bye, little brother!" answered the soldier and shook the little boy's hand . . .

Now the soldiers began to sing a song I had never heard before, which suddenly drowned all else. I could only understand a few lines:

> The little woodland birds
> Sang such a wonderful refrain:
> In the homeland, in the homeland,
> There we'll meet again.

It wouldn't have taken much for me to burst out crying. I went home by a roundabout way. I held in front of me the hand that the soldier squeezed. As I went up our poorly lit steps, I stared at the palm of the hand. Then I quickly kissed it. Silly, wasn't it?

AUGUST 6, 1914

Copenhagen: Denmark has declared its neutrality.
Constantinople: The Turks have declared their neutrality.

Bern: Switzerland has declared to the powers its neutrality.
Bucharest: Romania has declared its neutrality.

Troops are constantly passing through the station. They come in end-less trains. We once counted fifty wagons on one single goods train. The soldiers and reservists laugh and sing. They arrive cheering and leave again cheering. The Red Cross ladies distribute coffee, lemon-ade, and sandwiches to the soldiers. When a train has left the station, the baskets are empty. But there are fresh gift parcels waiting in our house, and our maid Marie and I run to and fro, bringing one basket after another. As it is very hot there, I had some of the soldiers' coffee too. I drank the large mug empty in one gulp. I pretended I was a sol-dier being well looked after, and I was very happy.

On one railway wagon it said: "Merrily to Russia! Japan is helping too!" But we haven't really got as far as that; Japan hasn't declared which power it supports and whether it is willing to take any part in the war. A few days ago we thought the whole world would stand by us. But see how things are now!

There was another slogan that I liked:

Every Prussian shoot a Russian,
Every German clobber a Frog,
The Serbs'll get what they deserve.
Whether they're Serbs or Russian fiends
We'll smash 'em all to smithereens.

I should like to go with them! I don't want to stay behind and be a child! I am so sorry for the soldiers and the horses!

AUGUST 7, 1914

THERE IS talk of an outbreak of famine in Russia, and it is said that the rebellious population are being driven into battle with whips. If famine is already prevalent in Russia, the war will soon be over. Per-haps instead it would be better if it were already over. There is so much corn standing in the fields that needs to be harvested. The mobilization has taken the farmworkers away from the harvest. But with God's help the corn will not be spoiled, so that we have enough to eat in the winter. The older children in the grammar school have offered themselves for harvest work. Eighteen members of my brother's form, the upper third, have already been detailed for land work. I asked Mommy to write me too a note giving me leave for harvest work. She wrote:

> I give permission for my daughter Elfriede ("Elfriede!") to do such harvest work as may be suited to her strength.
> Yours faithfully

This afternoon I went to our headmaster's house and gave him the letter. I was very frightened. He read the note and said: "But you are still much too young, Elfriede."

"No, not at all!" I said. "I am really much older than I look."

"Really!" answered the head, pouting. "And how have you come to be so much older than you look?"

I knew very well what he was getting at. He was thinking of the incident two years ago when I was nearly chucked out of the school. (I will tell you why, later on.) I looked at him coldly. But before I could make any further reply, he said: "Go back home, you naughty, horrid-looking child! Girls like you are no use to the Fatherland!"

This evening, while we were on the veranda eating baked potatoes and pickled herrings, a man in the street called loudly, "Luttich has fallen!" We all jumped up, and Willi upset the basin of pickles. "Children, children!" said Mommy, and tears were running from her eyes. We could hardly grasp the fact that we must have gained the first great victory. Grandma threw the window open and called out: "Please come up here for a moment!" She ran down toward the newsman and bought a copy of the special news sheet. There it was in black and white!

We went into the street, none of us wanting any more to eat. There was great rejoicing in the town. People were dancing on the pavements, there was singing and whistling, and people were calling out to one another, "Luttich has fallen!"

In the midst of all the joy I was seized by a terrible aching sadness. The 149th! When we were sitting on the veranda again, I collected up the melted grease from a candle and formed it into a little cross on which I scratched with a darning needle the words: "Luttich fallen, 7.8.1914." I hung the cross on a cotton thread next to the ears of corn by my bed.

AUGUST 14, 1914
OH, AT LAST!

"The powers involved in the European War have so far made eleven declarations of war and in the following exact order:

1. Austro-Hungary v. Serbia
2. Germany v. Russia
3. Germany v. France
4. England v. Germany
5. Belgium v. Germany
6. Austro-Hungary v. Russia
7. Montenegro v. Austro-Hungary
8. Serbia v. Germany
9. France v. Austro-Hungary
10. Montenegro v. Germany
11. England v. Austro-Hungary"

There are whispers in the streets that preparations are being made for a great battle both in France and in Russia. In France we are drawing up our troops around the stronghold of Belfort. In Russia we are pushing on toward St. Petersburg. The Russian government has to try and win over the Poles for the Russian cause. German and Austrian columns of cyclists are now sticking notices on the walls in Polish towns and villages that say, in the Polish language, "Poles, rise up and bring yourselves under the orderly German regime."

Our railway station bridges are now barricaded too. You come up against sentries everywhere. Notices are hung on bridges, saying, "Drive Slowly!" Every driver is questioned and every vehicle is searched. No one crossing the bridges is allowed to loiter. Military trains rumble through under the bridges. You suddenly have the feeling that the enemy is quite near.

People are becoming uneasy. We heard that some families have left town. Our Marie is not the only one who wants to escape. Fresh refugees have arrived from East Prussia. This time I have seen them myself, mothers, children, old women, and old men. Some well-dressed, others badly. They all carry bundles and cases, bedding, coats, and cloaks all tied together. The refugees are looked after by our Red Cross depot on the station.

One woman with noisy children kept crying out, "Just where can we go? Where can we go?" I wished her good luck and said, "Don't worry, the emperor will look after us all!" "Dear child," said the woman (pronouncing it in her funny way), "a child like you can have no idea what it's like, can you?" And tears ran all over her chubby red face.

August 20, 1914

The news sheets giving the names of dead soldiers are called "Casualty Lists." A black Iron Cross is printed at the top, and below this are the words "Fallen on the field of honor. . . ." Then follow the ranks and names of the dead, the army unit, the battle, and the date of death. After the killed, the wounded are listed, and again after these the missing. Above the missing it says, "Reported missing."

Every soldier carries an identity card. The soldiers call it the "death ticket." The medical orderlies who search the battlefield for the dead establish the names of the fallen by means of the identity cards. We are afraid every time we see a casualty list. We always expect to find sons, brothers, or husbands of people we know among the fallen. The war had better be ended.

Yesterday it said in the paper that the emperor has been to the

Western Front. Someone had written a poem, the last verse of which ran like this:

> *O Emperor, proceed with joy*
> *To the battlefield;*
> *By you the whole world's destiny will be sealed*
> *Above your brazen armies there arise*
> *Golden clouds of glory filling the skies.*

How can the emperor proceed "with joy" to the battlefield? If he walks over the battlefield and hears a dying man at his feet calling "Mother!"—what then?

Willi laughed when I said this to him. "Do you really believe that the emperor goes walkabout on the battlefield?" he asked.

"It says so there though!" I cried, and pointed with my finger to the newspaper.

AUGUST 23, 1914

MOMMY GOES back to Berlin the day after tomorrow. Then we shall feel like a dog who has lost his master. The war will seem even sadder. There will be no one to talk to about it.

Willi and I are always running about after Mommy, and if it doesn't bother her, we like to watch her closely. At all events we don't want to forget what she looks like when we think of her during the winter.

In the evening, when Mommy and Willi were sitting in the summer-house working on Willi's own poetical composition, "In the Land of the Ringing Stone," my sadness became so great that I ran out. In the Guterbahnhof Strasse I encountered three trucks that were slowly turning the corner. The trucks were carrying stretchers on which wounded soldiers lay. They groaned when the wheels rattled over rough stones. Women in the street stood watching, and one working-class woman called out: "There go our boys now!" pointing to the bandaged soldiers. The material was covered with encrusted blood. One soldier was sitting up on the edge of the second truck. His left arm was missing from the shoulder. His chest was like a four-cornered box of dried bandages. His lips were drawn up so that you could see the teeth behind them. His head kept drooping to one side. The woman suddenly grasped me by the arm, tugged me this way and that, and shouted: "It's your fault that they're all dying! Your fault!"

I tore myself free and struck the woman's hand. Then I ran down the street, while the woman went on scolding behind me, shouting, "You toffee-nosed little snob!" When I reached our yard, I sat down on the sand heap under the cherry tree and began to cry. Gretel came out of the door and asked, "Why are you crying?"

"A woman said it's my fault that the soldiers are dying."

"She's absolutely mad," said Gretel indignantly, "Think nothing of it! She's quite mad!" She sat down by me and prodded the sand. Then she asked: "What about the soldiers, then?"

"Oh, the wounded. They were badly wounded, coming from the east. On trucks."

"Did you see them?"

"Yes."

"Were they very bad?"

"Very bad. Some looked almost dead."

"And are you to blame for that?" Gretel began to laugh. I poked a finger in the sand and said, "Perhaps I am partly to blame. Perhaps I have committed some sin. You never know."

During the night, while Grandma was asleep, I got up quietly and stood by the open veranda window. The stars were shining brightly; I had to keep looking at them. If every dead soldier were to become a star in the sky, it would be so bright that we would no longer need the sun and the moon. Then it struck me, what rubbish that was, because stars get their light from the great constellations. In any case a dead body can't become a star. Then I thought of the working-class woman's words and became furious. I considered for a long time whether I shouldn't creep secretly to the station and smuggle myself into a troop train. It would be best for me to die with the others. I dreamed of how our headmaster would make a speech in the school hall: "Our comrade Elfriede Kuhr has given her life on the field of honor. Honor the young girl who truly became a brave girl at the end of her days!" At the thought of how difficult it would be for him to utter these words, I had a job not to explode. I would have shamed the head.

AUGUST 30, 1914

Now SUDDENLY the members of Granny's sisterhood are complaining about the Jews and are not going to shop at Jewish people's businesses anymore. It has become obvious to me that that working-class woman recently took me for a Jewish girl. I was just going to tell this story to Granny's sisterhood ladies when a messenger brought a gigantic basket full of wine, fruit, bread, and sausages. It just happened to have been sent by a Jewish shopkeeper's wife for the soldiers. Her name is Frau Edel, and she lives in our Alte Bahnhof Strasse. We do a lot of shopping at Edels.

Fighting is raging all the time on the Eastern Front. Along the whole line of nearly 400 kilometers [250 miles] there is furious fighting. If you stand quite still and pay attention, you can feel the ground slightly quivering beneath your feet. It is an uncanny feeling.

Whole columns of East Prussian refugees came through the town. Many are crying. But some are quite quiet. There are mothers with quite tiny children. They put their infants under their shawls and let them drink. The little ones' behinds are bloody because the mothers haven't enough nappies to lay them out to dry. We have torn up old sheets and shirts and given them pieces to wrap the babies in. Gretel and I now play a game in the yard in which her old celluloid doll is a refugee child that has no more nappies. She has painted its behind red, indicating soreness.

The girls of the Schneidemühl schools come together in the afternoons in their particular classes in order to knit stockings, scarves, head-warmers, knee-covers, mittens, gloves, and earmuffs for the soldiers. Field-gray wool is bought by the pound out of various collections of money. A scarf is not difficult to knit—always right-hand stitches and left at the back. But you have to be a wizard to knit the foot of a stocking. When I have with great difficulty finished both legs, Grandma takes the stockings with her to the station, and between making soup and pouring coffee she knits the feet on.

SEPTEMBER 4, 1914

IN THE train a woman is detained who suspects every person of being an enemy who is going to shoot her dead. She is shrieking, raving, and praying. There are five children with her, also shrieking. Medical orderlies carry out a fourteen-year-old boy from the same train. During the journey he kept trying to jump out of the train. Now he is put in a cab and taken to the municipal hospital.

"Has he no parents then?" Frau Annchen asked the refugees. They don't know either; the boy was all on his own in the train.

"Where we were living there is not a single stone left on another," said one countrywoman. "Everything is burning. Not a single head of cattle is alive. Some bedding and clothing and a little money is all that we could bring with us."

We ran around, serving bread, coffee, and soup. On average 400 kilos [900 pounds] of bread, ½ hundredweight [56 pounds] of coffee, 100 liters [26 gallons] of milk, and 1 hundredweight [112 pounds] of fat are consumed each day at the station. Sometimes three or four troop trains, with 1,500 men each, arrive in a single hour. In between these come trainloads of refugees and passenger trains that have been converted into hospital trains. Yesterday evening a soldier burst out of a hospital train screaming at the top of his voice. All he was wearing was a gray woollen shirt, his identity disc around his neck, and tattered military trousers. He ran up and down in front of the Red Cross depot, tearing his hair, and struck his forehead at least ten times against one of the iron lampposts, yelling: "I heard them shrieking! You've never heard anything like it! I heard them shrieking, heard them shrieking!" Then he himself, with wide open mouth, roared, "Aaaah . . . aaaah . . . aaaah," until some orderlies came running up and held his arms firmly behind his back. He had thoroughly battered his face against the lamppost, and blood was trickling from his forehead. We ran up to them too and Grandma asked in horror, "What is the matter with the lad?" "He's gone mad," said one of the orderlies. "He was present at the fighting in Masuria and went crackers. There's nowt else wrong with him."

"Don't squeeze his arms so much," ordered Grandma, and she went up to the bleeding soldier and just stroked his cheek. The soldier cried "Oh, Mommy, I actually heard them shrieking!" and looked at Grandma with wild eyes. Grandma said, "No, my lad, you're dreaming. Come to your senses, my boy, and I'll give you some coffee."

And he drained a whole pot of coffee that Grandma held to his mouth while she and Frau Annchen kept smiling at him. When he had at length been taken away, I said to Grandma, "They were really shrieking, Granny! You see, they were shrieking in the swamps. The soldier wasn't telling lies!"

But Grandma suddenly became angry and said I mustn't keep sneaking around among the soldiers but should make my way home and get my homework done. At this I also got angry, tore off my coffee apron, and swept off without saying good-bye.

SEPTEMBER 7, 1914

SOMETHING HAS happened. I got into a fight with a boy because he was calling Sibylla Lowenthal "Jewish sow!"

"Take that remark back at once!" I cried and stood stock-still. It was in Milch Strasse right in front of the Diaconate House, which my grandfather had built just before he died. A deaconess with a blue hood and a blue gown with blue shoulder-bands was walking up and down in the garden, cutting asters. "Jewish rabble!" cried the boy. "War hoarder!"

We immediately went for each other. The boy struck me on the face, and I gave him a punch under the chin. He knocked my school hat off, and I knocked his cap off. Then he seized my hair and nearly pulled my pigtails off. If the deaconess had not run out of the garden gate, we would have hit each other a lot more. She said "Now, children! Aren't you ashamed of yourselves? Don't you want to behave like German children?" I pointed to Sibylla, who was pressing up against the garden fence. "He called my friend a Jewish sow, sister."

Then the boy ran away. I ran a few steps after him and called out: "You wait—we'll meet again!"

SEPTEMBER 14, 1914

THE LITTLE cemetery is the burial place for our enemies. A few Russian prisoners who have died in transit and several spies who have been shot rest there. The Belgian husband and wife are also buried there. Frau Annchen and Grandma have asked me to show them the cemetery. As they were not on duty at the station today, we went there together. Gretel Wegner came with us too.

As we stood in front of the barbed wire fence, Grandma suddenly looked around her in a pained way and cried: "Now that beats everything! It's our own land!" We were really amazed. The strip of sandy ground that immediately adjoined the cemetery was the last piece of land that we owned. As the ground was infertile we had never been able to sell it. Our former coachman Schultz had once tried to sow potatoes there, but it was never worthwhile. Frau Annchen thought Grandma ought to be pleased. She would now certainly be able to sell the land to the town, for there would be many more enemies dying and needing graves. Then the council will soon buy additional land in order to enlarge the cemetery. Besides, the fine sand is good for burials.

Gretel and I broke off pine twigs and threw them onto the nearest mounds. We secretly decided to look after the Russian cemetery. It was to belong entirely to us. Gretel would even bring a little rake, for we had found a hole in the barbed wire through which someone must already have crawled. The wire was twisted and bent down outward; you could just manage to squeeze through. We would tie the rake up in the top of a pine so it couldn't be stolen. Then we would rake between the graves every week and lay little bunches of wildflowers on the mounds . . .

SEPTEMBER 15, 1914

WHEN WE had had supper, there was a ring at the door, and Frau Schön (the councillor's wife) was standing there in tears.

"God in Heaven, what has happened?" said Grandma. "Dear Frau Schön, come in and sit down on the sofa and calm yourself!" But Frau Schön couldn't speak at all and just cried louder, until we gathered that her youngest son, who was serving as first lieutenant, had been killed at Tannenberg. Just before that he had been awarded the Iron Cross, Class II. Councillor Schön had just gone to the family of his eldest son, so Frau Schön was all alone when she received the sad news. She had just hurried to Grandma in her misery because she knew of no other earthly comfort. Grandma and Frau Schön cried together for some time. Frau Schön kept calling out, "If only I knew just how he was killed! Whether he had to suffer much . . . and whether he remained whole, without losing any limbs." It was so sad that she worried herself as to whether her boy remained whole in all his limbs, when after all he was dead.

SEPTEMBER 16, 1914

LAST NIGHT I heard Grandma crying. She was crying so much that it greatly distressed me. The young First Lieutenant Schön is the first of our friends to be killed. I buried my head in my pillow so that Grandma would not hear me crying.

This morning there was a letter from Mommy. "Now my dear pupil Dahlke has been killed at Maubeuge," she wrote. "The best pupil in my singing class, a heroic tenor, who could have become a second Caruso! You can't imagine my grief, I go around as if I had a stone in my chest and another in my throat." That is the second friend! Mommy then goes on—"Thank you, dear Piete, for the first pages of your diary! How busy you have been! It is already almost a book! But you ought to see the war in a more heroic light—not so much of the 'down' side. It clouds the view of the greatness of an event. Don't let yourself be overwhelmed with sloppy sentimentality. Our enemies want to rob us of our country and our honor. Our men are defending both. And Siegfried Dahlke died the death of a hero! Never forget that!"

I certainly will not forget it. Indeed I cry, not because our soldiers are dying the deaths of heroes, for there is something great about the death of a hero. I cry simply because they have died—just died. No more morning, no more evening—dead. When a mother's son is killed, she will cry her eyes out, not because he had died a hero, but because he has gone away and is buried. No more will he sit at the table, no longer can she cut a slice of bread for him or darn his socks. So she cannot say "Thank you" that he has died like a hero. (Please, please, Mommy, don't be angry!)

OCTOBER 2, 1914

A COLD, horrible day. The leaves on the trees are already yellow and red and in some places are falling. They will not last much longer, and then everything will be bare and empty. To follow this weather there will be a mild and dirty winter. We shall therefore be twice as busy knitting. When I have finished the second pair of mittens, I want to knit knee-warmers. The soldiers at the station have said that the rainwater in some of the trenches is half a meter deep. Wet through to the skin, the soldiers paddle in water as they fire. The damp penetrates right into the dugouts. There is much bladder and kidney trouble among the soldiers.

NOVEMBER 2, 1914

THERE IS no chance of peace by Christmas. Otherwise they wouldn't be hustling us so much at school about Christmas. Every day they say: "Every pfennig for the soldiers." Grandma says we are making her bankrupt with the school collections. We now have a big Iron Cross made of wood hung on the wall at school in which we have to knock 1,000 iron nails. When all the nails have been knocked in, it will really be an "iron" cross. Every girl can hammer in as many nails as she likes. The black nails cost 5 pfennigs each, the silver ones 10 pfennigs. I have so far knocked in two black nails and one silver. It makes a bit of fun. The proceeds are devoted to war purposes.

The snow has gone again. It is raining. In the west all operations are ruled out by floods. In other battle areas, too, the trenches are under water. Perhaps they will be unable to shoot at Verdun because of the dampness.

A soldier has written the following poem:

> *Our hair grows like a mane*
> *And we are strangers to soap*
> *Our teeth uncleaned remain;*
> *A change of shirts? No hope!*
>
> *Our clothes are sopping wet,*
> *Our stomachs often empty.*
> *No wine or beer we get*
> *Gone are the days of plenty.*
>
> *We've really got mud in the eye,*
> *Our shoes and our socks are afloat,*
> *We've nothing left that is dry*
> *Except for our humor and throats.*
>
> *And yet this heroism*
> *Does earn its special coin;*
> *We display our patriotism*
> *Through rheumatics in the groin.*

The soldier has certainly not exaggerated, although there is one thing I can't imagine—that their stomachs are often empty. For the best meat, best preserves, and all the best foodstuffs go to the army supplies. But in the turmoil of battle it must often be the case that the field kitchens cannot come forward. Then the soldiers' stomachs must rumble. Ours too will soon be rumbling, for many provisions in the home country have become still dearer and there is no longer as much meat. Everyone talks of scarcity . . .

NOVEMBER 5, 1914

I RAN to Gretel in the yard, and because of the rain we sat under the roof of the drying room. There I told Gretel that Paul Dreier had not written for three weeks. I said: "Grandma prayed to God to protect Paul. If God granted all our prayers, no soldier need die. But he hardly hears them at all. He has probably become stone deaf—through the thunder of the guns!"

Gretel begged me not to commit sin. "Something will happen to you afterward, you will become ill and might have to die," she said.

"Believe it or not," I said, "it wouldn't matter to me at all. Before, when there was yet no war, it did matter. But now it doesn't. And then I'm going to tell you something else. . . . I can no longer play with dolls. Such small dolls, you know—they have no place in war."

Gretel asked me what I would like to play then. I said, "Soldiers." Gretel was sad because she loves her dolls so much. But I can no longer play with dolls.

DECEMBER 24, 1914

IT IS about to strike midnight. I am writing secretly in bed by the light of Grandma's war torch.

Christmas! It is Christmas now!

We exchanged presents at six o'clock. Before that Grandma, Willi, and I went to the old Town Church for Christmas service. The market was quite full of silent people. The bells rang and then stopped, we went through the porch and sat in our seats. Suddenly the organ began to play, first a voluntary, but the tune of "Silent Night, Holy Night" could definitely be recognized. Everybody bowed their heads, as if an order had been given, and began to sob and cry. Then the melody was brought out clearly, and we sang as well as we could. Then our senior minister Schammer went up to the altar, gazed for a time at the Christmas tree with its lighted candles, and said: "Peace on earth! And goodwill to men!" Then everybody sobbed and cried still more.

The whole church was full of people wearing black clothes and black mourning veils. For a long time we couldn't speak as we came out of the church. Our military band was playing Christmas music in the marketplace. If anyone met any friends, they just shook hands in silence.

Then we went to the station for the soldiers' Christmas festivities. Our old disused fourth-class carriage stood on the platform, handsomely decorated as a gingerbread house. It was brightly lit inside. The little Christmas tree stood on a long table, which was covered with a white cloth and laid out with Christmas packets. On the wall there hung a large picture of the emperor surrounded by a garland of fir. Also hanging on the walls were our soldier-puppets, pairs of braces, and thick shoe-stiffeners that the soldiers like so much.

As we walked in, they all cried "Aaaah!" as though we were the life and soul of the party. The Red Cross ladies had been expecting Grandma, as had also the soldiers. Grandma now lit the lights on the Christmas tree. Our gramophone, which we had lent them, played "There Is a Rose in Bloom." Nearly all the soldiers present sat or stood in silence in front of the lighted candles, some of them crying bitterly. A lieutenant sidled up to the carriage door. He took off his cap, kissed Grandma's hand, and listened thoughtfully in a corner. One of the soldiers was as lanky as a lath and as dark as a Gypsy. He squinted horribly as he cried. Another, a young wounded dragoon, was ceaselessly writing postcards "home" with lightning speed, wiping his nose and eyes with his fist all the time.

Now we are all in bed. The house is dark. In the rear quarters also, where the Wegner and Zuhlke families live, it is all dark and quiet. Gretel will certainly be asleep now.

What are they doing out there . . . all of them?

Please, please, dear God, do bring the war to an end!

DECEMBER 31, 1914

WHY AM I not with the soldiers! Why am I not dead! Why on earth am I still living this life? For a long time I have got no enjoyment out of it, first school, then the war. I just can't write otherwise. No, I can't; do you hear, Mommy? And I won't! Life with us here is like that, and if I am to describe it differently, then I've got to tell lies! I would definitely rather not write any more at all.

MARCH 1, 1915

THE SOLDIERS sing this marching song—

Musketeers are a cheerful lot
A happy brotherhood.
They shout and sing their cheerful songs,
To the girls they're really good.

The young lieutenants are even more cheerful than the musketeers. (Incidentally, nobody speaks of "musketeers" nowadays; they are called "infantrymen" or "footsloggers.") The officers often make whoopee in the officers' mess. Although this is quite a distance from our house, the sound of the lively music reaches us. That is when a so-called Regimental dinner is taking place. Sometimes ladies attend them, officers' wives and invited young girls from the town. There is dancing and a good deal of drinking. The merriment increases more and more. Recently it developed into a riot that was, however, hushed up.

Who wants to die! You would at least like to have a quick taste of life. Life is beautiful, in spite of war or anything else. The grass is lovely, the trees, the open air, the sky, the moon and sun. And the animals too—all these things are lovely.

MARCH 11, 1915

ANOTHER COLLECTION has been announced at school. This time it is again for copper, but also for tin, lead, zinc, brass and old iron. Out of this are to be made gun barrels, cannons, cartridge cases, and so forth. There is keen competition between the classes. Our class, the fourth, has so far collected the greatest quantity. I have turned the whole house upside down, from top to bottom. Our Marie doesn't half complain! "Miss Piete is robbing us of everything!" I took old spoons, knives, forks, pots, kettles, a tray, a copper bowl, two brass lamps, old belt buckles, and I don't know what else. Grandma clapped her hands and cried, "The wench will bankrupt me! Better give your lead soldiers than take the last of my possessions!"

So my little army, with which Willi and I had so often played, had to meet their deaths. To avoid all the soldiers being sacrificed, I drew lots for the candidates for death. Those on which the lot fell, I took out from the four rows and laid on one side. When the drawing of lots was all over, I placed the unlucky ones two by two in a large metal spoon and held it over the gas flame. The heroes in their lovely blue uniforms melted to death for the Fatherland, the lead became silvery, heavy and fluid.

"Into cold water, quick!" exclaimed Willi. I let the lump sizzle in a basin of cold water, while I sang "The Little Woodland Birds." "The others too," cried Willi cruelly. "There's no point in keeping them."

It was awful! I melted the last of them too. I could easily have cried. But instead I laughed with my brother.

JULY 29, 1915

ZEPPELINS FLY over our town nearly every day; they look like gigantic silver cigars. I am now so accustomed to the sight that I hardly look up any more. "Zepp 35" often comes over. The zeppelins are frequently engaged in bombing raids over England and Paris; they cause great destruction.

I am sitting writing in the garden. The sun catches me on the neck beneath my broad-brimmed panama hat. The hat belonged to Grandpa. How good the summer is! I am looking at the old apple tree—"my" apple tree—I look around in my garden at all the pretty flowers, the stripped strawberry plants with their green leaves, the red currant and gooseberry bushes, the robust potato plants. This year I am going to take all my garden produce, both fruit and flowers, to the soldiers in the hospital.

DECEMBER 24, 1915

CHRISTMAS EVE! I have tied a sky-blue ribbon round my cat Minka's neck. Mommy has come from Berlin for the festival, as she does every year. Willi and I are very happy and hardly let her out of our sight. She wears a dark blue woolen dress that fits closely at the hips and is fastened with a million tiny buttons. When I showed Minka to her, she was delighted. Minka behaved really splendidly. She performed all the clever tricks that I had taught her. First—"Minka, how do cats go?" whereupon a long "Meow!" follows. Then—"Minka, make yourself look beautiful," whereupon Minka goes up on her hind legs with both front paws high in the air and reaches for my outstretched hand. And then still more, until Mommy said, laughing, that was enough and Minka was ready for the circus.

Nighttime. I am writing in bed with the light from a pocket flashlight; Minka is rolled up in a ball by me, purring. All the household is already asleep. Oh, our Holy Night!

The scent of Christmas tree and extinguished candles comes from the drawing room. I think of the hundred thousand snow-covered trenches and dugouts and the Holy Night of all the soldiers. I am sad and happy at the same time, and could cry. Oh, not now that song from the station, ". . . in the homeland, in the homeland, there we'll meet again!" Oh no, not that!

APRIL 25, 1916

TODAY IS my birthday; fourteen years!

I can never quite decide what is right and what is wrong in this war. I cheer for our victories and am beside myself because there are dead and wounded. I heard yesterday that, hidden away in the forest, there is said to be a military hospital where soldiers live who have had their faces shot away. They must look so frightful that ordinary people cannot look at them. Things like that drive me to despair.

JUNE 10, 1916

OUR KITTEN is dead. Shot by a wicked neighbor. His own daughter told me about it on the way to school. Willi and I are inconsolable. Minka was evidently playing with the neighbor's pigeons on the roof of the shed, that is to say she sprang in the air after them as they took off. Then the man got his gun and shot her dead. I cry and cry. Willi sits at the piano and plays out his grief for Minka in hymns of praise and sorrow. When he played Minka's little lullaby that I often used to hum to her in fun, I slammed the piano lid down. After a while we searched all Minka's favorite places, sofa, rugs, bedcovers, cushions, for white hairs that she had shed. We soon had quite a bundle of them. Then we dug a token grave under my old apple tree. Gretel helped with the grave and shed floods of tears. With Grandma's sharp kitchen knife we suitably carved a wooden tablet, which we placed on the grave. On the tablet in thick ineffaceable letters was the following—

> Here lies our sweet little Minka
> Born 7.14.1915
> Shot 6.10.1916
> Sleep, dear Minka, sleep!

That evening I was feverish—38.4 [101°F] degrees. That night we swore revenge on the man who had killed Minka.

SEPTEMBER 1, 1916

I'VE FINISHED with the war diary! I really cannot bear it any longer. The war is never-ending. I can't go on writing when my hair is gray. Now on August 27, Romania declared war on Austro-Hungary. Just a day later we on our side declared war on Romania. Then on August 29 our ally Turkey followed suit, declaring war on Romania, and today comes Bulgaria's declaration of war on Russia.

In former times, when we were something like "a great family," there was a silver bowl in our drawing room in which visitors put their visiting cards. That's how it seems to me with these everlasting declarations of war—every one declaring war on every one else. The only thing missing is the bowing and kissing of hands. "Allow me— please—my declaration of war!"—"Respectful thanks! Allow me— here is mine!" . . .

NOVEMBER 20, 1916

MOMMY AND Granny are writing to each other a lot, because they are afraid that Willi will be called up next year. A few boys from his class have already been enrolled.

DECEMBER 23, 1916

WE HAVE bought a tiny fir tree and dressed it with our old Christmas decorations. On top is placed our only candle. The third wartime Christmas.

The German admiralty wants to extend the so-called "total U-boat war round the whole world," as a giant fence against the attacks of the Allies. No one speaks of peace anymore.

DECEMBER 25, 1916

MOMMY THINKS I have become as thin as a lath. But who has not gone thin in this war? Gil has legs like a stork. We stand in line for one loaf of bread.

MARCH 16, 1917

RUSSIA NO longer has a royal family. On March 2 Czar Nicholas "surrendered the throne," as it says in the paper. A so-called Provisional Government has been formed.

I am not yet quite fifteen years old. How can I know whether the royal family should be shot? According to Jesus, you definitely shouldn't shoot them. "Thou shalt not kill!" Definitely!

MARCH 19, 1917

WE HAVE only a few potatoes in the cellar now. When we come to the end of those, what then?

JULY 17, 1917

I DON'T understand much about the revolution and the working classes. I just always feel sorry for the soldiers, the wounded and those who have to die. How many millions have there been already? I don't know, no one knows. And the horses get shot in great numbers, and poor dogs like Prince tremble when a farmer cracks his whip.

AUGUST 20, 1917

DEAR DIARY, I must tell you something that really shook me. I came back from a walk today as it was getting dark. I went up the stairs, opened the door into the hall, and crept on tiptoe into the kitchen to see on the quiet what food I could lay my hands on. There I saw an old woman sitting on the coal box crying; she was sitting all bunched up, her head on her knees and her hands covering her face. Her thin white hair was gathered into a meager bun and she looked so hopeless, so terribly sad, like the refugee women from East Prussia, who used to pass along Zeughausstrasse, and she seemed lost. I didn't recognize the woman on the coal box at first. Suddenly I realized it was Grandma. I was paralyzed with shock; then I crept quietly out and back to the front door. Outside I acted as if I was running up the stairs, whistling loudly. I deliberately made quite a lot of noise, called out, "Granny, I'm hungry!" and rang the door bell to give her time. Grandma acted as if nothing had happened. She just said, "The door wasn't locked, child!" I pretended to be surprised and said, "I hadn't noticed. I am so hungry. Can I bake some potatoes?"

"Oh," said Grandma, "the potatoes are all gone. I've only a crust of bread and a few apples." I said that that would be wonderful, I was just dying for bread with apple.

I shall never forget how Grandma sat on the coal box crying. And I have often behaved so badly to her, and when Willi and I were alone we have referred to her as "the old girl," or "oldie," because at school everything is so up-to-date. Oh, Grandma! I do so love you!

Now I can't help crying myself.

SEPTEMBER 2, 1917

I MUST confess something else. Gretel and I recently from sheer greed stole from Frau Zahl in the baker's shop. Some kind of delicious-looking sugar-snails were laid out there; they made both our mouths water. When Frau Zahl went into the back room for a moment, I seized a snail as quick as lightning and hid it in my old shopping bag. Then Gretel did the same, quick as the wind; so we had two. Frau Zahl didn't notice anything, and we ate the snails later in the summerhouse. With delight! We kept gazing at each other and laughing as we ate. We felt no remorse at all. As I was licking my fingers, each tasting better than the other, I said to Gretel, pointing at myself, "Look—a snail eater!" Gretel clapped loudly and said, "We children have got to look after our nourishment." I am of course no longer a child, and stealing is stealing. Perhaps I shall regret it later.

WHITSUN 1918

PRESSED CLOSELY against each other, we [Piete and her grandmother] looked at the Bible. There it read, "But thou child, shalt be called the prophet of the Highest: for thou shalt go before the face of the Lord, to give light to them that sit in darkness."

My heart nearly stood still. Grandma told me to read the sentence again. Then she closed the Bible and said, "Take note of this. You will always find this text again, every time you open the Bible. It is God's will that you walk in that path. Don't forget that."

I leaned my face against Grandma's hand and rehearsed the text with her until I knew it by heart. I asked Grandma whether it would also be a part of my task to tell people that they should never go to war again.

"That too," said Grandma.

"But why has God permitted the war, Grandma?" I asked.

She answered, "You must never hold God responsible for the war. It is mankind that has made the war. We alone commit all the evil in the world." "But surely not natural disasters!" I said. "Earthquakes, storms, floods, hail, and so on."

Grandma said these were God's punishments for us, but we simply took no notice of that and just complained about everything. But Moses and the prophets had always recognized God's punishments and warned mankind.

"And was it of any use?"

"None at all."

Terrible. We never learn.

WHIT TUESDAY, 1918

VISITED GIL in the Flying Corps barracks. An NCO (very friendly, probably because I am a girl) asked me whom I wanted. But even before I could answer, he said, "It's Airman Kuhr, as I can see." "How can you see that?" I asked in astonishment. "By the resemblance," he said, smiling all over his face.

So I was allowed to pass. I had to wait in the rather cold guard-room, in which a sergeant sat at a long writing table rummaging among papers; there was also another older NCO there.

I waited quite a long time; then my brother came. But what did he look like! Was this Gil? This long, pale being in loose-fitting uniform with concertina trousers, thick boots, and a crazy-looking helmet? And his lovely soft, dark hair cut short? Oh, Gil, my brother Willi! I gazed at him flabbergasted. I was roused by the fact that he didn't cast a single glance toward little me, but clicked his heels together in front of the table, his hands pressed against his wretched trousers, his backbone straight as a ruler, his head held stiff and high, staring vacantly into space. Oh boy, oh Diary! Like a corpse! I have myself played the part of Lieutenant von Yellenic like this and so drilled my boys in the yard, until they mastered the rules just like Willi now.

But that was in a play. This is reality. My brother, the soldier!

AUGUST 17, 1918 [PIETE IS NOW WORKING FOR AN INFANTS' HOME IN SCHNEIDEMÜHL]

NOW THE poor little worm that was all skin and bone, and whom the doctor injected with a saline solution, has died too. He had become my darling. I devoted every spare moment to him, and he would look at me continually with his overserious eyes like a wise old man. He never smiled. This dear little boy died in my arms too; he simply laid his head, which looked much too big for the skeleton of a body, on my arm and died without a twitch or a rattle.

I bedded him down in the nicest possible way under the net covering after arranging round him as many flowers as I could find in the meadow behind the Catholic Church of the Holy Family. Surrounded by these, he looked horribly like a very old dwarf, who had been dead for a hundred years.

NOVEMBER 4, 1918

I SHALL soon finish my war diary. It will be the last war diary that I write in my life, for never again must there be a war, never again. If only the armistice agreements could just be signed, for fighting keeps flaring up again. On the south front the Italians have even seized Trieste and are advancing on Innsbruck. They encounter no real resistance anymore; it is said that the Austro-Hungarian army is in complete disarray. The Hungarians in particular want no more fighting, but want to get back to wives and children and rebuild their country. They want no more truck with the Emperor Karl . . .

Tomorrow we will take [a garland] to the prisoners' cemetery because it is my day off. Gretel asked if we wouldn't do better to take it to our "heroes" cemetery. But I said, "No—the others have no one to bring them a wreath."

NOVEMBER 29, 1918

GRANDMA GRUMBLED a bit when she heard that we intended to go all the way to the prisoners' cemetery and said we would get our feet wet in the snow. I put my slippers carefully at the back of the warm stove and looked into the oven to make sure everything was all right. There stood the blue tin can of coffee; so we were well prepared.

It was not still snowing, but everything was white, and the air misty and gray, a typical last-but-one day of November. Gretel trudged along beside me; she looked pretty, though, in her old thin coat. I looked at her sideways and declared, "Your cheeks are blue with cold." I rubbed her face with my woolen gloves till it was warm and rosy again.

The way to the prisoners' cemetery had never seemed so far to us; it was never-ending. Our shoes were soon full of snow. I could no longer feel my toes for cold. I had hung the wreath over my left shoulder; it pricked me in the face whenever I stumbled. We hardly made any headway, for we sank halfway up to our knees in snow. Although we had started out before three o' clock, it was already beginning to get dark. The sun hadn't once been visible all day. Gretel said that many of the pupils at her council school were ill with 'flu; also two teachers were away. The school is to be closed for fear of infection. Gretel said I must on no account get 'flu because I have become so thin and couldn't offer enough resistance to the illness. I laughed and answered that I would however resist it with my energy; besides, I had no time to be ill, for the sake of the poor little ones at the Infants' Home.

"And for my sake too," said Gretel, falling full-length in the snow. We laughed because at least thirty crows were so startled by Gretel's fall that they streaked, croaking and grumbling, across the snow field. "Shall we soon be there?" asked Gretel. "We have been so long on the way. Do you know the right path in the snow?"

I pointed ahead; there was already the first of the barbed wire that surrounded the graves. The low mounds were hardly recognizable under the mass of white; only the black wooden crosses stuck out a bit. And the trees suddenly appeared much smaller because the lower parts of their trunks were buried in the snow; everything looked uncannily different. When we reached the fence, we were amazed. So many crosses! We hadn't been for a long time; and now the prisoners' cemetery had suddenly become so big—enormous!

"Look," said Gretel, "they lie there so still!"

What can they all have died from? But in fact typhus and influenza had been around; there had been many cases of dysentery too, and some perhaps died from homesickness.

"Or hunger," whispered Gretel.

"Or hunger!" I agreed sadly.

"And now?" Gretel eyed the thick expanse of barbed wire . . .

So I climbed over the gate in spite of the barbed wire. While doing this, I grazed the skin on my legs, but I quickly dragged myself onto the wooden parapet and jumped down. "Wasn't so bad!" I assured Gretel, involuntarily softening my voice, although there was no one in the vicinity. "Give me the wreath. And wait here!"

"I'll wait," she whispered.

So many dead—! It was really already dark, but I could still read the names of the dead, not only Russians, as at the beginning of the war, but also French and English. There were even names in strange lettering, perhaps a Mohammedan. How did they come to be in our Schneidemühl camp? . . . How on earth was I to distinguish from the other graves? They were all just alike. In death all are, so to speak, just like the others.

AFTERWORD

After the war, Piete changed her name to Jo Mihaly. She achieved her ambition to be a dancer, and was already renowned by the time Hitler came to power in 1933. Piete initially spent her youth working in the sick children's home in Schneidemühl. In 1920, exhausted from this work, Piete joined her mother in Berlin and used all her extra cash earned as a typist in the city to fund secret dancing lessons. Three years passed before her ballet skills became so pronounced that she decided to confess to her mother and dedicate her life to dance.

In 1927, Piete married the prominent Jewish actor Leonard Steckel. They lived, together with their infant daughter Anja, in the notorious "Red Block," a Berlin colony for left-wing bohemians. Leonard was out rehearsing when the Nazis brutally raided the colony, removing many of the residents for transportation to prisons and concentration camps. It was not this, however, that prompted the family to flee Germany, but the unexpected arrival of an SS officer, who invited Piete to become a so-called cultural dancer for the Nazis. Many of Piete's dance routines contained an antiwar message. When Piete asked if she would be allowed to retain dances that expressed the persecution of the Jews, the officer politely suggested that she leave the country. She and Leonard left the following morning for Switzerland.

During the war, she was involved in activities to help the refugees in Switzerland. Besides this (she had to give up her dancing because of a heart condition that worsened during the occupation), she found creative expression in new forms: she wrote many books, stories, and articles for newspapers up until her death in 1989.

WORLD WAR II

1939–45

Voices

Nina Kosterina

Well, then, I am ready. . . . I want action,
I want to go to the front . . .

Born in 1921, Nina was a child during the difficult and uncertain postrev-olutionary years. Her father, a Moscow journalist, offered an account of his daughter's early life as she slept in a rudimentary cradle improvised from a trough, swaddled in his old partisan jackets. Although they strug-gled financially at first, family life was intimate and happy, with sum-mer holidays spent on the Volga, sitting around a campfire, listening to Mr. Kosterin's reminiscences of the heroic revolutionary days.

In the early part of the twentieth century, a left-wing political group called the Bolshevik Party led the revolution that eventually secured the party's control of Russia. Several of the key leaders were Vladimir Lenin, Leon Trotsky, and Joseph Stalin. The Bolshevik Revo-lution intended to overthrow the ruling elite and shift the balance of power in favor of the working classes. Consequently, a series of laws abolished rights to private property, permitting the seizure of lands by peasants; workers were given control over industry, while inheritance and similar class privileges were suspended. During this time, a work-ers' army was also established. Eventually, the party split into two groups, those who favored Leon Trotsky and his ultra-Communist stance, and those who favored Joseph Stalin, whose primary aim was to construct a new economic order, divergent from original Bolshevism. When the

Bolshevik leader Lenin died in 1924, Stalin rose to power. Trotsky was exiled to Mexico and eventually assassinated in 1940.

By the 1930s, Stalin's political control seemed dependent upon a strictly controlled and highly paranoid form of government. In order to control unrest and remove those who opposed his leadership, Stalin launched "the Great Purge," which involved the arrest, exile, or assassi- nation of millions of individuals deemed a threat to the ideal state he envisioned. High-profile trials were held in Moscow, through which So- viet officials of various ranks were brought to court under fabricated charges and often executed. However, many of those who opposed Stalin's regime were not brought to trial but simply "disappeared" without public- ity. As the child of a Communist, Nina was enrolled in the Young Com- munist League (Komsomol) at a time when Russia was in the shadow of the coming World War II. She witnessed her father, and other members of her family, "disappear," either to prison or into hiding, only to return when all individuals, sympathizers of the nation-state or not, were needed to fight the Nazis.

When the shadow of Nazi Germany appeared, Stalin underestimated Hitler, assuming that he would be able to negotiate a deal that would avoid outright war. Initially it appeared as if this would be achieved, as Stalin reached several agreements with Germany, including the 1939 German-Soviet Nonaggression Pact. Meanwhile, Hitler suspected that Russia was unready for war and saw fit to exploit this weakness. Hitler made the decision to invade Russia in December 1940, amassing troops on the borders of Russia throughout the spring of 1941. At dawn on June 22, 1941, German soldiers crossed into Russian territory, and war officially began. The initial weeks of war were devastating for the Russian troops, who lost over 2,000 planes in the first couple of days.

The courage of individuals like Nina resulted in a strong counteroffen- sive on the Moscow front, which pushed the German army back more than 200 miles. Germany had assumed a quick victory, and underestimated the impact of the Russian winter during the Battle of Stalingrad. The stoicism of the Russian people during the war years is almost unparalleled in history, but it came at a bitter and heavy cost. By the time they took Berlin and

*secured victory over Germany, upward of 15 million soldiers and civilians
had lost their lives, and countless others had been severely injured.*

JUNE 20, 1936

EXAMS ARE over. I am an eighth-year student! And suddenly, out of
nowhere, came the feeling—I shall keep a diary. Said, and done. But
what shall I call it? I thought about it for a long time. I began to ask
myself: Who am I? What am I? I have no talents of any kind . . . and,
thinking of how untalented I am, I decided to call my diary "Diary of
an Ordinary Girl." Completely ordinary. I don't even dream of anything special. Other girls dream of becoming doctors, engineers. To
me, the future is utterly hidden, in a fog.

I want to begin my diary with a date that is most vivid in my
memory. It was April 8, my fifteenth birthday. I gave a party, and my
guests were Alik, Boris, Volodya, Volya, Lusya, Tonya, and Vitya. Before the party, I was terribly nervous, afraid that everybody would be
bored. But the evening went beautifully—I've never had so much fun
at a birthday party. Also, this was the first time that I "ventured" to
dance with boys—with Alik and Vitya. When Alik put his arm around
my waist, and I put my hand on his shoulder, a shiver ran through
me—it was such an exciting and happy feeling. I have been dancing
for a long time, I love to dance, but I have never enjoyed it so much
before. Alik was fooling around and lifted me up in the air. My heart
stopped, I could not catch my breath, and my cheeks flamed . . .

Afterward, we played forfeit games, and Alik and I kissed. The
first time, he kissed me; the second time, I kissed him, when he was
saying good-bye. We also played "flirt of the flowers." Volodya and
Lusya turned it into a flirtation between themselves. I did not like the
game and stopped playing. There were other games too. Everybody
stayed late, until eleven o'clock.

It was a good party. It reinforced my friendship with the boys, but cooled off my relations with the girls. Oglobina was especially angry and later called me a "toady." There were many arguments about that, and finally she was transferred to another class.

The May Day celebrations were very gay. We marched in demonstrations across Red Square; I saw all the leaders. We sang, danced, shouted . . . And in the evening we went to see the operetta *The Bird Seller*. I loved it.

I must tell about the visit to the Museum of Fine Arts. I went with the whole family. But in the museum I went off by myself: I wanted to see whatever I felt like, and to look at it alone as I felt like. There were many things I liked, but best of all was a certain French painting: a seacoast, ships in the distance, beautiful, branching trees on the shore, and a crowd of people stretching their arms toward the sea in panic and despair. There was also an English painting—a woman in a gray dress, with a riding crop in her hand, standing on a veranda.

But the conclusion I drew from this visit to the museum was that I must go again, and next time with a guide.

Now I must make a record for myself of the important events of the period: Gorky died, and a draft for a new constitution has been published. The constitution is something I understand very little, although I feel that this is an event of great importance for our country. But Gorky's death was like a personal sorrow to me. We have his complete works. I've read many of them, and some stirred me so much that I could not sleep. And now, Gorky is gone. . . .

There was also a lot of anxiety in connection with my admission to the Komsomol. I have, generally, been reading the newspapers, but all the same I had to go to Father for help. He talked to me for two hours, reminding me about many things and explaining others, especially about the constitution. After the talk with him, I went to the District Committee, and everybody was nervous. I did not like the District Committee office: dirty, with smudged, dingy walls, nowhere to sit down. It seemed to me that I was calm, but others said that I came out of the office white as chalk. They gave me a membership card, tiny-tiny, white.

At home I showed it to Papa. He caught me in his arms and threw me up and kissed me. "Good girl, Ninok!" He said it in such a way that I was filled with joy and pride . . .

Let me list the books I have read lately. I read Kolchin's *Peasant Girls*. I liked it very much. Hugo's *The Man Who Laughs* almost made me flunk the physics test—I got so absorbed in reading, I forgot that I had to prepare for the exam.

During the examination days I went twice to the Kamerny Theater and saw the movie *The Circus* three times. Orlova is marvelous!

During exams Papa made a promise: if I did well, we would go to Khvalynsk. Yesterday was the last exam—geography. I passed. I've graduated from the Seven-Year School. Hurrah, we are going to Khvalynsk!

OCTOBER 20, 1936

WE SAW Papa today. He even shed a tear or two before starting on his long journey, and everybody's eyes were wet.

Yesterday Papa bought me a guitar. I was so happy I threw my arms around his neck and wouldn't stop kissing him. Such a pity he had to go. For two years now we shall be without the companion of our frequent surprise outings in the country, which Father was so clever at thinking up. A fire somewhere in a clearing, *shashlyk* roasting on the coals. For himself, he would bring some vodka, for us—a soft drink. We'd eat the half-raw bits of meat—they smelled of smoke—wash them down with a drink, and start singing, "Glorious sea, sacred Baikal . . ." Mobs of people came to our house these past few days—Father's friends and colleagues.

Now I am sitting and strumming the guitar. I have already gone through four lessons in the instruction book.

Yesterday we had a Komsomol meeting. Mulka reported on his work as organizer. A committee of three was elected. My assignment to work with the Oktyabryata group was confirmed, despite my fervent refusals.

November 7, 1936

At last, the holidays! We'll have some fun now!

Last night I was in a dreadful mood, I don't even know why. I cried all evening and wanted to die. I fell asleep in tears. But today everything is singing inside me. I jumped up early, feeling marvelous. We had tea with Grandmother's cakes. Then off to school. Stayed there until eleven, then went to the Institute of Law. The students were no longer there, but we managed to find them later in a kind of dead-end block off Hertzen Street. We sang and danced for an hour and a half to the music of an accordion.

At two we went to Red Square. I saw Stalin. There was some confusion beyond the square. We were caught in a crush in a narrow street and were swept along. Lidka, naturally, started screaming, and we shouted at her. When we were dragged out to a wider street, things eased up, but the militiamen blocked the way and began to force everybody into a wide detour. Suddenly we heard cries, "They broke through, they broke through [the militia chain]!" . . . We rushed there. The militia were pressed to the wall, everybody was running, and we ran with them.

In the evening, Sima came to pick me up. Stella and Lelya pestered us and we had to take them along. First we went to Arbat Square, where the children's exhibits were. In all the show windows there were marvelous models of the Artek Children's Sanatorium, of characters from Pushkin's fairy tales, and so on. Mobs of people in the street. From Arbat we sent Stella and Lelya home, and went on to the Manege, where they'd built a stage and a platform for dancing. We looked at the stands of the food industries, then we wanted to dance, but there was too much of a crush. We went on to Theatre Square. I liked Stalin's portrait, about as big as the Mostorg Building. On the way back we stopped off at the Manege Square and danced our fill. I came home at eleven, with aching feet.

You must have heard that Nikolay Ostrovsky died recently. We went to see him in his coffin. He died at the age of thirty-two. Did you read his book *How Steel Was Tempered*? If you didn't, read it. It is a marvelous book.

Verochka just woke up and will probably start bawling. She is a good baby, everybody loves her. She laughs so hard, as if she understood things.

I have many girlfriends at school, but my best friend is Lena Gershman. We sit at the same desk.

We are decorating our tree. We made lots of toys, bought twenty-five candles, beads, shiny balls, and so on. We shall also go to parties at Stella's and Irma's—they're our cousins.

I have a pretty new dress, blue, with a white collar and white belt. I'll wear it today. They also bought me high-heeled slippers and new stockings. Now I am considered a young lady. Our Lelya has eczema. It is spreading to her face. She is as skinny as ever.

Good-bye,

NINA

JANUARY 25, 1937

I HAVE neglected my diary—my first entry this year.

Briefly, about January: the twelve days of vacation passed very pleasantly, although I did not go away to the country. I often go to the skating rink, and also to the theater. During January, I saw *Woe from Wit, The Marvellous Alloy, Princess Turandot,* and *Floridsdorf.* School-work is going badly. To heck with it, I am tired of school . . .

The second Trotskyite trial is going on now. Frightful revelations. All of them will probably be shot.

JANUARY 31, 1937

OUR POOR kitten died. She wasn't given a chance to live, somebody poisoned her. And we don't know who could have done such a vile thing. She was always so gay and playful, but the last few days she vomited and did not eat. Yesterday Lelya and Margarita went to the doctor. He gave them a medicine, but "kitty" died before it came.

I remember the day we brought her home. She was so tiny, so helpless! All she did was lie on her yellow cushion. Such a darling kitten! The whole house is sorry now. Yet, when we collected the money for the doctor, all we got was eighty kopeks. The rest—to make up the three rubles—came from me and Lelya. We contributed our entire savings.

FEBRUARY 7, 1937

THE TERRIBLE trial is over. Of course, they will be shot. How could it have happened that old revolutionaries who had fought for decades for a people's government became enemies of the people? . . .

At school, things are picking up. We play volleyball and go skiing. A few days ago there was a funny incident: I climbed up on the window to close the transom. Suddenly Svetlov ran up to me, caught me around the waist, and lifted me down. Everybody gasped, and I was so embarrassed that I ran away. Afterward they all laughed at me and Svetlov. But generally, Svetlov is disgusting; he is always trying to put his arms around you or something else of the kind. I received a letter from Nastya and still have not answered it. She asked me to send her a hat, but, to be frank, I have no patience to bother with hats.

FEBRUARY 21, 1937

GRIGORY KONSTANTINOVICH Ordzhonikidze is dead. Lida, Svetlana, Lena Gershman, and I went to the Hall of Columns at the House of Trade Unions.

Loss after loss: Kirov, Kuybyshev, Gorky, Ordzhonikidze—our old guard is dying off . . .

Today Mulka, Vovka, and I went with the TETs workers to Red Square. We saw all the leaders on the reviewing stand.

On February 7 we had a costume ball dedicated to Pushkin. I was dressed as Masha, the captain's daughter, in a long orange dress with white lace around the throat and on the sleeves. And, of course, I wore a mask. I felt wonderful all evening. The costume was very good for dancing. Svetlana was the Queen of Shemakha, and Valya was a Circassian girl. My costume was judged the best.

Today I finally answered Nastya. I wrote her about the New Year's

Eve parties, the skating rink, the hat, the skis, the Institute, Ordzhonikidze, and so on.

I received her letter February 1, and only answered it today. So that's how things are!

MARCH 25, 1937

SOMETHING FRIGHTFUL and incomprehensible has happened: they arrested Uncle Misha, Father's brother, and his wife, Anya. Irma, our little cousin, was sent to a children's home. They say that Uncle Misha was involved with some counterrevolutionary organization. What is going on? Uncle Misha, a member of the Party from the very first days of the Revolution—and suddenly an enemy of the people!

MARCH 27, 1937

I CAN'T understand what is happening to Mother. All she does is scream and scold.

Today I scrubbed the floors, bought bread, went to the hospital for her, washed all the dishes, and took care of Verochka all day. Then I happened to touch Lelya's toys, Lel'ka began to squeal (her tears are never far), and Mother swooped down on me like a hawk to defend her. I got smacked too. And she screamed at me—I'm nasty, I'll be an old maid, and so on, and so forth. All right, to the devil with her. Mother always takes Lel'ka's part.

MARCH 29, 1937

I CRIED again today. It's all Mother's fault. She scolds me all day. What does she want? Life has become a daily torture. . . . I wish I could go to Father in the Far East.

APRIL 16, 1937

MY BIRTHDAY passed unnoticed. Only Tonya gave me a present—a little red purse. Everybody has forgotten us and our mother.

And now another dreadful thing. It's beyond understanding.

Stella's father was arrested. He was a department chief at the People's Commissariat of Heavy Industry. They say he was a wrecker. . . .

Yesterday I had a fight with the boys. One of the kids began to throw sand at Denisova, and she was scared and kept quiet. She hasn't got a bit of self-respect. The girls were playing volleyball, and the game broke up. I was just standing and waiting. Then I saw one of the boys bending down to pick up some sand to throw at me. But before he had a chance to raise his hand, I rushed at him and pulled at his collar so hard that his shirt tore, then hit him in the face. And . . . stopped! That was my mistake. I should have given him a thorough beating after I started, but I stopped. The kid took advantage of it and punched me in the nose and the eye. I saw sparks, and he, naturally, ran away. . . .

Now I laugh at it, but yesterday I was furious—most of all at myself. I ought to know how to fight properly.

AUGUST 22, 1937

A DREADFUL misfortune has hit our landlords.

Today our landlord unexpectedly came home from work at noon. Marusya, his daughter, thought he was sick, he was so upset and pale. But two other men came in after him and began to search the house. They went through the landlord's rooms, then started on ours. These people were full of an odd icy courtesy. I was so stunned, I could not move. The landlord's linen closet stood in our room. After they looked through the closet, the two NKVD agents wanted to search our things too, but the landlord told them that we were summer visitors. He was chalk white and so confused that when they pointed at me and asked, "Is this your daughter?" he said "Yes!" Afterward they all went to the landlord's part of the house and talked about something for a long time. Then we heard the landlord saying loudly, with a break in his voice, as if keeping back his tears, "Well, good-bye. . . ." Then everybody burst out crying, and loudest of all, Marusya. She rushed to her father screaming, "Daddy, Daddy . . . Where are they taking you? . . ." The landlord could no longer restrain himself and started crying. Marusya clung to him so desperately that I began to cry too. He finally tore himself away from her and quickly walked out. The two polite, cold men walked out after him.

They went. And everybody, including us, cried. I went to the landlord's rooms and tried to console Marusya. When she calmed down a little, she suddenly jumped up:

"I'm going after him!"

After lunch Marusya came back with her mother. As soon as her mother entered, she began to wail. Grandmother tried to console her, and the landlady said that her husband had been arrested on suspicion of Trotskyism.

I thought about it for a long time. I remembered the arrests of Irma's and Stella's fathers. Something strange is happening. I thought and thought, and came to the conclusion: if my father also turns out to be a Trotskyite and an enemy of his country, I shall not be sorry for him!

I wrote this, but (I confess) there is a gnawing worm of doubt.

SEPTEMBER 13, 1937
DEAR PAPA!

How are you out there? Lelya and I miss you very much. I am doing well at school and taking part in all the activities. I work with the Pioneers in Lelya's class. She is also good at school. Her eczema persists despite all treatment. I was elected to the Komsomol committee. Recently we took up the case of one of the girls. Her mother and father had been arrested. At first I disagreed with the motion to expel her, but later the others convinced me, and I voted for the expulsion. Still, I am not certain that she should have been expelled. The girl cried, she did not want to leave the Komsomol, but at the same time she said that she loved her mother and father and would never repudiate them. After the meeting, I felt terrible, and when I came home I cried for a long time. How is it her fault if her parents were arrested for something?

Come back soon, Papa, if you can. It is dreary and lonely
at home without you.

Many, many kisses,

Your loving daughter,

NINA

NOVEMBER 30, 1937

THE DAY before yesterday was very foggy. The fog lasted all day and all
night and all day yesterday until evening. Lena and I ran through the
streets, observing the life of the city in the fog. The whole city, so
familiar since childhood, all the streets and squares and alleys were
changed as in a fairy tale. All the sharp, angular lines became blurred,
the buildings seemed taller and wider. Even the sounds were drowned
and muted. We walked, listened, and looked. It was very interesting:
even the sidewalk across the street was invisible! Cars moved slowly
with their headlights on and blew their horns continually. Streetcars
and buses inched along cautiously, their bells ringing. And yet there
were many accidents. Pedestrians looked like shadows two or three
steps away, and then melted into the fog.

Yesterday, Lena, Grisha Grinblat, and I came to Tatyana Alexandrovna's to work. We are preparing an exhibition for the Twentieth
Anniversary of the Revolution. The members of the history circle are
taking an active part in it. I worked with enthusiasm—writing, cutting
out, pasting. Tatyana Alexandrovna was very pleased with my work. But
I also found time to flirt with Grisha. Tatyana Alexandrovna said I had
a crush on him. Of course that's nonsense. After we finished, Tatyana
Alexandrovna served us tea, and I acted as hostess at the table. She is a
remarkable person, and I wonder why she is not a Party member.

DECEMBER 15, 1937

I RECEIVED a letter from Father:

DEAR NINA!
Forgive me for not writing you. I am not in a letter-writing
mood, and I'll tell you why. I was expelled from the Party

and, consequently, dismissed from my post. I shall not go into details: at your age much will still be unclear to you. But you must remember one thing: you will need a great deal of calm and endurance now. I do not know as yet how events will turn for me. But even in the worst case, you must be sure that your father was never a scoundrel or double-dealer, and has never blemished his name by anything dirty or base. And therefore—be steadfast! Of course, these are difficult days, but we must not and should not lose courage. We shall live through and overcome all ordeals. Believe me that your dad still has "enough powder in his powder keg," and has no intention to bow before adversity.

Regards to Lelya and Verushka. Kiss Mama and Grandmother and all the rest.

YOUR DAD

DECEMBER 20, 1937

THERE WAS a terrible and ugly row at home today.

A friend of Papa's, Esfir Pavlovna, just came from the Far East and telephoned us. Mama was out, and I spoke . . .

APRIL 15, 1938

WELL! I have just heard a declaration of love! And from whom? Heavens, even the diary will be surprised and burst out laughing! Grisha! I don't want to and I cannot write about it now. I don't know how I got home after he told me. I cannot eat, I cry and I laugh. Lelya looks at me with alarm. I don't know what to do, and try to stuff her with candy. She is surprised and refuses to take it. I tell her I got excellent in school. She does not believe me . . .

APRIL 17, 1938

I'VE CALMED down a little, and now I can write down what happened.

When Lena told me she had a great sorrow, I decided to find out from Grisha how he felt about Lena. He was walking home, and I asked whether he had any sorrows. He said he didn't. Then I asked, was he suffering about anything? And he said, "One doesn't speak about such things." I persisted, and asked how he felt about Lena. He said frankly that he had stopped noticing her and had cooled off toward her. "Why?" I insisted, since I considered him a friend and nothing else. Then he said, "I like you, Ninka, I like you very much." I tried to turn it into a joke and said that he was still a kid, that Lena was a fine girl, and a pretty one, and that I could not imagine how he could possibly fall in love with me after Lena.

"You think Lena is pretty?" he asked. I said yes, and was completely sincere. Lena really is a very pretty girl. "And I would not like you to be like her!" said Grisha.

We walked for a long time after that, and I said to him in parting: "You may feel whatever you wish about me, but I still consider you only a friend." He held my hand in his and asked me to forgive him for blurting out his secret. "You insisted on it yourself." "Nonsense," I said, "don't get upset about it. How cold your hands are. . . . Good-bye, Grisha."

But when I entered the gateway, my legs turned to water and I pressed myself against the wall. . . .

Yesterday our meeting was a little strained. He was embarrassed and upset, and there was a guilty look in his eyes. Today he was calmer.

Lena is in a dreadful state. She does not do her assignments and sits at her desk, dull and apathetic. I feel very sorry for her, but I don't know how to help her. I am not in love with Grisha, there's simply a good, comradely feeling. . . . But then, who knows . . . if this goes on, I may even fall in love.

April 20, 1938

I had a strange dream last night.

Grisha and I were sitting at a table in some room, so near that our heads touched. Lena was also in the room doing something behind us. She asked, "What are you talking about?" We turned our faces to one another and smiled, without answering Lena. A strand of my hair fell over my forehead, and I wanted to put it back, but our heads were so close that my hand brushed against Grisha's hair, and I stroked it. It was very pleasant to touch his hair. Then Lena said, "Well, I'm going." And we went to walk her home. She seemed to be going to give birth to her second child. I wondered, "But where is the first?" But she did not answer. Somebody screamed, but Grisha said, "It's nothing to be alarmed about," and I calmed down. . . .

What silly nonsense one dreams of!

The radio was just playing Tchaikovsky's romance, "I do not know whether I love you, but it seems to me that I do." I've become amazingly romantic lately, I've even begun to love the moon. . . . Last night I looked for it, but I did not find it.

APRIL 22, 1938

LAST EVENING Grisha and I agreed by telephone to meet earlier today, to go to the museum. As we were walking, we bumped into Nina and Olga. They began to giggle and make hints about us, about our being inseparable, always together. We hurried away from them. I was so embarrassed that I could not say anything for a long time. When we came to the museum, we met a group of kids, Lena among them. It seemed to me that she gave me a probing look. Well, it's time for her to guess at the truth. After our visit to the museum, Lena went home at once, although I begged her to come up to my house.

I've lost a lot of weight these past few days, and everybody at home keeps asking why I've become so thin, am I in love?

Incidentally, Grisha confessed recently that he has begun to keep a diary again. I wonder if he'll ever let me read it.

MAY 2, 1938

ON APRIL 30 Grisha and I went to see the gala illumination. We walked to the center of the city, along the embankment, but there was nothing new. Our conversation was more interesting than the lights. We spoke of many things. Later, when we were already on the way home, I said that I would transfer to another school next year. "Why?"

"Well, perhaps I won't, depending on circumstances." He interpreted this as meaning that I was tired of him, and said quietly:

> I'm melting the windowpane with my brow.
> Will there or won't there be love?
> And will it be great, or will it be tiny?

"The latter seems more likely, I guess," he concluded.

My lips trembled, and my eyes filled with tears. It hurt me to think that he considered our love "tiny." I felt sad that all of this would soon be over. He noticed my tears and became upset, trying to find out what was wrong with me. I explained to him why I wanted to transfer to another school. "It will be painful for me to remain in this school if everything ends between us." He had thought that I was seeing him just "for lack of something better to do," that I was simply amusing myself with him. I was shocked, and told him in veiled words that I love him. He glowed with joy and begged forgiveness for his words. We parted reconciled and promised each other to avoid misunderstandings in the future.

May 7, 1938

I GAVE Lena my diary. She read it and said, "I expected it from him, but not from you."

We took a long walk in the evening. It was raining, but we had an umbrella and we walked disregarding weather and time. At first Lena said, "After this, I do not love him anymore." But then she repeated again and again that she loves him to the point of madness. For a long time I tried to console her and to assure her that the situation could be mended. She complained of her lack of character and envied mine (found something to envy, really!). Lena confessed that when she was with Grisha, she suddenly became tongue-tied and could not say anything. She also said she was jealous, and that it would be hard for all of us to be at the same school.

Today the three of us remained after classes to arrange certain materials. Lena was in a wretched mood. Grisha asked her why the funereal face. "It's nothing at all." She did not walk home with us.

I must admit that when we three are together, I find it doubly difficult: first, because I feel guilty, and second . . . because I am jealous! What a character. I am no longer sure that Grisha feels indifferent toward Lena.

But why should I care? After all, I don't love him. That's the whole trouble—I no longer understand myself. Now it seems to me that I do love him. He was so extraordinary today. He took a red ribbon I used as a bookmark from my book and would not give it back. He also scowled and returned it. But how handsome he was at that moment!

Yesterday Lena assured me that I would come to love him, that he was a wonderful person and we were very well suited. She almost cried, called herself an idiot, and accused no one but herself for his cooling off. She had always been silent with him, he was bored, and the flame went out. . . .

May 10, 1938

Yesterday Grisha and I went walking, and suddenly he began to insist, "Tell me, tell me what you feel." I said, "I don't understand myself anymore. I don't know whether I love you or not." He said that he wanted to be alone, and we said good-bye. In parting, he asked me not to think about it and to leave everything to time.

I feel rotten. All I long for is to get through with the exams and get away, as far as possible.

May 11, 1938

Dismal mood. I want to cry.

It's a strange thing. When I see him, it seems to me that I don't love him. And when he's away, I go mad with longing for him. . . .

Mama scolds. Uncle Misha came yesterday from Baku. He had a few drinks with Grandmother, and today he went out somewhere and disappeared. Grandmother went to the militia to report a missing person. She came back even angrier, now she just sits there and drinks.

May 22, 1938

Yesterday Grisha called and invited me for a walk. I refused, saying I was going to study. But two hours later I called him myself. I waited for him on the boulevard and watched the children. I love children. . . .

Then we went wandering through the streets without aim or direction. It began to rain. We hid under a canopy and stood there for a long time without speaking. And silently we said to one another more than we could have said with words. He took my hand and pressed it hard.

And at home, unexpectedly, there was something terrible and beyond understanding. My lost Uncle Misha was back. It turned out that he had come to Moscow to seek protection for his brother, arrested in Baku. He had gone to the NKVD to ask for justice and protection, and there he was arrested. Now he looks altogether confused and frightened. He was telling us about the shocking goings-on in Baku and kept looking over his shoulder and talking in whispers. At the NKVD they kept him all these days, and when they let him go, they advised him to keep quiet about his brother. In the evening, the family had a celebration—at least, he was free. We sang "In the Wild Steppes Beyond Baikal." Grandmother started crying. I went to the other room, feeling terribly sad. Now they are singing "Glorious Sea, Sacred Baikal" once again. Papa sings it especially well. . . . Soon, soon I shall see him at last. . . .

SEPTEMBER 7, 1938

WHAT OMINOUS darkness has shrouded my whole life. Father's arrest is such a blow that it bends my back. Until now I have always carried my head high and with honor, but now . . . Now Akhmetov can say to me, "We're comrades in misfortune!" And just to think how I despised him and despised his father, a Trotskyite. The nightmare thought oppresses me day and night: Is my father also an enemy? No, it cannot be, I don't believe it! It's all a terrible mistake!

Mother is calm and steadfast. She tries to reassure us; she is forever going somewhere, writing to someone, and feels sure that the misunderstanding will soon be cleared up.

SEPTEMBER 10, 1938

DESOLATION AND gloomy silence at home. Nobody is doing anything. Grandmother cries all the time—our father was her favorite
son-in-law. After all, he was a friend of our grandfather, her husband, who died in the Civil War. After Grandfather's death, Father
never broke his ties with the family. He married Mama soon afterward, while he was still fighting. To top it all, there is no news of Uncle Ilyusha. He should have been here from Transbaikal by now,
but he has disappeared. We have decided that he was probably
arrested too.

Mama is looking for work. With Father here, we never knew
want. Now everything is falling to pieces. . . .

I have no one to share my troubles with. It seems to me that Lena
is too preoccupied with some problems of her own, but she does not
confide in me. She has become secretive and draws away from me into
her own world like an oyster in its shell.

And I am sunk in a deep, gnawing depression. Everything
is either repulsive or meaningless. Yesterday, Lena, Zhora, and I
saw *On the Banks of the Neva* at the Maly Theater. It was a very
good play, and the acting was good, but I watched with cold indif-
ference.

I think I shall probably have a fight with Grisha soon. We are
both to blame. He is closer to Lena, and calls me "Ninka." And I flare
up at every word I don't like. The cleft between us is widening and
deepening.

That is my character: at night I'll cry and curse myself for my
rudeness and quick temper, and in the morning I'll be still sharper
and more rude. A savage character.

Father used to say, half joking, that we have stormy Slavic blood
with a Tartar streak. "Yes, we're Scythians . . . with slanting, greedy
eyes . . ."

And now all the young Kosterins—my father and Uncle Misha—
are supposedly enemies of the people. How can I, their daughter in
flesh and blood, believe this?

SEPTEMBER 13, 1938

LENA SPOKE to me about herself. Grisha had said to her, "I tore the old love out of my heart with the roots, and I love you—but it is not a great love." Lena accepted it and wrote him a letter, saying that she loves him. I involuntarily burst out laughing and told Lena that it was nonsense— a man could not so easily stop loving one girl and begin to love another. Whoever tells a girl that he loves her "a little"? Grisha is an idiot, and Lena does not understand that he is simply "playing a game."

SEPTEMBER 26, 1938

WHAT A fool I am, how I despise myself for calling Grisha—twice in a row. Of course he was home, but they told me he was out. He's probably thinking, "What a pest!"

And today he suddenly handed me a note offering his friendship, as he sees that I "do not have enough" friends. At first I almost burst into tears, then I flew into a rage and wrote him a rude and sharp reply.

And still another unpleasantness: Lena is leaving our school. Her father transferred her to another one. I got dreadfully upset. . . .

Generally, I am in a terrible state of mind. Something is badly wrong with me lately. We're studying chloroform in chemistry, and I had a sudden nasty little thought: it would be good to put an end to everything all at once. I quickly stopped myself, forced myself to think about something else.

OCTOBER 2, 1938

AUTUMN. Foggy drizzle and mud. Where is Papa now? How is he?

Someone is playing melancholy, mournful music on a violin. I think of these desolate days of my life. I have not lived yet, but I keep thinking: Is there any sense in going on?

My friendships are breaking up.

My note to Grisha also made our break final. He is turning away from me. I feel that I could still make things right if I wanted. But I can't. I seem to do everything as if to spite myself. I approach him intending to say one thing and say the opposite. What is this? Why?

Lena has been at the new school for two days. She likes it there. I miss her very much. All these days I feel with particular sharpness that I have no one else, that she is my only friend. . . . And she is so far away!

OCTOBER 7, 1938

THERE'S A stony weight in my chest. In such a mood I don't have much control of myself and may do something bad. I went to see Tatyana Alexandrovna. She told me things that convinced me even more what a vile, nasty creature I am.

Yesterday I called Grisha and asked him to come to the reading room. He came. Then he walked me home. And today he telephoned and we went bicycle riding. He is very calm. I did not notice my agitation in him . . . or any feelings.

There were moments yesterday when a heavy, empty silence fell between us. Between friends silence is often more expressive than words. With us, there is only emptiness. But why does it trouble me so? After all, I repulsed him. Or am I really a monster who tries to get a man to fall in love only to repel him rudely? Tatyana Alexandrovna is right in suspecting that I have some very bad traits. But all of this is not intentional, I do not want to do what I am doing. Why, then, does it turn out like this? It sometimes even frightens me . . .

I told Grisha that I needed friendship, and therefore rejected his love. Before I sat down to my diary I said to myself, "I love him." But I was afraid to write it down, because it would lead immediately to "I don't love him." What is he: a toy, a rubber ball? I may be losing something great and significant, but I must step aside.

What am I living for? What is ahead for me? It is frightening to think that so much suffering has come to me in just a few short months, and that it's breaking me up so badly. And time crawls like a long sleepless night—a sticky, tormenting night without rest. . . .

By chance, I came across his poem, written last spring:

Tonight an autumn wind is howling,
Blinding my eyes with rain.

Today, for the last time, we parted,
With final words, not to be heard again . . .

I am reading these words, and tears fall on the page. . . .

NOVEMBER 1, 1938
I HAVE a strange premonition of still more disasters in our family. I often dream about Father. I did last night. It seemed that he came home—a gloomy stranger, and . . . wearing a tie. He never dressed like that. I woke and felt so bitterly wretched, I could have howled like a wolf. . . .

MARCH 25, 1939
VACATION TIME, and I am disgustingly lazy.

I have just come from Lena. Grisha was there too. I have been spending much time with Grisha lately, and our relations are excellent. He told me that he tried to fool himself and me. He loves me. My feeling toward him is also more than friendship. But it is altogether different now. Much calmer, but deeper and more serious. I don't show it, though, and don't intend to. Let it be friendship.

I am sorry for Lena. I am happy, and she is lonely.

Hurrah! A telegram. Ilya is free and asks us to send him money for the fare.

There is rejoicing at home, but I think of Father. . . .

MARCH 27, 1939
How DAMNED good life is, in spite of everything! I shall soon be eighteen! That's a lot, isn't it?

I am eighteen, I am loved, and I love!

Beautiful!

AUGUST 2, 1939
LENA CAME to see me yesterday. When I was walking her home, we ran into Grisha. And, of course, we went wandering through the streets.

And behaved as stupidly as usual when the three of us are together. I was fooling around, kidding Grisha. Now wanting to take him by the arm, now quarreling with him. Lena was furious because Grisha was not attentive to her. She loves him and expects more than simple, friendly relations with him. And he, the good-for-nothing, does not notice anything—neither her pain nor her love. Lena is generally kind and restrained, but yesterday she could not control herself and needled me.

DECEMBER 7, 1939

LATE EVENING. It's going on eleven. The weather—right out of Blok's "The Twelve": wind and snow, snow and wind.... As you cross the bridge near Gorky Park, you see the white snowy distance stretching along the Moskva River. Far, far away is a dark strip of woods, overhead—the powerful and at the same time lacy light structure of the bridge, and over everything—the heavy Moscow sky. It has a unique beauty of its own, especially in the evening hour when the setting sun sends up its purple and scarlet flares from beyond the greenery of Newkuchny Park.

YES, GRISHA, everything you said was true....

To part and go in different directions, to lose the best there is in life—friendship, love—you understand yourself that I will not be able to do it.

I have told you that life without you seems empty to me. Not dull—no, sometimes even more gay, but empty, devoid of deep, satisfying meaning. You bring into my life something better than the things people usually live by. You bring good feelings, you bring the genuine essence of life....

JANUARY 20, 1940

I LOVE Moscow. Last night I had insomnia. I turned from side to side for a long time, trying to fall asleep. Then I got up quietly and went out. It was after three. Silent, deserted streets, a fine, bracing frost . . . I walked without aim and without choosing direction. Crossed the center of town. Red Square, the Kremlin and the scarlet flag over it—I saw it all with new eyes and with a new feeling. I cannot even define what I felt at the time. There are no words. What a pity I don't know music. Only a solemn symphony could probably express the emotions, moods, and vague images that took possession of me at that silent hour before dawn.

Leaving the center, I immersed myself in the twilit stillness of the Zamoskvorechye streets and alleys.

Moscow! The very word stirs me and fills my soul with pride, with the rhythms of ancient songs and epic tales. Thousands of years have passed over you, Moscow! Out of the ravages of fires, plagues, famine, out of the greedy paws of invaders and bloody internecine strife, you rose again and again, each time more beautiful, mightier, and dearer to the Russian heart. Thunderclouds are gathering on the horizon. But can they frighten Moscow? Moscow may be leveled by flames, but like the fabled Phoenix, she will rise from the ashes still mightier and more fair than ever.

FEBRUARY 24, 1940

IF WAR comes, I am ready for it. One thing is bad: I cannot learn to shoot well because of my nearsightedness, and I don't feel like saddling myself with glasses.

MARCH 8, 1940

A COLD, empty gulf is widening between old friends. I thought of Nastya in Khvalynsk. Something faraway and childish, but beautiful. . . . Long years apart have killed the beautiful childhood friendship. But Grisha and Lena? Especially Grisha? Love came to nothing, and friendship is also turning sour and moldy.

SEPTEMBER 22, 1940

I JUST read over last summer's notes, and felt sad.

Everything I dreamed of is gone: deep, strong emotions, sincerity in love. Something flared up and went out, like a will-o'-the-wisp.

I have lately begun to think more and more often of Grisha. And I regret the lost pure friendship and love. And Lena? I loved her very much, and still do. . . . How good it would be to meet as before, and talk and talk. . . . But all the paths are overgrown with grass. . . .

NOVEMBER 30, 1940

THE FIRST letter from Father, and what a terrible one: a special NKVD court pronounced him a "socially dangerous element" and sentenced him to imprisonment for five years. He spent more than two years in prison while under investigation. Twenty-six months! Yet it's astonishing how full the letter is of strength and freshness. To spend all that time in prison (perhaps under the same conditions as Uncle Ilyusha!), to be condemned to five years, and then describe with such zest the place where they had sent him for "reeducation." A wild canyon, a cold, crystalline, transparent, rapid forest stream. Papa was assigned as a work-team leader on a road-building project. His team consists of three former border guard lieutenants and two workers. All of them either "dangerous elements" or "active Trotskyites," etc. Father wrote a beautiful description of the taiga and his comrades in misfortune. And he sent us a song composed in prison by a Moscow operetta singer.

I liked both the letter and the song very much, but Mother flew into a rage. "Is he guilty, or is he not guilty? Why doesn't he appeal the sentence? Writes all sorts of drivel, and not a word about important things. . . ." She is planning to write to someone.

JUNE 23, 1941

DO YOU remember, Nina Alexeyevna, how you secretly dreamed of experiencing great and stirring events, how you dreamed of storms and danger? There you have it—war! A predatory black beast has suddenly swooped down from behind dark clouds on our homeland.

Well, then, I am ready. . . . I want action, I want to go to the front. . . .

JULY [DATE UNKNOWN] 1941

WE DON'T know what to do. Hysterical telegrams keep coming from Moscow: "Continue work . . . ," "Wind up . . ." And if we are to "wind up," where are we to go?

What is happening at the front is unimaginable—the Fascists have sliced into us like a knife into butter. . . . And everywhere—perplexed questions and shocked, puzzled eyes: are we so weak?

SEPTEMBER 1, 1941

THE FUTURE is dark and menacing. . . . But I shall go into this future, that's decided. . . .

The pale blue sky is covered with feathery clouds, the sun is hot, and all around me there are woods. I shall never forget the Tambov woods. Beloved forest! You were our friend, tender and welcoming, you shielded our love from inquisitive, sometimes venomous glances, you sheltered us with your dense branches and whispered fairy tales to us. . . .

And the meadows, carpeted in early summer with multicolored flowers—I shall not forget them either. I braided the field flowers into wreaths and crowned my beloved with them. . . .

The mowers have bared the land. Flowers and grasses fell before the sharp, ringing scythes, and haystacks now rise amid the gray, desolate fields. At first, the stacks were fluffy and aromatic. Now, washed by rains, they have darkened and shrunk. On my favorite clearing there is also a haystack—solitary and gloomy.

OCTOBER 28, 1941

I CAME to Moscow October 24, and was badly shaken by my first impressions. It began with our apartment—I found none of the family there. An empty house. I walked, utterly lost, from room to room. Everything was in its place—the bookcases, the books, and even all the knickknacks: the photographs in frames made of pebbles from the Urals, the clocks, the radio (speaks just as clearly, and the same announcer as six months ago!). But none of the family—neither Mother with my little sister Verochka, nor Lelya, nor Grandmother, nor my aunts. . . . Empty. Quiet. A letter from Mama on my desk: she writes that her office is being evacuated to the Urals. And advises me to come to the Urals too.

The empty rooms depressed me. I tried to divert myself and fight off loneliness with my beloved books. Alas, the dead silence was unbearable. I passed my finger over the bureau—leaving a clear line in the dust. I wrote: "Nina—Lena—Grisha!" And felt terrified—gooseflesh over my body—of the silence, and writing in the dust. I quickly wiped off the words and went out into the street. . . .

Why send away the young people when there are not enough forces to dig trenches around Moscow? With great difficulty they mobilize people from house to house for the labor front, yet hundreds of students, young and healthy, are being evacuated. What does it mean?

Outwardly, Moscow is the same, although the boarded-up windows in many houses jar the nerves. In some buildings, the doors and windows seem to have been forced out. A bomb struck the Moscow State University building; the heavy, massive shutters were blasted out; the sidewalk is covered with piles of glass and broken brick; all the houses nearby and across the street seem to grin with smashed and splintered windows.

And on Kaluzhskaya, barricades are rising at intervals. Their fronts bristle with heavy rails, slanting forward. Antitank "hedgehogs" stand in rows, and behind them, walls of sandbags with openings for guns. Our beautiful Crimean Bridge is mined, and pedestrians are no longer allowed to cross it.

How my heart aches for everything in Moscow: the damaged Bolshoi Theatre, the ancient Book Chamber. I walk through the streets and think with terror: another ton of explosives, and this magnificent building will disappear. Perhaps it is the last time that I am seeing the Lenin Library, where I have spent so many hours in the quiet, pleasant reading room, where I have thought and felt so much. . . .

NOVEMBER 2, 1941

YES, IT was a marvelous summer, full of tender caresses, love, forest fairy tales, and promises "to the grave." . . .

He was away when I took my "mad" step. I left a letter: "Don't feel sad, forgive me and farewell." I slung my knapsack over my shoulder and strode away toward the station along the forest path. I must go where my homeland calls me. And now everything is behind me—the forest smells, the whisper of the pines, the merry dancing birches, and the wreaths of wildflowers. . . .

Today I learned that Grisha is already at the front—he went as a volunteer. How I would like to be there with him shoulder to shoulder. I remember his poem:

> Late autumn. Wilted, sere
> The leaves of lilacs and roses.
> People have grown more sober and severe.
> Late autumn. Frost.

Yes, Messerschmitts are roaring over Moscow, my beloved native Moscow, blasting the dreams of my youth with demolition bombs, burning down everything that has nurtured and nourished me from infancy. . . .

So this is it, my dear Seryozha. Don't wait for an answer from me. These are other days, and other songs . . .

And Lena is not in Moscow either—she's gone somewhere. . . .

NOVEMBER 5, 1941

I WALKED a great deal over Moscow today, and saw a great deal. I was especially struck by one building. From the street, it seems intact. But it is only a deception. Only the facade is left, and behind it there is nothing! Behind the blasted windows you see nothing but the dazzling blue sky. Like a badly made piece of stage scenery . . .

The days are full of anxious expectation. Hitler is marshaling his forces, preparing to pounce on Moscow.

I must come to a decision, and quickly. I cannot remain an onlooker.

The streets are filled with the clatter of the antiaircraft guns. Today was a beautiful frosty day, and the Hitlerites did not venture to disturb Moscow. But now, in the evening . . . there's the siren! The announcer is repeating over and over, with a special intonation, "Citizens, this is an air-raid alarm!" From the next apartment they are knocking on my wall—"Air-raid alarm, air-raid alarm!" But the Moscow residents who remained in the city have become accustomed to the raids, and few of them go to shelters anymore. I did not go there even once.

Judging from the stories of eyewitnesses, many people have been killed in the raids. A few days ago a whole line before a store on Gorky Street was hit: people waited for raisins and got a bomb.

NOVEMBER 7, 1941

AND SO, this is the day when Hitler promised to review his troops on Red Square. But everything turned out somewhat differently. Yesterday Stalin addressed us. We all sat motionless by our receivers, listening to the leader's speech. And outside the windows, bombs were crashing—it was so extraordinary, so strange. Stalin's voice sounded calm, confident, without breaking for a moment. In the hall where he spoke, everyone shouted hurrah and greetings to him. Everything was the same as in the past, except for the booming artillery, which spoke of the extraordinary character of our time.

NOVEMBER 9, 1941

TODAY THERE has been a particularly heavy raid. The alarm sounded twice. There is endless firing.

"Tak-tak-tak"—the clatter of an ack-ack gun.

"Ooh . . . ooh . . . ," the heavy artillery is booming.

And now and then, infrequent but shattering, heavy explosions: somewhere a house was blown up, people are dead. Moscow! Moscow! How many years from Batyi's Golden Horde to Hitler? But never mind, Moscow is a phoenix. . . .

NOVEMBER 13, 1941

IN THE evenings, from seven o'clock on, the houses stand like huge, dark, lifeless mounds of stone. They fill you with a deadly cold and loneliness. Cars move like blind creatures, tooting their horns in short, low blasts, afraid of disturbing the lifeless gloom of the canyons in this city doomed to grave ordeals.

When the alarm sounded last night, I was on Karetny. Somebody ran into the streetcar and cried, "Air-raid alarm! Get out!" The light in the car went out, and we piled out into the street, hurrying and stumbling blindly. Dozens of searchlights glided over the Moscow sky, studying it, crossing and uncrossing, gathering in sheaves. The stars of war flared singly and in groups, going out quickly. Tracer bullets spun long green threads across the sky. And the entire menacing picture was accompanied by the clattering of the ack-ack guns, the chatter of machine guns, and the pealing, deafening boom of demolition bombs. The streets became totally deserted, and I walked with tapping heels, pressing my handbag to my breast. And despite the shattering noise of the war, the patter of the heels was for some reason especially distinct.

NOVEMBER 14, 1941

OH, NO, I am not flinty, not even hard as stone. And this is why it is so difficult for me now. There is no one around, and I am spending my last days here. Do you think that I am not tempted by all sorts of slippery little thoughts, that I am not reluctant to leave my comfortable rooms and face the unknown? Oh-h, it isn't so, it isn't so at all. . . . I feel so lonely, I need my friends so badly these days. . . .

I walk through the empty rooms, and all around me images of the past arise and vanish. Here is my childhood, my youth, here is the place where my mind matured. Lovingly, sadly, I look through my books, my letters, my notes, reread the pages of my diaries. And fragmentary quotes copied on slips of paper.

Good-bye to all of you—books, diaries, dear trifles that have been parts of my life since childhood: the inkwells made of Ural rocks, the stool and table in old Russian style, Khudoga's paintings, old photographs which contain the childhoods of Father and Mother, and mine, and Lelya's, and the Volga, and Moscow . . .

I say good-bye to my diary. How many years now it has been my silent companion, the confidant of my sorrows, the witness of my failures and my growth, remaining with me in my most trying days. I have been truthful and sincere with it . . . perhaps there will be days, after the storm, when I'll return to your faded and yellowed pages. Or perhaps . . . No, I want to live! It seems like a paradox, but it is true: this is why I am going to the front—because living is such a joy, because I want so much to live, to work, to create . . . to live, to live!

MY WILL
If I should not return, give all my personal papers to Lena.
I have a single thought: perhaps my action will save Father?
LENA!
To you and to Grisha, my only friends, I leave all my personal belongings—my diary and letters from my friends.
Lena, dear Lena, why did you leave, I want so much to see you.
NINA.

DECEMBER 28, 1941
DEAR ANNA MIKHAILOVNA
   Please let me know where Nina is today. I received one letter from her, when she was still in Moscow, but then she became silent. I am terribly worried. You know Nina's character. We, her friends, were always a little afraid of her flare-ups and outbursts. I am afraid that, with her hot head, she will think up something wild. Keep her from doing anything reckless and let me know her address. I shall soon try to get to Moscow and will attempt to find her. Tell her the sad news: Grisha, our mutual friend, with whom we studied together for several years, was killed at the front.
   With all my best wishes,
   Your daughter's friend,
   LENA.

JANUARY 20, 1942
USSR PEOPLE'S COMMISSARIAT OF DEFENSE GENERAL HEAD-
QUARTERS OF THE RED ARMY

January 20
TO KOSTERINA, ANNA MIKHAILOVNA
NOTICE NO. 54
Your daughter, Nina Alexyevna Kosterina, native of Moscow,
died in December, 1941, in the fight for our Socialist Home-
land. Faithful to her military oath, she showed heroism and
courage in the performance of her duty.
COLONEL KUPRIANOV
Chief of Army Personnel

AFTERWORD
*Nina died at the Russian front at the age of just twenty. Grisha was also
one of the early casualties of the war, unknown to Nina as she walked
the streets of their former haunts. The once tight-knit group of family
and friends had become so fractured by events that Lena's letter to
Nina's mother, Anna Mikhailovna, dated December 28, 1941, in which
she expresses her wish to "Keep [Nina] from doing anything reckless,"
came several weeks after Nina had sworn her military oath and forfeited
her life at the front.*

Inge Pollak

I don't think I can bear my homesickness much longer.
When I die I want written on my tombstone: "Here lies a
child who perished miserably from homesickness."

Inge was born in 1927 to a Jewish family in Vienna, Austria. Following
the 1938 Anschluss (the incorporation of Austria into the Greater Germany by the Nazi regime), the conditions became increasingly difficult
for Austrian Jews. Inge and her sister, Lieselotte, left her family and
traveled as part of the Kindertransport to Cornwall, England, where a
solicitor and his wife had guaranteed to give them a home and pay for
their education up to the age of eighteen.

The Kindertransport (Transport of Children) was devised to save
young Jews from the extermination policies that threatened the Jewish
populations of Europe. The Nazi persecution of Jews began in earnest on
November 9, 1938, named Kristallnacht (Night of Broken Glass) because mobs smashed the windows of Jewish businesses and synagogues,
as well as physically attacking and intimidating Jews.

A plan of action was immediately mooted to allow at least the
children of European Jewish families to find safety elsewhere until the
situation improved. Initially, the British Jewish Refugee Committee
alerted sympathetic members of Parliament to the issue, which resulted in a debate in the House of Commons. The outcome of the debate was that England would allow an unspecified number of children
between the ages of five and seventeen the opportunity to enter the

country. This opportunity would have to be secured by a £50 bond. Once this had been confirmed, children traveled in sealed trains. These trains operated up until two days before war broke out. By the time the start of World War II had put an end to the Kindertransport, around 10,000 children had left their homes by these means. Germany never succeeded in advancing into England, but life was not without risk for the young evacuees, as many towns and cities were heavily bombed.

Children arriving in England were fostered by willing families where possible and otherwise placed in orphanages or special homes. Many of the older children sought and found work. For most children of the Kindertransport, their dreams of being reunited with their parents never came to fruition, as parents, grandparents, and older siblings were interned and murdered in the concentration camps. Nevertheless, many enlisted in the British Army once they turned eighteen and fought to free both their homelands and their families from the Nazis.

JUNE 30, 1939

I AM twelve-year-old Inge Pollak, and you are my darling diary to whom I'll tell everything, and you'll of course keep it all to yourself. I hope you won't be too shocked if I complain too much.

I'm in England! In Falmouth, Cornwall, to be precise, at the house of Mr. and Mrs. Robins. The house is large and very nice and the journey was quite good but something traveled with me, something I didn't want and which here too is my constant companion. It is home-sickness. Not a pleasant feeling. Do you know it? No, of course you don't.

We have a private tutor (like in books). She teaches us English, among other things. She told Mr. Robins that I don't work hard enough. I do try, but everything is so strange here.

It seems to me that I've been torn out of my own warm nest, and it hurts terribly. But nobody must know this, only you and I. And do you know who is the cause of all this? Hitler! He has ruined my youth, but I'm sure some good will come out of it and Hitler will one day get his just deserts.

I'm tortured by homesickness. If only I could be back in Vienna, going for walks on Sunday mornings with my parents. I wish Austria could be a monarchy and that Hitler didn't exist. Dreams! Childish wishful dreams. Everything is destroyed. But I must keep telling myself that everything will be all right in the end.

Now I must explain to you the meaning of the word "melancholy." It is when one doesn't feel like doing anything anymore and believes that nothing will ever make one happy again. It is wanting to cry all the time. It is looking forward to nothing and suffering from homesickness and memories of the past. But then it passes—I hear music or eat something nice—and, hey presto, I'm cheerful again. Or perhaps I hear you comforting me and telling me that everything will be all right in the end.

JULY 2, 1939

I'M WAITING for the breakfast bell and will tell you a few things in the meantime. The "Miss" still thinks I'm lazy. I'm still homesick, but I tell myself that everything that happens here is only a fleeting dream, and then I feel better. I don't like Mrs. Robins, but Mr. Robins is nice. Yesterday we had a picnic on Maenporth beach with two other refugee children, Lisl Gutfreund and Georg Müller. It was lovely to hear German again. Here's the gong.

JULY 3, 1939

I'M IN a foreign country and no longer at home. If someone corrects me, I immediately think the worst; they want to annoy me, they hate me. Then I tell myself: "These people are strangers. What have they got to do with you? This is not your country. You weren't born here and consequently you don't belong here." But then I feel a bit guilty and ungrateful. After all, the Robinses have done a wonderful deed, taking two strange children in. If you are miserable you see every-thing in a bad light.

How I envy English children! They're able to live at home with their parents. I'm sure there are many in Austria who envy me, but they needn't. Homesickness is terrible. Last night in bed I remem-bered how I used to pray and pray and long and long, in my bed at night in Vienna, for my visa to come to England. My wish was granted. Now I'm lying here in bed and pray and long to be back in Vienna. When I'm bored and don't know what to do, horrible thoughts go round in my head. To think I may be here for months, years! I feel I shall die of misery. But then I fetch you out, darling diary, and tell you everything. If Mama had the slightest suspicion, how upset and un-happy she'd be. She must never, never know! It hurts me to lie to her in my letters, but one mustn't only think of oneself, must one? No-body knows how unhappy I am here, only you.

Daddy wrote from Paris to say if anything is wrong we can write to him or to Uncle Hans. Shall I? Dare I? Better not.

How I long for freedom from homesickness!

JULY 4, 1939

MR. R IS much nicer than Mrs. R (not because he's a man—honestly not). He's so charming. Otherwise I've nothing much to tell you. This afternoon we're invited out to tea at friends of the Robinses' and I'm very nervous. Are you surprised that I have so many moods and am sometimes like this and sometimes like that? I can't explain it myself.

JULY 5, 1939

LAST NIGHT Lieselotte and I had a serious discussion. She doesn't believe in God. She's quite the opposite of me in every way. She tells her best friend Muschi Redlich everything, but I couldn't possibly tell everything to another *person*. That's why I have you. We were very worried because Mama's letter was three days late. I thought she might have been taken to Dachau, but then her letter came, and I cried with relief.

JULY 6, 1939

AGAIN SOMETHING unpleasant has happened. This morning, during our ten-minute break from lessons, we went up to our room, Lieselotte and I, and who is standing in our room? Mrs. Robins. She shouts at us that we didn't do our room properly this morning, commands me in an awful tone to go and fetch the broom, accompanied by an incessant "Quick, quick, quick," and Lieselotte to fetch the mop. I could have strangled her. Lieselotte must sweep the carpet, I the floor, then she accuses us of scratching the furniture (not true), and then she tells me I must open the door for her and always let her go first. I thank you, Mrs. Robins, for trying to replace my mother. Am I to be grateful to you for this? It makes me laugh. Only I can't laugh. I cry instead. Mrs. Robins has got worse and worse. Poor Mama, you know nothing of how unhappy your darling child is, and I feel for you so because you worry about us and you may suspect. But I won't tell you, I won't be an egoist. One day everything will come to light.

I feel as if I were in chains and cannot free myself.

JULY 7, 1939

TODAY MR. R said he'd send me away if I don't soon learn to speak English. Lieselotte and I mustn't talk German together. They listen at our door.

I've become indifferent to everything here and just keep thinking of the future and longing for my mother to join my father in Paris, so we can all be together again. It must happen soon. I'm no longer an optimist of course, but I don't want to be a pessimist and so I've become a fatalist.

Why does Mrs. R ask Lieselotte to clear the table, when there are two maids in the house? Is everything really so terrible, or does it only seem like it to me, consumed as I am with longing for my family and home? Lieselotte says I mustn't keep thinking of home.

JULY 8, 1939

MR. ROBINS HAS written to Mama saying I should try and learn English soon. I'm so happy he didn't say anything worse about me!

Mrs. Robins was in a very bad mood yesterday. She always asks me where my handkerchief is, and she keeps correcting my English in front of other people. But she's only a hated inhabitant of a hated place, there will never be any room for her in my heart, and so I remain cool and uncaring. Only hope sustains me, hope that I shall soon be united with my family. The fact that I am envied by the thousands of Jews who so long to be out of Austria and Germany is really ironic. It's so sad that the Jews are being chased out of their beloved homeland. English people rave about their fatherland. Lucky people! They can rave. We can't. We're rejected by our fatherland. I only know now what that really means. When I return to my beloved Vienna in better times, I'll love it properly and be a good Austrian.

JULY 11, 1939

I HAVE such strange thoughts and feelings that I never had before. For instance, I've been thinking about one's mother tongue, and how beautiful it sounds when one hasn't heard it for a long time. So evocative. English hurts my ears. When I am in the Robinses' car driving along and think about such things, tears come to my eyes. I don't think I can bear my homesickness much longer. When I die, I want written on my tombstone, "Here lies a child who perished miserably from homesickness." And you, darling diary, shall be buried with me. I've no pleasure in anything. I've lost my sense of humor. I've no interest in learning or entertainments. I just want to go home. What worries did I have when I lived at home? What did I think about? School, friends, dolls, films, food, boys. That's all I knew. I've lost my youth now. And who is to blame? HITLER.

Mr. Robins took me to the doctor's because of my blocked nose. The doctor prescribed something. Perhaps the Robinses do care about us and just can't show it?

JULY 12, 1939

I OFTEN think: Why did I leave Vienna, when so many other poor Jews are still there? If they can stand it, so could I. After all, I'm not free here, either. On the other hand, perhaps I'm doing them some good; the more depart, the better for those remaining.

What shall I look forward to? Nothing. Do you know how I feel today? I feel like lying on the floor in some dark corner where nobody can find me and staying there till this ghastly period ends.

I can't stand Mr. Robins anymore either.

JULY 15, 1939

I HAVE a new and terrible fear: that I may be here for years and years, that I may have to finish school here, that I won't see my parents for a long, long time. Please God, don't let that happen! I could not bear it. I have no wishes or desires left, only to be with my parents again.

During lunch yesterday there was some beautiful music on the radio and I suddenly began to cry. No one noticed. Anyway, they didn't say anything if they did.

There's a chance that my father may come to visit us from Paris. I can hardly believe it. To tell you a secret—a dead secret, which nobody in the world knows—I love my mother better than my father. Now you must forget this secret.

The Robinses keep on about my blocked nose. I must try and breathe through my nose and not through my mouth. "Inge, your mouth is open!" Mrs. R says to me the whole time. I have to take some medicine. I'm beginning to believe my body is as sick as my soul, but I know that the doctor, the medicine, breathing cures, the Robinses' good intentions—all are useless. And why will nothing help me? BE-CAUSE I AM UNHAPPY!

Can you hate somebody and yet be a little in love with them? Well, I have another confession to make to you—that's how it is with me and Mr. Robins!

JULY 16, 1939

THE ROBINSES say I can't take my entrance exam to the high school until next summer. Next summer! Another year! What do they think? That I'll have my great-grandchildren here? Oh, why did you snatch

me away from my home, Mr. and Mrs. Robins, why didn't you leave
me where I was? You just wait, one more year and you'll have a sickly
child on your hands, not a fresh and healthy one, with only a blocked
nose.

Mr. Robins can be so charming. Yes, I can see your shocked and
amazed face. I can't help it. But—imagine it—Mrs. R has discovered
that I have YOU! I've no idea how. I'm glad she can't read German. I
think both Mr. and Mrs. R prefer Lieselotte to me. She's a much less
naughty girl than I am.

JULY 17, 1939

LAST NIGHT I dreamed that my dearest wish came true—I was together with my parents and grandmother again. But of course, this
dream was too lovely to be true. What do happy English children think
or worry about? Is there anything more wonderful for a child than living in their own country with their own family? I too had that happiness once, but I didn't value it. I must remember that for the future,
Annemarie Breuer is homesick too, and she's in England with her parents! I think my longing for home has gone to my head, I'm going mad.

I didn't tell you that Mr. Robins was annoyed with us because we
made a noise in the evening, firstly because at that time I didn't love
him yet and so didn't much care, and secondly because Lieselotte hadn't
yet told me the terrible thing he said to her. Listen carefully. This is
what Mr. Robins said: "Even the dogs know that there is only one
master in the house whom they must obey, and I hope I won't have to
show it to you in the way I did to them." As Lieselotte spoke these
words, they seemed to pierce my heart. True, he regretted them afterward, as Mrs. R told Lieselotte, but I can never forgive him for them.
The hole these sharp and cruel words made in my heart will not heal
so long as I remain here, and many pleasurable things will slip through
it without affecting it. Only one joy will heal it, and that will be my re-
union with my family. If Mama knew this!

Yesterday we spoke about Hitler and Germany with the Robinses.
Mr. R asked Lieselotte, "Didn't you have anything to eat anymore?"

Lieselotte: "Oh, it wasn't as bad as that. Only no butter, no meat, no fruit, and not very good milk. But enough to live on."

Mr. R: "Then why did you come to England?"

This might have been interpreted as a reproach, but he said it unsuspectingly, and of course he meant all Jews.

Lieselotte: "But we couldn't live there—haven't you heard about the tenth of November? (I'll tell you about the tenth of November some other time.) We couldn't go into a park, a theater, or use a tram. In the street, anybody could do what they liked to us, the men were being imprisoned, we were thrown out of our homes. . . ."

Mr. R: "Oh, I see."

He found it impossible to understand, but he looked sad and seemed to sympathize with us. I must say I don't blame him, I wouldn't understand or believe it either, if I hadn't experienced it.

Mr. R again: "I expected to find you very nervous. My wife and I were surprised that you weren't."

I must say he's at times a little tactless. Lieselotte was furious afterward, and she hates him now, but loves Mrs. Robins—exactly the opposite of me! She says she has lost her faith in human nature, and that the British are only Hitler's enemy because they are afraid for themselves, not because of the Jews. Very sad, if true. We couldn't sleep that night.

JULY 19, 1939

OH MY goodness! Every day brings something new that's terrible. I can hardly keep up with telling you about it.

Over breakfast today, Mr. R told us that they are going away for three weeks—and we are staying here! Not in this house with the maids, but at someone else's house, with a lady who teaches English and who takes in children for holidays. It was the last thing Lieselotte and I expected. We are very upset. My heart may now be of stone, but these torments can bore painful holes even into this hard texture.

Last Sunday we went to the Lizard with the Robinses in their car, and Mr. R bought me a little glass duck. I sleep with it every night, and of course I kiss it often. It won't disappoint me as people do.

How can such different people as Mr. and Mrs. Robins love each other? She's hardly ever nice to me and keeps correcting my English (although it is really much better now) and never praises my progress. Yesterday she got it into her head that I have a cold, but I haven't. Then there are all the rules we must obey.

JULY 22, 1939

WHO WILL change with me? I'd love to be somebody else. I was so happy once, laughing and playing in my parental home. Now I'm in CHAINS. And those chains hurt. In moments of my greatest despair I'd prefer to be a prisoner. At least prisoners know when they'll be free.

A few days ago we went for a walk with Mr. Robins. I may not have mentioned it before, but he has very bad posture. Imagine my astonishment when he suddenly said to me, "Inge, walk with your head up, not down, so that you get some fresh air into your lungs. Shoulders back, hold yourself straight." What do you think of that? I said before that a prisoner is better off than I. At least he can walk as he chooses. Soon the Robinses will sit at my grave and tell me which way to turn! And if they accompany my coffin, they will think: "So that's all we get for our goodness in saving her from Hitler." I have no more time to write now, but tomorrow I'll tell you about Tommy Müller.

JULY 23, 1939

WELL, YESTERDAY we were invited to the house of Tommy Müller's guardian for tea. It was wonderful! Two other refugee children were there. We played games and spoke German as much as we wanted, and I felt quite at home. Tommy told us that he doesn't like his foster parents either. Poor Tommy. How I felt for him. When I saw Mrs. R again after that lovely afternoon, I got a real fright.

On the first of August, Ruth, my best friend, is coming to England on a children's transport!

JULY 24, 1939

TODAY I must say good-bye to you, because we're going to Miss Davis's for three weeks. I think it's disgraceful to take in two children and then dump them on somebody else, especially without a word to the parents. But the time will pass, and you and I will be together again. I won't have time to write there, but I'm taking the key so no one can interfere with you, and I'll keep praying, to relieve my feelings.

AUGUST 14, 1939

I'M BACK. I enjoyed myself very much at Miss Davis's. She wasn't nearly as strict as the Robinses and there was a happy-go-lucky atmosphere. While there, I promised God that I wouldn't be as unkind about the Robinses anymore, and I hope to keep that promise.

Mr. R was going to visit us between Friday and Sunday, but he didn't come. On Monday he came and fetched us back to "Penhale." My fleeting love for him has disappeared, though sometimes, when I look at him, it comes flooding back for a moment. When he is not here for meals I hardly say a word, but when he is, I chatter away all the time (in English, of course). On the whole, both of them are much nicer to us since our return.

Sometimes, when I look out of the window into the far distance and see nothing but fields and sea and a few houses, and nowhere where I belong, I lose courage, and inside me I scream, "Aren't you coming to fetch me home? Your child longs for you, she's wretched and lonely here, have you forgotten her?" No reply. All in vain.

AUGUST 17, 1939

TODAY, I must tell you another secret that nobody but you must know (unthinkable for me to tell secrets to a person, not even to Ruth, as Lieselotte does to her friend Muschi). I'm very ashamed of something I've done. Listen. When we were alone at home with the cook today, I saw an open letter from Mama to Mr. Robins lying on the table. What did I do? I read it! Just as well, really. I shall never love Mr. Robins again now, never, never! I read the following: "Dear Sir, I am very glad that my children are well and happy with you. They write such glowing letters. I am pleased that you like Lieselotte so much, and I hope this will soon be the case with Inge, too. She is an affectionate, bright, and cheerful child and usually very popular."

So now I know. How could Mr. Robins write to my mother saying he didn't like me, or not as much as Lieselotte? It must have hurt her terribly. And why is it so? Am I such a bad specimen of humanity? I never knew it, and nobody told me. Am I so bad, Mr. and Mrs. Robins, that you can't love me? Of course, you wouldn't understand how a refugee child feels away from home in a strange country. . . .

It seems I can't do anything right. But today, Mrs. R actually said that I've begun to speak English very well. I hope she'll write and tell Mama, and that it will make them like me better.

My heart is so heavy that it feels as if a gigantic stone was attached to it, weighing 2,000 pounds. All my sorrows are in that stone: Will I ever see my parents again, will I pass the entrance exam to the high school, shall I ever speak English properly, will the Robinses ever like me? Sometimes these fears and worries feel as if a million worms were gnawing away in my stomach.

AUGUST 19, 1939

MR. R CAN can be very nice. For instance, yesterday, Mrs. R said something about the Stone Age. I'd never heard this word before and asked innocently: "Did you say 'sausage'?" They all burst out laughing. The one person who politely declined to join in was—Mr. Robins. He only smiled sweetly and said: "It is very bad manners to laugh if somebody makes a mistake." And he explained to me what Stone Age means.

Relations of theirs were here for a week. The lady gave us 6d [6 pennies] each, and Lieselotte asked Mrs. R if we could accept it. She said, "Of course. You are her adopted nieces." That means we are the Robinses' adopted children. It's very nice of you, Mr. and Mrs. Robins, but please never say that again, never. You can think it, but don't say it, because it hurts me nearly as much as if you said, "We hate these children." WE ARE NOT YOUR CHILDREN. We belong to our parents, and they won't give us to you, not ever.

AUGUST 20, 1939

I HAVE very bad manners. I am spoiled. I am lazy. These are the only observations I have to make today. We're going to the beach now, and anyway, it's so hot that my thoughts have all melted today.

AUGUST 21, 1939

THE PRESENT is a luminous ball. Behind it—the past; in front of it—. the future. The whole soars in total darkness and reels to and fro, now gently, now vigorously. Below there is an abyss, above vapor. It is pitch-dark. Either the ball crashes, then all is lost, or it glides into the future, and that means hope. Which way is it going? We mortals are helpless and can't influence it. We await our fate. That's how I see things, anyway.

All the Robinses ever think about is dogs, garden, weather, entertainments. Think of it—a twelve-year-old-girl has more worries than a grown-up man and woman! When I was at home, Mama always kissed and comforted me if I had something on my mind (what on earth could I have had on my mind?), but now there's nobody. Perhaps it's good for me to be hardened. Perhaps the second half of my life will be easier to bear, if I ever reach it. If a person is unhappy from morning till night, day after day, they may not live long.

AUGUST 22, 1939
MY JOURNEY TO ENGLAND (TOLD BELATEDLY)
I'M NOW going to describe to you, belatedly, the journey from Vienna to England on the Children's Transport on which Lieselotte and I came on the twentieth of June.

On the evening of our departure I couldn't eat anything except a piece of apple. I was terribly excited. Everything seemed like a dream—saying good-bye to Granny, going through our apartment for (presumably) the last time, driving to the station in the taxi for the last time along the beautiful Ring, the Stephansplatz, the Opera, with Mama and Aunt Anna. On the station we were each given a cardboard number on a string, to hang round our necks. As I lay in Mama's arms, saying good-bye to her for heaven knows how long, I still didn't realize what was happening. We were told to join a line with hundreds of other children, and stood about for a long time. Then suddenly we were on the train and waved good-bye to Mama and Aunt Anna until the train took us out of sight. I looked at the other children near us, and they were all talking and shouting and running about. Naturally, we couldn't sleep much that night. We sang Viennese songs, and some of the children cried. The train left at 11 p.m., and it was now past midnight. Some of the children unpacked the food we had all brought to last us the whole journey and started eating it. Lieselotte tried to disown me for most of the time and teamed up with older children. Boys and girls were in separate compartments. A lady was in charge of us who put in an appearance from time to time and told us to go to sleep. When we crossed the border into Holland and freedom, a great cheer went up. Some Dutch people handed each child a bar of Nestle's milk chocolate through the train window. On the boat crossing over to Harwich, Lieselotte offered to look after a little girl aged six and shared a cabin with her, instead of with me, which upset and annoyed me. I shared with another strange girl. In the night I felt seasick and got up to go to the lavatory but ended up in a sort of linen cupboard and was sick there. We arrived in Liverpool Street Station in London on Thursday, June 22. The Müllers met us, and we stayed the night with them. For breakfast I had toast for the first time and thought it was burned bread. Lieselotte must have done too, because she took the only piece that didn't look burned. The Breuers called to see us later. I still felt giddy from the ship and thought I must be dreaming everything. In the afternoon we were taken to Hyde Park, and I heard English spoken all around me for the first time, even by children, which seemed very strange. The next day, we were put on a train to Exeter, and there Mr. and Mrs. Robins were to meet us. They were late, and I was in a panic. I couldn't speak a word of English, and when a taxi driver asked us if we needed a taxi while we stood waiting for the Robinses, I thought he wanted to abduct us! Lieselotte knew better because she understood some English. The Robinses arrived about fifteen minutes late.

"Are you 'Lieselotti' and 'Ingi' Pollak?" they asked us. We got into their large white car and drove to Falmouth, which took many hours. I was still in a dream. At last we arrived at "Penhale." The two maids were at the window. They had probably been waiting there with great curiosity to see what the Robinses were bringing home. The dogs ran out, barking. And that was the beginning of my new life. Little did I know what was ahead of me.

AUGUST 23, 1939

MRS. R HAS an unpleasant habit. If I don't understand something and ask for it to be repeated, she says crossly: "Why don't you listen? I've just said that." Or: "This was explained to you yesterday, you don't pay attention."

But all this is nothing when compared to my new huge worry—namely WAR! Everyone is talking of war. Hitler, that rotter, has made a nonaggression pact with Russia and is demanding Danzig. And he calls himself an "angel of peace"! Why does he want more land? Why do people fight? Please, God, let there not be war. I go to bed with old worries and get up with new ones.

Mr. and Mrs. R asked me if I didn't like them, because I don't join them in the drawing room after lunch.

I haven't told you much about the political situation in Austria. Jews were forbidden to go into certain shops, into cinemas, theaters, the Opera, parks; were taken in their thousands to Dachau, from which only 1 percent came out alive. The rest had their ashes sent to their families, usually with a letter saying something like: "We regret that your husband (or father or son) slipped on a banana skin and died." They were treated and addressed with utter contempt, in the "Du" form, by the Nazis. They were made to stare into blinding light for six hours; they were made to do heavy work regardless of age, and often shot as they walked in the street. I was terribly afraid of the Hitler Youth boys because they often teased me. We were even afraid to go to places that *were* allowed to us. At any moment, someone might exclaim, "It stinks of Jews here," and you might be killed, anywhere, at any time. A Christian dog, if there is such a thing, was more valuable than a Jewish person. Swastikas hung from every window. All conversation among Jews centered around emigration. "Well, have you got your visa yet?" "Where are you going?" "Will we get out before there's war?" "My wife is domestic help in England." "Yesterday I was at the Kultusgemeinde,* tomorrow I'm going to the passport office." And so on. Quite small Jewish children played at emigrating.

The worst day of all was the tenth of November. A Jew in Paris killed a German official, out of anger against Hitler. Hitler revenged this deed by punishing all Jews with renewed intensity. In the morning of that day, Mama, Lieselotte, and I went to the dressmaker's. We saw crowds in the streets and knew something was up. We went home quickly. In the afternoon I went to bed with a bad cold and a temperature. By then thousands of Jews were being fetched out of their houses or rounded up in the streets and taken away. Occasionally also women. At about 5 p.m. our doorbell rang. We heard men's voices. Mama said, "Here they are. They've come," and went to open the door. I wanted to jump out of bed but lay frozen and rigid with fear, unable to move. A few minutes later Mama returned. "They only wanted to know about the business," she said. "I told them Daddy was in France, and they left." We all relaxed, although none of us slept that night. Granny said to me later, "It was your mother's charm. Even those brutes couldn't resist it. Otherwise they would have taken her." Many of our friends were taken to prison.

It is now 10 p.m., and I'm dead tired. I'm going to sleep now, to dream of being at home again in Vienna, with my parents, in better

---

* A Jewish organization.

times. But first I'll pray for a letter from Mama tomorrow. Good night, darling diary.

AUGUST 25, 1939

MRS. R AGAIN told us off for not doing our room properly. "We give you a home," she shouted, "but you must keep it tidy." And if not, you'll throw us out, I suppose! I think it's Alice, the less nice maid, who tells tales about us. We sometimes go for a walk with her, but I don't trust her. Mary is much nicer.

I can be justly proud of what I've experienced at only twelve years old, I think, and all the other Jewish children, too. I'm sure we've all become more mature, sensible, and clever. Unfortunately, also sadder. Sometimes, when I chat and laugh at mealtimes, I suddenly stop and ask myself: "What reason have you to laugh? Your situation is much too terrible for you to laugh. So STOP!"

Just imagine, Lieselotte has become homesick! No wonder. She is missing parental love and our home. She says she has had enough of living in strangers' houses, riding in their cars, and taking their charity. The further the good old days slip back into the past, the more vivid their memory becomes.

Yesterday, in a shop, the shop assistant asked me how I was getting on with my English. Before I could reply, Mrs. Robins said, "She's a bit lazy." This really hurt me, because it was so unfair. Everyone else says how well I speak English now. She's so unjust. I hate her.

I'm still in love with Mr. Robins—but not all the time.

AUGUST 28, 1939

MRS. ROBINS (A CHARACTER DESCRIPTION)

I'M AFRAID I've more bad than good things to say about her. She's terribly moody, unjust, strict, and usually scolds me for things I'm not guilty of. She has no feelings whatever for refugee children—probably no deeper feelings about anything. She has the nasty habit of criticizing everybody she sees in the street, never saying anything nice about them. Sometimes she's quite funny and tells jokes, but that's all I can say in her favor. My last sentence is and remains: I hate her.

MR. ROBINS (A CHARACTER DESCRIPTION)

MR. ROBINS is the exact opposite of his wife—and yet, they love each other! He's sometimes not nice, but never as nasty as she is. It's quite obvious that they have no children of their own. He seems to care more about us, sometimes even in an exaggerated way. He's strict too, but he's fun. As you know, often I'm really in love with him. As my feelings for him are not consistent, I can't really judge him properly.

SEPTEMBER 2, 1939

GERMANY AND Poland are at war. It can't be long now till England and France join in. I'm sure you're thinking, how can I write that down so calmly? Well, I'm *not* calm. I'm in a terrible state. But my imagination fails me for once. What will war be like? If there is really a war, will I ever see my parents again?

Hitler, I hate you even more than I hate Mrs. Robins!

SEPTEMBER 3, 1939

IT'S SUNDAY morning. Lieselotte told me that Mrs. R told her a secret that only she and Mr. and Mrs. R know. She says I'll find out what it is in a few months. She swears it is nothing to do with me, and she had to swear to Mrs. R not to tell me. I think it was really horrible of Mrs. R to come between me and my sister. But God has punished her a little, because her favorite dog died a few days ago.

Later. Heaven help us! My eyes are full of tears, and my heart is pounding. It is WAR! It has come at last, the specter of horrors I feared for so long. Mama, Daddy, shall I see you again, and when? Up to three-quarters of an hour ago I was still hopeful. Now all hope has gone. I should like to die for all the innocent people who will be shedding their blood who have so much more to live for than I. I know that thousands of children are suffering the same fate as I, but it doesn't help me.

SEPTEMBER 4, 1939

I WAS too upset to write more yesterday. This is what happened: Lieselotte was downstairs listening to the news on the radio in the morning. I was upstairs in our bedroom. Then I too went downstairs, and met Lieselotte running up to our room.

"Do you understand what has happened?" Mr. Robins asked me as I came into the drawing room.

"No," I said.

"War has been declared," he said. I ran out of the room. In the bedroom Lieselotte is lying on the bed, crying hysterically.

"It's war, isn't it?" I cry. No answer. "Isn't it?" I repeat. I begin to cry too. At last we both stop. Then we talk for a long, long time, and we both look at the photograph of our parents with the same thought in our heads: Shall we ever see them again? Then I go to the calendar and look at the date. Sunday the third of September. The first day of war. At 11:00 a.m. it was declared, and at 11:45 a.m. I was informed of it. I mark the date with a black ring round and ask myself, When I shall be marking the last day of war?

SEPTEMBER 6, 1939

FIRST DAYS of war. No sign of it here yet, except that we get no letters from home. I don't know what has happened to my parents in Vienna and Paris. If I'm unoccupied for long, the wildest thoughts oppress me, and I get headaches and stomach cramps. I think the same thoughts over and over again, but too much philosophizing is not good for you.

SEPTEMBER 8, 1939

THE OLD woman (you know who I mean) is cross with me again. Mr. R has also been very moody and unpleasant. I usually bring him the ashtray in the evening, but last night I didn't. Served him right.

Because the Robinses are such loving and caring foster parents and so concerned about us, they took us to the optician's yesterday (they'll have our behinds examined next). Lieselotte has to wear glasses, and I must see a specialist because there might be something wrong with my eye muscles. Mr. R says it's my fault because I don't move my eye muscles enough and always turn my head to look around in-stead of my eyes. To think that a forty-year-old man can talk such nonsense. I am sure you are laughing and I almost hear you say: "Well, even Inge wouldn't say anything so stupid." Am I right? I think they only do these things to torture me.

SEPTEMBER 14, 1939

LIESELOTTE STARTED at the high school today. She passed her en-trance exam in the summer. My turn next, but I'm sure I'll fail.

Darling diary, I've nearly come to the end of you—only two pages left. We must say good-bye. I'm sorry I had to begin and end in such an unhappy mood.

SEPTEMBER 17, 1939

APPARENTLY I don't pronounce the word "toast" well, so Mr. Robins decided to make me ask for it every morning instead of passing it to me. I wouldn't do this, so for three days I've gone without toast. Better starve than give in, I told myself. On Sunday, that is today, I was pre-pared to go without again and was curious to see what would happen. And do you know what did happen? He passed me the toast! Then we had a long chat and he was quite nice to me again. The funny thing is, each time he is especially nasty to me my love for him returns more vigorously.

I'm starting school at Miss Davis's on the twenty-fifth. She's going to coach me for the entrance exam to the high school, so I won't have much time to write. Lieselotte has decided only to speak English from now on. The war goes on, but there's no sign of it here. Sometimes we hear airplanes overhead, that's all.

Now I've reached the last page we really must say good-bye. I don't know when I shall continue writing, but one day I will. I've loved you very much and am sorry I had so many sad things to relate. I kiss you good-bye now. Good-bye, my darling diary. Then I shall lock you up and put you away where nobody can ever find you.

OCTOBER 9, 1940

I HAVE just escaped death by a hair's breadth. This is what happened: Connie and I were going for a walk as usual after homework. We felt a bit hungry and were going to buy a pennyworth of chips. We were just passing the Wesleyan chapel on the moor when we heard *sssssss*, the unmistakable whistle of a bomb. There had been no air-raid warning. We heard no bang. But suddenly all around us there was rubble, and people were screaming and belatedly diving for shelter. One woman and her little girl under an umbrella came running toward us and seemed hysterical. We didn't know where the bomb had dropped until someone shouted, "It's the chapel!" Then we saw that it was in ruins—and we were not a stone's throw from it. How had the bomb missed us? One minute we were exactly in front of the chapel, the next we were ten steps away, and in that split second the bomb fell. Thank you, God, for saving my life. But the ginger-haired son of our air-raid warden, who had been inside the chapel, was killed.

We were too excited not to tell Miss Davis and Miss Kitty what had happened, although we never tell them when we've been to town in the evening, as I'm not allowed there then because of the sailors and soldiers. Connie's mother doesn't mind—she's more broad-minded. At first no one believed us. Then Miss Davis said: "What were you doing in town at that time?"

"I was nearly killed, Miss Davis!" I cried.

"You shouldn't have been in town. You see what happens when you disobey," she said.

I still think God meant to save me, not punish me.

APRIL 3, 1941

TODAY WE broke up for Easter holidays—hurrah! After tea Moira and I went for a walk with Denzil and he wanted to give us 1d [1 penny] each, but we refused it. He shared his bar of chocolate with us instead. David is home for the holidays. He has been here to tea with his mother, who is a tiny woman who lisps and speaks Scottish instead of proper English.

I have joined the public library.

Tomorrow my father is coming to visit us again.

One day when it was raining, Connie, Moira, and I went to the museum. We thought the exhibits rather dull. Suddenly I had an idea: there was an old chair standing there, for people to sit down in case they felt tired. "Let's make people think this old chair is an exhibit, too," I said to Connie and Moira.

"How?" asked Moira.

"It hasn't got a label," said Connie. I took a piece of paper and a pencil, which I always carry with me, from my pocket, and I wrote in large capital letters:

This Chair was Used by Judge Jeffreys at the Bloody Assizes.

We put the piece of paper on the chair and left the museum. We were laughing so much that people were looking at us as we sneaked out.

The next time we visited the museum, the piece of paper—and the chair—had gone.

March 2, 1942

If ever I have grieved, I cannot understand why now. I grieved about such small things that matter so little in life. Today I had some very sad news. I have been through three miserable years, been unhappier than most English girls or boys of my age have probably ever been. I don't say that during these three years I have known no happiness. I have, generally speaking, come across only kind people apart from Mr. and Mrs. Robins. I have spent many happy hours at parties or walking with friends and having fun with boys. I don't complain of continuous unhappiness, but all this doesn't change the fact that my situation during those years has been sad and miserable and all the little pleasures merely diversions. But today, when the terrible news arrived, I felt all joy had vanished from my life forever and that I would never be able to recover my sense of humor. When I came home from school at dinnertime, I found a card from my uncle in Switzerland, informing us that my mother, my darling mother, has been—sent to Poland.

We have feared and feared it. I have dreaded it. Now it has happened. While I was reading the words my face grew very hot and my heart seemed to stand still. Millions of terrible thoughts rushed through my mind that I have not enough paper to write down. I threw myself on my bed and then seemed to turn to stone—but the first word of sympathy from kind Miss Davis made me burst into tears. I had wanted to avoid crying because my mother doesn't like me to be sad, but it was unavoidable. I have so much here to make me happy, but what has she got now? I have always loved life, and quite little things have helped to make it happy, and she loves life too, but what can make her happy now? When I was about six years old, our maid once said to me, "It is always good people who suffer and are unhappy, but they'll be happy in heaven. Bad people are happy on earth, but they'll go to hell." Poor comfort, but was she right? If so, that evil Hitler, those wicked Nazis, will one day get their deserts. They are not human—though what are they then?

I cannot bear to see people around me carry on as though nothing had happened. My mind is occupied with only one thought: my mother in Poland. I didn't go to school this afternoon, and Miss Kitty took me to Flushings on the ferry. She bought me an ice cream and told me jokes, but nothing pleased me and I couldn't laugh. I can only console my sister. Oh, if only I could do something to help my poor mother, and my grandmother too. If only I could let them know that we are all well and happy! If only it was in my power! If only . . . if only . . . it had all never happened.

We are all human beings, and yet some human beings' only object is to bring misery on others. WHY?

I must stop now. Everything comes to an end, and so does unhappiness. Some day perhaps I will read these pages and will say: "I am too happy to remember how that felt."

AFTERWORD

Inge's mother and grandmother were transported to Minsk, where they perished in November 1941. Both Inge and her sister survived the war to remain in England, marry, and have families. Her father fled to England on the last boat before Paris fell to Germany, and also made a life there. After matriculating at the Falmouth High School, Inge left Falmouth for Oxford, where a distant relative lived, and worked in libraries, Blackwell's Bookshop, and Rosenthal, the antiquarian bookseller. She left there after marrying a research scientist at Oxford University, and ten years later they and their son moved to Sheffield when her husband obtained a lecturing post at Sheffield University. She then qualified as a teacher and taught modern languages to both children and adults until her retirement. She now enjoys her two grandchildren and writing her diary. Inge altered the spelling of her name to "Inga" to avoid mispronunciations. When her diary was first published in its entirety as My Darling Diary, *she took the pen name Ingrid Jacoby.*

William Wilson

NEW ZEALAND
1941 (21 YEARS OLD)

Hans Stauder

GERMANY
1941 (21 YEARS OLD)

*Through the rubble, I see only abandoned weapons,
burning cars, and dead bodies . . .*

William Geoffrey Wilson was born in Wellington, New Zealand, in 1919. He was a driver and storeman before being enlisted to fight in World War II in 1940. Hans Stauder was born in Germany in 1919. He became a soldier in 1939 and was enlisted to fight for the German Afrika Korps.

New Zealand entered World War II in the autumn of 1939, when it declared war on Germany simultaneously with Great Britain. In June 1940, Italy entered the war in an alliance with Nazi Germany and provoked a battle for control of the Suez Canal and the Mediterranean Sea, which were important trading routes. Egypt, which was British-held, was targeted first in the Italian campaign, but its defeat led to the arrival of German troops under Erwin Rommel (including the

*German Afrika Korps, in which Hans Stauder was enlisted). During the
years of 1941–43, a series of campaigns were fought in Egypt and Libya,
chiefly by New Zealand, Australian, and British troops against Germany and Italy.*

*These desert battles moved back and forth across the borders of
Libya and Egypt. The flat nature of the sandy battlegrounds meant that
fighting mainly revolved around the use of tanks and fighter planes. As a
result of this, victories passed from one side to the other, depending on
which army succeeded in mustering its tanks and planes first and fastest.
It was the famous second battle of El Alamein that allowed the Allied
forces to finally halt the advance of the German troops and force them
into defeat.*

*New Zealand suffered catastrophic casualties in the North African
war, at a rate higher than that of either Britain or Australia.*

WILLIAM WILSON, NEW ZEALAND MIDDLE EAST FORCES, 1941

MARCH 8, 1941

FINISH FINAL leave—16½ hours in train. Very lonesome for someone.
Gosh it was hell leaving Wgtn. [Wellington] station. Scotty kept talk-
ing all the time; all I wanted was to be alone and think. I wish Dad and
Joan hadn't come into town.

MARCH 9, 1941

BACK IN camp, what a life. May be going away at the end of the week.
Hiding out under the trees with Scotty, who does not want to see his
girl. Still lonesome.

MARCH 15, 1941

I HAVE just picked up a record, "Are You Lonesome Tonight?" What a
hang of a song. In bed about 9 o'clock, felt too tired to go anywhere.

March 29, 1941

Marched through Auckland today, great crowd to see us but they were a pretty dead lot. We got a bit wet, marched in sixes, looked pretty good. Leave in the afternoon. Went out in a car to Onehunga, lost our way coming home, didn't know where we were! We got a tram back.

April 5, 1941

Messed around camp all day, most of the boys have jumped the fence. Rang up home. Went to the pictures in the night. Camp very quiet.

April 7, 1941

On board *New Amsterdam* [ship] 9 a.m. Rotten sleeping quarters but great tucker. Saw Ma and Joan at wharf. Missed Freda. Felt miserable going out the heads. Warships in the convoy are the *Achilles* and *Hobart Australia*.

April 10–11, 1941

1,200 Aussies [came] on [board] today; plenty of gambling, good thing to leave alone and I intend to do so. Reached Sydney—great day, no leave. Some of the boys tried to make a break but no such luck. *Queen Bess* and *Mary* in convoy. I think we sail tomorrow for Fremantle. The heads look great coming into the harbor; there are many great cliffs outside. The harbor sprawls like Auckland. Saw the bridge. Aussie Govt wouldn't give permission to let us land.

Left Sydney this morning; it looks a great city. I'll come back some day and take a look at it. The harbor is very large; we left in the morning, so we were followed by swags of launches. Have just been joined by the *Queen Mary*, so that makes the *Elizabeth, Ile de France, Mauritania,* and the *Naura Amsterdam.* It's a swell day. I am going to church parade to get out of drill. Sitting in the sun now.

April 20, 1941

Going to the R.A.P. to see about my throat. There is a rumor that Japan has come in against us. The German radio reckons this convoy is sunk.

Been to the R.A.P., had to wait 2 hours before being attended to. One chap in our troop who is sick was told by the MO to stay in his bed until they sent a stretcher to take him to the hospital. He hasn't been picked up yet; the MO saw him 24 hours ago. I have to go back later for a gargle.

APRIL 21, 1941

THE WEATHER is getting warmer. My throat is still crook. Everyone on the ship seems to think we are going to Singapore first. Have been told what to do in case of action at sea. We have to carry our lifebelts all the time from tomorrow. We had an apple and a banana from the Patriotic Fund today. They reckon we will reach Singapore Thursday morning.

APRIL 23, 1941

WE WILL be leaving this ship Thursday in Singapore. I don't think we will get leave. The sea is like a mill pond. Saw a school of porpoises. There are bamboo markers showing the channel to take. The other 4 ships made a great picture going over the horizon yesterday. I will have to look Jack [friend] up in camp. 40 cigs. And tin of tobacco from the Funds. Had 6 showers and a swim today. Gosh it is warm. The officers had a cocktail party tonight.

APRIL 24, 1941
SINGAPORE

ANOTHER GREAT day; there are swags of flying fish. They sighted an island last night. Should reach Singapore today. 20 cigs. today. Can see land on the portside. Arrived in Singapore; looks a strange place, there is plenty of green around the bush. The houses are open and have wide arches; the boys are throwing pennies down to the natives. It looks as if some Indian soldiers are here. We don't know if we will be getting leave.

MAY 1, 1941

IN COLOMBO. The *Mauritania* and the *Ile de France* are in port too. Terribly muggy. The boats are anchored out in the stream. No leave today, the lousy cows. The other ships have got it. They have been in for 5 days. The natives are around the ship in boats selling pineapples, etc. I got 6 for 1 rupee. They have a poor flavor; they say you can get 20 for a rupee ashore.

MAY 9, 1941

A BIT of a breeze today. On guard we are traveling S.W. I wish to hang I was home; I am fed up. I don't blame any chap keeping out of it. The *Canberra* [ship] is well out ahead. There are Vickers guns all over our upper decks. One of the crew reckons this is the most moaning crowd there has been on the boat. The officers get chicken, fruit salads, ice cream; why can't they cut down their tucker and give us some decent stuff.

MAY 13, 1941

END OF SEA VOYAGE. 22 *TODAY*

ARRIVED IN port, think it is Suez. There are dozens of ships all shapes and sizes in port. The town is on the starboard side while on the port side there are hills like those at the entrance to Sydney; but no green to be seen anywhere. It's about 4 p.m. back home; I wonder if they are thinking of me now. We have been told we won't be going off ship so we will have to spend another day on this tub.

MAY 15, 1941

FIRST DAY IN EGYPT

GARAWI

THEY'VE DRAGGED us out of bed at 3:50; we are going off today. Just waiting around up on deck with our gear. We will be taken off in lighters, then we will catch a train, a 5-hour trip so they say. In camp—gosh it's crook. We arrived during a sandstorm. In tents. We are here for a week in quarantine. Have seen Jack; he arrived yesterday. Hell of a train journey. Took us right up to Cairo. Doesn't look so bad. The natives are terrible.

MAY 29, 1941
MAADI

GAS MASK drill today. They've dragged us out this afternoon to put up more tents; it looks as if there will be more troops coming in soon. They say we will lose Crete. Great news, I've got the measles, going to Maadi tonight. What a hell of a ride in the ambulance; they are as rough as can be. I thought I was going to a flash hospital with nurses but I'm in a tent and no nurses.

JUNE 1941, WRITTEN IN CAMP HOSPITAL, MAADI

[The following entry was written by William Wilson while he was recovering from measles at the camp hospital, Maadi, on a blank page at the front of the diary, dated June 5, 1941. His entry on June 5 suggests that Wilson was feeling down after not having received mail from home.]

I wonder if I will ever get back home. Sometimes I don't care what happens to me, then again I wish to God I was home living my old uneventful life again. It would be swell to be looking out the front window again at the hills as the sun sinks in the evening. I have a feeling I will come out of it safe, but should something happen it would only be fate; if I do go out that way nothing will stop it, but I don't think I will. I will try and think like with Ma. There may be something in it. I don't seem to be getting so homesick nowadays. I would like to be home though, gosh what a day when I sail into Wellington harbor.

[Gunner William Wilson was killed in action at Sidi Azeiz on November 27, 1941.

Hans Stauder found the diary lying in the sands of the desert and continued after Gunner Wilson's last entry. He understood no English.]

HANS STAUDER, GERMAN AFRIKA KORPS, 1941

NOVEMBER 1941

DAYBREAK STARTS—we are with the tanks. 9 o'clock enemy engagement—I catch up with provision supplies—food distribution. We capture 5 Tommies who were stuck with their car. Enemy encircles us.

At 12 o'clock shots are fired all around, in the sky English planes, enemy artillery attacks on us, wild running around—panic!!

We finish off eating the rations (obtained with previous loot)— One Hurricane is shot down—it's raining—we draw together and form the shape of a hedgehog. No orders—no contacts—fires all around us—rainy weather.

12:30 OFF toward the east in deep darkness. We push too far south, therefore have to push back north. Big rest from 9–14 hours. Then push on toward south following the Seventh Battalion. Shortly before nightfall, big fighting with enemy tanks. The fighting is fierce. We retreat, then we retaliate against the Tommies (we have the upper hand now), during the night the enemies (Tommies) surrendered. Still further horrendous tank attacks.

BIG FIGHTING day! Shooting from right and left—two trucks from the Ninth Battalion explode, I am used to it. In the English ambulance we found beer, whisky, and biscuits, as well as meat conserves. At 12 o'clock we move toward the west. Artillery fire hits flank—English positions right around us—heavy fighting all around us. I drive only very badly wounded from the front line back to us.

Through the rubble, I see only abandoned weapons, burning cars, and dead bodies. We march to Sidi Azeiz at approx. 15 o'clock. Ten Hurricanes attack. I am kept busy, many badly wounded.

AT DAWN, enemy fire from the left, battalion takes position. I drive into attack (with Lieutenant Kramer), meet at 13 o'clock at divisional battle position.

(*Situation*: we take English camp)—Division sets off at 15 o'clock and is immediately bombarded by tanks. At 17 o'clock I drive to a rise, where I discover the English camp, and we start shooting; tanks simultaneously free 850 German prisoners.

Big trouble and excitement within our division. I sleep in kitchen.

AT 13 O'CLOCK, surprise attack, but enemy too strong. Battalion to dig into attack position 1,000-meter [1,093-yard] distance from enemy line, strong "fire," and many losses.

DECEMBER 1, 1941

ENGLISH CAMP on fire—command position shifted ahead, passed burned cars, now toward Sidi Rezegh. Many dead. We are shot at and also attack enemy divisions. At darkness back, and still attacking.

DECEMBER 4, 1941

START AT 5 a.m., division toward Sidi Azeiz through the desert to Trigh Capuzzo. Arrived 13 o'clock Sidi Azeiz. Small battalion fires, not a lot going on, we turn south. At 17 o'clock division marches back.

In the darkness, crazy driving, I see nothing, short break, we continue alone, I lead. At approx. midnight we make contact with our group. Thank God there was a little moonlight!

DECEMBER 7, 1941

DEFENSE ESCALATED.

In the morning, we reach the Second Infantry and dig in the hills to defend position.

At 10 o'clock, tank attack warded off. Now we are under the command of the rifle-infantry. Enemy artillery keeps us covered, constantly, English tanks are circling around us. From 15 o'clock we are in readiness for an attack but only a few people of the group assigned. I race around the terrain for about 2 hours, and search for the 15cm cannon battery. At 18 o'clock return to base, get beer. Once again night move—sometimes snail pace, then at racing car speed!

DECEMBER 9, 1941

THROUGH THE ravines of Cirenaica, up and down, crazy terrain! Broke differential due to stone, drive without oil, terrain is getting worse and worse, drive through narrow gorges and ravines. No enemy planes! Often long waits, as vehicles had to be pulled through one by one. At approx. 5:20 a.m. we arrived at our destination for the day. I direct battalion and command. Received mail—in the kitchen by the light of candles, I read my letters.

DECEMBER 22, 1941

AT ABOUT 4:30 a.m. in the distance we could hear heavy bombardment. 6 o'clock night, rest abandoned. We dig holes for cover, vehicles spread out, Arab settlements all around us, it's raining—shit weather!! I wash and shave myself (for the first time in 5 weeks).

DECEMBER 25, 1941
X-DAY (CHRISTMAS DAY)

GOT UP at 7 o'clock, reported at 8 o'clock, speech for Christmas by major. R.A.F. in the air. I sleep a bit under a free sky. At 12 o'clock we drive onward and stay there until 4 o'clock (move on in columns to meet together at via Balbia, there enter the desert—after 28 km [17 miles] stop and form for firing position). In the trucks celebrate a bit of Christmas. Every man receives 3 bottles of beer. We receive telephone connection in our car. Sleep 22 o'clock.

DECEMBER 28, 1941

8:30 MOVE on to rifle regiment. After a few air-raid attacks on the English by our Stukas, we move east, reach the height, and position our battalion to open fire. Immediately powerful counterattack by Tommies. I dig a hole in a great hurry. English explosions getting very close—big tank fights in the valley.

English retreat and we follow—the tank cannons firing well—I with commander and regiment's radio car in the lead, pass many tanks in sand traps, I also get stuck.

At 6 o'clock brigade returns—today we have no losses—at least 50 tanks destroyed.

DECEMBER 29, 1941

AFTER YESTERDAY's battle, today apparently quiet.

On daybreak we spread out the vehicles, we are on a big flat ground—receive cream and skin oil, Stukas greet us—shortly afterward eleven English bombers. They discharged their bombs in the distance. We get mail and parcels. I install a swastika flag on the bonnet of the car for the first time after a long while. At 3 o'clock we move out, every 100 meter [100 yards] stops, every time many cars get bogged through the sand fields.

(*Situation*: Enemy retreats after yesterday's loss, apart from vehicles, they also lost 58 tanks.)

DECEMBER 31, 1941

7 O'CLOCK KITCHEN arrives—I drive car a bit farther on—drank coffee—a bit of peace and quiet is lovely—wrote a letter, ate, ate, ate . . .

At 11 o'clock 6 bombers and 20 Spitfires throw single bombs, two Spitfires shot down.

13–14 o'clock at binocular periscopes. Constantly Spitfires in the air.

At 16 o' clock once again bombardment—powerful detonations.

At 17 o'clock air battle.

At 18 o'clock—kitchen (dinner) for officers "roast lamb."

I must leave the car, the "gentlemen" dine.

At 12 o'clock all around us flares and firing of shots—A NEW YEAR HAS STARTED.

AFTERWORD

The diary was found in the sands south of Tobruk. William Wilson's last entry is on October 11. Hans Stauder begins his first entry on No-

vember 19, eight days before Wilson's death. Several decades after the war, Hans attempted to trace the owner of the diary, or his descendants, so he could return it: "After many years I spoke to some acquaintances who also were soldiers in Africa about the diary which I came across again." *In 1994, Hans discovered that his fellow diarist had been killed in action.*

Eventually, in 1999, he sent the diary back to New Zealand. In a letter dating from this time he wrote, "It is in my interest that the diary must go back to where it started from N.Z. It makes me very sad to read that there aren't any relatives and the writer of the book (diary in North Africa Libya) died and on that hill 'Sidi Resghi.' I can still remember very clearly the battles on Nov 4 15 miles S.E. of Tobruk."

Sheila Allan

SINGAPORE
1941–45 (17–21 YEARS OLD)

*I think I grew old, very old and
very frightened during that short time . . .*

Sheila Allan was born in Malaysia in 1925. She grew up in Singapore,
the daughter of an Australian father and a Malay mother. In February
1942, when Sheila was seventeen, the nationalist regime in Japan seized
Singapore.

Japan's involvement in World War II came in response to its
previous clashes with China throughout the 1930s and its regional ambitions of controlling countries such as Korea and Singapore. From 1937
Japan's military leaders employed its army to wage a war of conquest in
China, which cost the lives of millions of individuals, mostly Chinese
civilians.

Japan's war in China brought it into conflict with the Western
powers in Asia. Throughout 1941, tension increased between Japan and
Britain. Japan held ambitions to expand its empire to access raw materials such as oil, rubber, and tin, which Britain vehemently opposed.
After many tense months, Japan launched a surprise attack on the European colonies in Asia and the Pacific. In December 1941, Japan made a
further attack on the U.S. naval base of Pearl Harbor in Hawaii.

The Japanese secured extensive victories and seized the British base
of Singapore in February 1942, capturing tens of thousands of British,
Indian, and Australian troops. After the fall of Singapore, Sheila and

her parents, along with two thousand other citizens of the British Commonwealth, were marched into the infamous Changi Jail on the Changi Peninsula, on the eastern side of Singapore. Initially, prisoners at Changi were free to roam throughout the area, but in early March fences were constructed around the individual camps, and movement between them was limited. Toward the end of August, Japanese POW staff arrived, and security became much stricter. Prisoners were forced to sign a statement declaring that they would not attempt escape. Day-to-day life in the camp was organized by the prisoners themselves, who mounted concerts and other forms of entertainment to pass the time.

Outside of the camp, Japan was moving toward defeat. The Allies reacted to the Japanese conquest of Asia by launching counteroffensives against Japan's possessions in Burma, New Guinea, and the islands of the Pacific. In August 1945 the Allies were preparing to invade Japan itself; however, the entry of Russia into the war and the atomic bomb attacks by U.S. forces on the Japanese cities of Hiroshima and Nagasaki, which resulted in unprecedented horrors, forced Japan to surrender. Changi was liberated by troops on September 5. The Pacific war cost the lives of about 11 million Chinese and almost 2 million Japanese.

DECEMBER 8, 1941
The idle life I lead
Is like a pleasant sleep
Wherein I rest and heed
The dreams that by me sweep,
And still of all my dreams
In turn so swiftly past,
Each in its fancy seems
A nobler than the last;
And every eve I say,

Noting my step in bliss,
I have known no day
In all my life like this.
—*Robert Bridges*

ALAS! How true the last two lines, for today marked the beginning of the "Malayan War"!

War? Impossible! It can't be! My whole being cried against it for shattering the peace of my holidays up in the hills; for intruding into my calm uneventful life, for making me feel both afraid and excited. In fact, I resented it for causing an emotional upset that was so strange to me.

Up in these hills [Cameron Highlands] I have been happy, away from the crowds and bustle of town life. Here, have I enjoyed the quiet mountain air and stream; here, where one can be free to indulge in one's own thoughts with no outside interference. And what happens? War! Presto—the whole atmosphere is charged with that little three-letter word! . . .

Leaving the house, I went my way to that tiny bubbling brook that dances over the stones, laughing and leaping at the secrets it only knows. My whole being drank in the sweet morning fragrance. Here, in a world of dew whose crystal drops beaded more heavily each dropping blade of grass, I had knelt in body and spirit. Here, I guess one could easily forget the petty annoyances and disappointments of life.

But could one forget War? Could one, I wonder.

Returning, I had gathered a posy of the mountain flowers. Those delicate, exquisite blooms lasting only until the sun got too strong for them. But this morning, poor things, they saw little of the sun as they were crushed and bruised by my hands when upon my ears fell that fateful word, "War"!

I had met Dad, feeling strong and wholesome in spirit after my morning's excursion, to be confronted by his grim face as he announced the news that Singapore was bombed this morning by the Japanese and that this meant we are now at war with Japan.

Bewildered, I had uttered that word to myself and looked at my stepmother, whose face showed traces of recent tears. Dad walked away in silence. Vichim, my stepmother, collapsed in a chair and started sobbing—from what? I know not.

All I knew was that I found myself wandering back to my little stream where I stood and only heard the rushing of the waters. Was it trying to tell me something earlier. I wonder.

Then I remembered the blossoms, still clutched tightly in my hands. I looked at them—no longer fresh but lifeless and broken. Dead! The word leapt before my eyes. I let them fall from my fingers into the water and watched them being carried away, away. Gone!

Death! War! Only then did I begin to realize what it meant. Those flowers—some of them only buds, died before serving their time. I had killed them; not thinkingly, but it seemed symbolic of what War is. Before me, I imagined deaths and sufferings—all caught in the web of war. And what is war?—a fight for freedom or power? A battle of one's right to peaceful living. War has reared its ugly head here to shatter our peace, and we must fight to keep our Peace.

Again I returned to the house. Thoughts revolved inside my head—how best to serve my country.

There was a time I had envied other girls in the services and wished I was one of them. Now here was my chance to do my duty. Suddenly I felt brave and excited at the prospect of having to fight.

Alas! for my high hopes of being useful to my country. When I told Dad of my decision to join up, he promptly told me that I was too young. . . .

Dad is a strict authoritarian and what he says goes. So, I bowed to his wish, feeling bitterly disappointed. . . .

This evening before turning indoors, I watched the sun slowly setting behind the mountains. I watched its almost level rays reaching into the valley. The evening light is kindly and soft as I write all this down and promise myself that I must keep a record of everything that is going to happen.

I look toward the stream, gliding and flashing shields of silver and gold where the sun shines on it. I sigh and with Wordsworth I write his lines:

> *I heard a thousand blended notes,*
> *While in a grove I sat reclined,*
> *In that sweet mood when pleasant thoughts*
> *Bring sad thoughts to mind.*
> *To her fair works did Nature link*
> *The human soul that through me ran;*
> *and much it grieved my heart to think*
> *What man has made of man . . .*

Good night, dear Diary.

DECEMBER 14, 1941

PHEW! WHAT a day! At last we are back home [in Kampar] and do I feel tired! We left Renglet this morning. Tears were in my eyes as I silently bade farewell to our holiday home. Wonder how long it will be before I go back there again. . . . Nearing Kampar, I heard a most peculiar sound—an unearthly wail seemed to echo through the air, again and again. That was the first time I heard what Dad called the "Alert." What a weird noise, and I'm sure I'm not going to like the "Alert" at all! We had to stop and take cover among some bushes along the road but only for a few minutes. The air was again startled by another sound—the "All Clear." I think I prefer this noise to the first one! . . .

In Kampar we stopped at Luan San Store to buy some tinned food. There were two trucks there as well, and I saw for the first time soldiers who appeared tired, unshaven, with their uniforms covered with mud and blood. They did look grim. I stared at them with wonderment of teenage hero-worship! Dad spoke to them and they gave him the latest news of the war—it was not good—the Japs are coming down from the north and the civilians are leaving their homes as the Japs advance. . . .

The soldiers were very hungry, and as they could not speak the language, made signs indicating that they wanted food and drink. . . . From afar I looked at them with admiration. I was too shy to go up to them and help them. To me they were men from another planet. Apart from my father, I know little of man and his ways so I guess I wouldn't know what to say if one of them had spoken to me. . . .

Mom is all scared and worried. As for me—I don't exactly know how I feel. It seems so unreal.

It is so quiet here that I can't believe there's a war on.

JANUARY 19, 1942

"SNATCHED FROM the jaws of death," as it were! That's exactly what happened yesterday. . . . Dad was with us—he had decided not to go out that morning. So, there were Dad, Mom, and I just sitting in our room doing nothing—just waiting, waiting, and waiting. . . . When the air raids were on, and we had plenty each day, we went down to the second floor under the staircase for shelter. From our room we can hear the warning whistle from the roof spotter on the VHQ before the official wail of the siren is sounded. The first and second raids came and went. Bombs were exploding in the distance. There we were, crouched under the staircase, our hearts beating rapidly and our thoughts running wild—will we come through this one and so on it goes.

The All Clear whistle from the spotter was heard. We got out from under the shelter and proceeded upstairs to our room. Of course, the official All Clear hadn't sounded yet.

On our way up I heard the droning of the planes (I have already learned to know the sound of the bombers) approaching nearer and nearer. There was no warning whistle, but it could have been given and we failed to hear it. Something prompted me to return to the shelter. I shouted to Dad and Mom to come down. Dad said the All Clear whistle had gone and he heard no warning signal. I grew frantic and yelled for them to come down at once. They hesitated, then thought better of it when the planes drew nearer and ack-ack guns started firing.

We reached the shelter just in time as the first bomb exploded. We flung ourselves flat on the floor and *whiz-shiss-ss-ss, crr-crr-rump, crash* came the bombs one after another. I heard the whistling of each of them as they hurtled down from the sky and waited for the rest—and explosion—to follow. The building rocked beneath us. An orange flame from the bursting bomb flashed in a downward streak as it passed an open window. Screams of human fear and pain penetrated through the sound of the crashing force of the bombs. Smoke and acrid smell assailed us through cracked and opened windows. There was dust everywhere. Mom had her head buried in her arms, sobbing. Dad had his arms around her. I, for that split second, closed my eyes and thought "This is it!" The danger had passed—no sounds of planes or firing. The All Clear rang through our fuddled minds as we lay on the floor, shaken and white-faced. The raid was over and we were alive!

We got up, rather dizzily, dusting ourselves and feeling ourselves all over to ascertain if any bodily damage had been done. No, we were safe and sound in limb and body. Mentally and emotionally, I'm not sure. I think I grew old, very old and very frightened during that short time when I had my face down on the floor!

We made our way through the debris of plaster, splinters, broken furniture, and dead bodies—poor souls, they hadn't reached the shelter in time. Dust, smoke, foul-smelling fumes seemed to fill the atmosphere as we choked and gasped for a breath of fresh air which was nonexistent!

It was too much for Mom. She was on the point of collapse as we helped her upstairs. . . .

Beach Road was closed to us, so we decided to go through North Bridge Road. We came upon the dead and dying. Many were badly injured. Ugh! It was awful seeing them lying around covered with blood that was still warm, and from some, the blood seemed to flow steadily on, making a pool of red. In fact, crimson seemed to be the dominant color. No matter where we looked our eyes rested on dead bodies, dying people—men, women, and children, and so many of them with horrific injuries. How could I describe such a scene? I've never read of such things, let alone seen them before now. I can't find the right words to convey the pitiful sight of this human life ebbing away; of the useless loss of life; of the young children crying either in pain, fear, or loss; of the agony some of them must have felt and are still suffering. What a tragedy.

So, this is War! This is what War does! Dear God! What a waste of life! What devastation! A destroyer of the young and old! Who wanted to glorify War? Why do we have to fight and hurt each other? So many thoughts go through my mind as I look around me. It is so senseless. No longer am I a happy-go-lucky child but a frightened, uncertain girl of seventeen whose life before had been serene, innocent, and joyous. Now I am stripped of my sensitive covering—I feel naked—I have no place to hide my tearful face, my knowledge of the evil that has erupted in this world that I am born into. I want to take flight from all this—I don't want to know that this is happening, but where do I go? Oh, Lord, help me to understand.

My stomach gave me a lurch as I stumbled across an old woman. She was dying, blood oozed from her head and mouth. One leg was doubled under her; her innards were laid open in the sunlight, and flies were already feasting on them. One of her arms was missing. What a picture to remember! Her eyes stared at me. I tried to close them, but the lids kept retracting. I shuddered—the smell of burned skin was getting to me. I must have looked pretty green, as a cup of steaming black coffee was pressed to my lips. I gulped down the hot fluid and felt the burning sensation go down my throat. It brought me around. I felt better and thanked the young Chinese man in his brass helmet—he was one of the MAS [Medical Aid Service.] They were here, there, and everywhere, helping the people, dead and alive.

FEBRUARY 15, 1942

THIS AFTERNOON we received the good news that we had driven the Japs back. Everyone in the shelter gave a mighty cheer. An Irish sergeant then quietly said, "Please don't be too happy—the danger is not over yet. Far better to be calm and steady, taking any good news when it comes; likewise the bad news. Let us rejoice by all means but not too extreme. We must also be prepared for the worst if it comes."

10:30 P.M. SURRENDER! THE FALL OF SINGAPORE

WE HAVE surrendered to the Japs. It happened at 8:30 p.m.

We were in the shelter all day. When evening came, it brought in about half a dozen injured soldiers—their injuries were slight but enough to put them out of action for the time being. No one spoke much as we listened to the shells as they whizzed overhead. The terrific burst of them deafened our ears and rendered it impossible to carry on normal conversation. When we did talk, it was mostly about the boys, lying in there with us. We asked them about their lives before the war. They seemed eager to discuss their home life, their families, their sweethearts, and what they were going to do when all this "hell" is over. . . .

At a quarter to ten we heard an officer commanding his men to line up. Not long after, one of them came with the shattering news, "We've given up!" "Boss" came in, dazed-looking. His face working up as if he wanted to cry. He kept repeating to himself, "I can't understand it—it's not true. We were told we were pushing them back. I can't—" Tears ran down his cheeks. He sat down and unashamedly buried his face in his hands and wept as if his heart would break. We tried to comfort him, but what was the use—what words could we say. We, too, felt like sobbing our hearts out. There are no words to describe how I felt; how any of us feel! Shocked, disbelief, horrified, anger perhaps. Then there's fear as to what is going to happen. All at once, everybody started talking—trying to convince ourselves that this nightmare is not true.

The firing has ceased. The night air was no longer shattered by the bursting bombs and shells. In fact, the silence is quite frightening. For the first time in weeks, there was no throbbing droning of the planes; no sirens; no guns. I found this silence from the artillery fire more threatening and unnerving to say the least. . . .

We slowly trekked upstairs to our flat with some of the boys. . . . One of them spied the piano. "Who can play?" he asked. I answered, "Mr. M." They pushed him on the piano stool and started to sing "Rule Britannia." Mr. M soon picked up a tune on the piano. Everyone started to sing. It seemed weird that—here we were—capitulated into Japanese hands—singing song after song till we were hoarse.

FEBRUARY 16, 1942

THIS MORNING we woke up feeling quite fresh after a night free from bombs and shells. I wonder if our boys had any sleep, or did they stay awake, thinking! The Japs are still marching in, on foot and riding on tanks. From our balcony window we saw them yelling, singing, and shouting in their triumph. What's going to be our Fate now? I felt fear, as I've heard about the Japanese brutality and the atrocities they had done in Shanghai and elsewhere. People had been shot for no reason except that they were there at the wrong time. And the women population—are we going to be safe from them? Who knows!

FEBRUARY 17, 1942

I SAW our soldiers going on their way to the concentration camp at Changi. Waved at them. They shouted back, "Keep your chins up"—"It won't be long," we heard someone else say. Saw our soldier friend among them. We gave him a wave. They looked so brave, marching and singing. I had tears in my eyes—looked at Dad—he stood straight and tall but tears were running down his cheeks. I went to him. His arms around me—so tightly that I could hardly breathe. No words were spoken.

Now the soldiers are out of the way, the civilians are going to be rounded up next—sounds like a herd of cattle! Military police everywhere—orders given that we must bow from the waist down whenever we see them!

Internment began for most of the Europeans today—Europeans mean "married to one"—"children of such union"—or if you profess to be a "British subject"!

FEBRUARY 26, 1942

DAD AND Mr. A went out yesterday. Returned afternoon with news that they had succeeded in obtaining passes from the Japanese envoy, who told them that we could be interned with these passes in Changi. Told to take enough for ten days, also enough clothes for those ten days.

Dear God! I am scared for all of us. Everything's packed—now we wait!

MARCH 8, 1942
CHANGI PRISON

WELL, WE are going after all—everything packed. Hustle, bustle, hither, thither—everyone dashing around and getting nowhere fast! Children crying, women shouting, orders given—nobody takes much notice—nobody seems to know really what's going on—just a mad scramble trying to get organized! Given three tins of sardines and two loaves of bread. We walk to Changi Jail—only the very sick, the very old, and the very young are allowed to be taken in trucks. . . .

Left Katong Camp in the true "British spirit"—singing along the hot, dusty road—whatever each of us felt inside was disguised by our cheerfulness, and in spite of what awaited us at the end of our pilgrimage, we kept our heads and spirits up. Ah! It takes a lot to daunt the "British spirit"! . . .

At last here we are—tired, hot, and dirty from the dusty road, hungry and very, very thirsty we slowly dragged our feet through those iron gates—glad to see the end of the road. Saw Dad and some of the men standing in the courtyard of the prison.

The iron gates clanged shut as we trooped through. Inside, there are rows and rows and iron stairs to the cells—imagine a 9-by-12-foot cell with a concrete slab in the middle—that's our bed, and who's the lucky one to get to sleep on it? We drew lots to see which of us sleeps on the slab. Mom had the honor of being the lucky one—I took one side of the slab, and Mrs. Kitts had the other space. For toilet purposes there is this Chinese lavatory or "squatters" at one end. The walls are high and above the slab a tiny window with bars across—could be about 10 feet above the slab. You wouldn't want to be claustrophobic here, or you'd go raving mad!

March 10, 1942

First General Meeting held in the Carpenter's Shop. Didn't know there are so many women interested in running and organizing of our camp. . . .

Chores for everyone and changes in roster every fortnight. Men allowed (under guard) to come over to help with the heavier work. The men and women are separated by the courtyard. Menu stinks! Rice and water—called "bubu"—tasteless and looks like dishwasher water. Porridge, maybe twice a week. Bread or buns every second day if you are lucky. Rations consist of about five sardines, a quarter tin of bully beef, with half a dozen tins of soup to feed about 100—some diet!!! Any extras of sugar and salt—I must carefully save for emergencies!

March 19, 1942

Miss Foss's birthday—had a little party for her on our floor. Each floor has its own doctor now—ours is Dr. Jeannette Robinson. LMO [Lady Medical Officer] is Dr. Helen Worth.

There are now over three hundred women and children in our camp. The men have been cooking our meals for a week, but now the kitchen has been built, and we do our own cooking for the whole camp. I help with the early morning teas and also the first drain sweeper in A Block. The men still can come to help with the heavier tasks, but we are not allowed to talk to them—the Jap sentries always accompany them.

One of the things we have to learn is to bow to the Japs whenever we see them. Heaven help us if we forget—a clout on the head, a bayonet threateningly thrust in front of you, or even a kick on the backside that could send you sprawling onto your face—so, don't forget to bow-wow-wow!!! And no whisperings please, or to gather in groups is also a no-no!

APRIL 14, 1942

SAW DAD yesterday. Being Easter Sunday—only children of seventeen and under were allowed—for an hour. Had no service, but I think the Japs will allow soon. Beginning to know a number of people—what a wonderful opportunity to study them—so many different characters—like in a storybook and what lessons you can learn from them!

APRIL 20, 1942

THE EMPEROR's birthday! Wow! We were ordered to face toward the sun at 10 o'clock with "two minutes" silence! When it was ended there were sounds of chains being pulled!!! As a special treat we were given a tin of pineapple to every three women and a box of Rinso to be shared between four women. Some celebration!!!

MAY 20, 1942

LIFE IS still the same old routine. The men have taken over our cooking—the place looks more cheerful. . . . Diet still terrible, and suffering from the effects of my first illness in January. Was carted off to hospital three weeks ago—how I hate hospitals. But Dr. Worth very nice, and so are the sisters, but still I was most anxious to come out. Dad came to see me about three times while in hospital. We had a Red Cross concert on May 2. It was a great success. I did a recitation and a dance. Mrs. Angela Kronin arranged it all—what style—what talents—Hollywood style no doubt!

OCTOBER 24, 1942

AM IN my cell and listening to the music from the men's side. They are playing lighter music. Mrs. Eisinger also planned this concert. Oh! Listen to that music—I am carried away from this existence to another world—a beautiful work of music as I wander dreamily through its strains. For just a while, all cares are forgotten. The concert's finished and I am brought to earth again. Short as it was, I felt refreshed. Music, music! The very word itself stirs my emotions and makes me forget for a while all weariness and sadness. . . .

FEBRUARY 4, 1943

EVER SINCE we first landed in internment, we've thought that things have to get worse before they start to get better. Have we accepted the fact?—I would say so as we seem to make the best of things—especially the children—there's the schoolroom where we can learn and study (that does while away part of the time!). There's the Rose Garden where we play and spend time entertaining in the Carpenter's Shop. The older boys lend a hand in helping too. The older girls (that means me too) look after the very young. Somehow we manage to keep up a high standard of health, conduct, education, and some measure of happiness.

With poor food, hardly space to move, nature and beauty are sadly missed and the worse part of it all, there is no home life—that family life which is the birthright of all. Despite that, we are managing to survive and grow into as fine a group as can be found anywhere.

Looking around me, I see all this is possible through the sacrifice, hard work, and cooperation of every woman here. There are mothers who worry about us. The doctors and nurses look after our health. The teachers take care of our mental development, and the entertainment committee gives us the humor to cope with our depression. Praise goes also to all the sweepers, drain workers who work tirelessly to keep the camp clean—not forgetting our Kitchen Squad, who manages to feed us best as they could with what they are given—we, the children, are their responsibility, and it's responsibility they take seriously. How wonderful they are, and I hope that I will never forget them when we leave here—end of my musing!

MAY 3, 1943

SOMETIMES I look up at the sky—clear sky—and that Milky Way—how I wish I am up there looking down and seeing women and children sleeping every which way and I ponder what is to become of us—how much longer can we stand being here and with each other. Already there are cracks in our community. Starvation, dysentery, beriberi, and malaria—just about everything is slowly taking its toll on our integrity, especially when we see our loved ones slowly fading away. . . .

This is war, and war seems to change people, and being in here in close proximity to other human beings can easily destroy our good intentions.

I look around me and take in everything that goes on—I look at the people here and the friends that I have made—friends like Jeannie Summers, Mary Winters, Joyce Edwards, and Nellie Symons—all around my age—we are in this together and we depend on each other to boost our morale and strange to say we seem to be blessed with a sense of humor!

AUGUST 1, 1943

HAD NEWS that Dad has gone into the hospital. Dr. Worth said not to worry too much, but I know it's more than that. He hasn't been well for weeks but refuses to see the docs. I noticed his legs swelling up and he had difficulty with his breathing. I hope the doctor keeps him in hospital for a while.

AUGUST 21, 1943

HEARD DR. E. S. Lawrie died around 6 this morning—suicide apparently. Afternoon in the Red Cross Hut saw many nurses and doctors attending the funeral. I wonder how many more will go the same way? Sometimes it isn't easy to be cheerful—especially when the "bug" hits you and you feel as if your inside is coming out in bits and pieces.

Dear God, please end this war soon and get us out of here before we slowly die from hunger.

AUGUST 26, 1943

ANOTHER SPELL in hospital—feeling rotten—no appetite! Got into trouble for not eating the "bubo"—horrible stuff! The doc warned if I don't eat the stuff I'll end up getting beriberi! I don't think I'll want to look at "watery rice" when I leave this hellhole of a place. Still losing weight—won't win in a beauty contest—I look at myself and what do

I see—tummy that sticks out—arms and legs—well, I think a spider's legs would look thicker than mine. Skin yellow with "atebrin"—yak! indeed and don't laugh.

JANUARY 1, 1944

COFFEE PARTY till 12:30 a.m. Greeted the New Year with singing and dancing and a few tears flowing freely from us all. Wonder what is in store for us in 1944—freedom?

Oh, God, deliver us from all this soon, soon. After a lot of hugging and wishing we went off to our respective resting places. I was too keyed up to go to sleep—just sat on the steps looking out at the stars, thinking my own thoughts.

JANUARY 14, 1944

JOYCE'S BIRTHDAY and she's 21! I wonder if I'll have my 21st birthday here too! But that's 2 years away—surely we'll be out of here then, or will we? Had a quiet birthday treat for Joyce. Later I sat with Pauline, Xenia, and Kyra and we started talking about spiders, fairies, and our war experiences. Xenia spoke of the two men who were under a truck that caught fire—they were covered in oil and they implored their mates to shoot them before the Japs could get to them. After, saw some of the prisoners with their hands bored and screwed together—how dreadful!

Then I told them what I had seen the day after we surrendered—a dying Chinese woman lying on the road with her tummy gashed open and her baby lying not far away with its head almost severed from its body—both of them just alive!

I think the bombing did that. Later I witnessed a Jap sentry plunge his sword into a baby's tummy to kill it, and he had a smile on his face! It was horrible! I couldn't help shivering, remembering that look on the man's face—as if he was enjoying what he was doing to that baby. Horrible vision to have before my eyes—can I ever forget—can I? Will I?

We sat in silence for a while.

January 26, 1944

Feeling sick today—off food and aching all over. Had to see the Doc to get permission to be off work tomorrow and instead got carted to hospital—malaria again!

April 8, 1944

Dad's birthday—55 today—gave him hankies that I had made. Told him that I have decided to take up nursing when we get out of here.

Men had a concert in their yard—very pleasant listening. More rumors of repatriation.

May 7, 1944
Sime Road Camp

New camp! Left Changi Jail about ½ past 2 this afternoon—in 7 trucks—men helped with luggage—gave hot tea to drink. A lovely, cool ride but not long enough. Fresh air—green, green everywhere—everything looks so normal! Volunteers needed for tin shed—Hut 16—separated from Mom—with Aunty Maude. Men ready to help us when we arrived. A bit of shifting about—first to go to the tin shed, then told to go to the "Flying Dutchman Hut." . . .

Got turfed out of that to go to Hut 16. Later told to go to Hut 14, then back to the Flying Dutchman, again to Hut 12—talk about moves on the chessboard!

Finally settled in Hut 5, but for the night! Evening told to be ready to move to Hut 16 in the morning.

May 13, 1944

At last moved (officially) to Hut 1—it's smaller than the others but it has a veranda and I've claimed a space there. Hope there won't be too much windy, wet weather—I could get a bit wet but at least I won't be disturbed by too many people and I'll be able to write without too many questions being asked. I think I shall sleep well tonight.

JULY 15, 1944

STARTED WORKING in the garden today—while digging to plant sweet potatoes found a worm—fat worm—picked up the wriggling thing and a thought came into my mind—wonder what it would taste like? Didn't fancy swallowing the squirming creature—threw it away—then found a clod of earth with more of the pink worms—had an idea—collected a tinful and later took it to the hut—decided to cook the worms and see what happens—well! All that was left after the cooking were thin strips of dried-up skins—not appetizing—but hunger took over—took a bit of a piece—not that bad—a sprinkle of salt and it tasted like bacon rind—well, I imagine that's how bacon rind would taste—crackly and salty! Did I tell anyone?—No way! They might think I've gone "cuckoo"—eating worms indeed—what next?

JULY 20, 1944

DID A dreadful thing today—thoroughly disgusted with myself—I swallowed a baby mouse! Found a nest of baby mice in the lalang—so tiny and pink and helpless—I was so very hungry after working in the garden and food was getting scarce. Without thinking I scooped up one and popped it in my mouth and before I realized what I had done, I swallowed it. Immediately I stuck my finger in my throat to make sick, but it was gone, and I did feel a bit green after that. Afraid I was very subdued little person and felt really awful about the incident—how could I have done such a thing and I couldn't even tell anyone about it. I don't even want to think about it, and even the worms have lost their attraction—I feel sick!!!

SEPTEMBER 5, 1944

DREADFUL DAY—6 girls and Mother Begg on their knees in front of the Flying Dutchman—apparently one of the girls was slapped and the girls were seen stealing.

Begg dismissed at lunchtime, but the girls had to stay without lunch until 3 p.m. "Blue stocking" arrived unexpectedly—told Mrs. Chowns to call the father of one of the girls. Thrashed the poor man and broke his stick. Then told him to get down on his knees and had him whacked dozens of times till he fell on the ground—still "Blue-stocking" hit him—the daughter was in hysterics and she screamed each time the stick fell on the man—Mrs. Chowns pleaded for him, and at long last at her request told the man to go. Was assisted back to his camp—body covered in weals. Eyewitnesses, including myself, in tears—we felt so helpless—to strike a helpless man and especially when lying on the ground—it's so brutal, so inhuman—how could one human do that to another? Dear God, what have you let us in for? How could you let it happen—how much longer?

This incident made us all wary, and I must be very, very careful that I don't get caught writing this. In fact I don't know how much longer I can continue to write—am having trouble getting another exercise book and have to resort to writing as small as I can—no more ink so looks like I will have to be writing in pencil again.

APRIL 15, 1945

CAME OUT of hospital yesterday. Went in on Friday the sixth. Thought malaria, but it was dysentery—lost weight again and feeling weak in the legs. Dad went in hospital too but came out two days ago and is now in the Convalescent Unit. . . . I saw Dad—he had a cut on his forehead, a black eye, and a sore hand—asked what happened—could not remember.

This evening Anna asked what happened to Dad—told her he had fainted and hurt himself. She made a wry face—"I wonder if I should tell you. . . ." Caught a note in her voice and knew something was wrong. "Tell me what, Anna?" I asked. She was reluctant to continue. . . . "I think you'd better tell me, no matter how bad it may be," I said gently. . . .

"He was given a bad hiding," Anna whispered, fearful of the walls around us whose ears are always on the alert.

"A hiding? But whatever for and from whom?" I asked.

"From one of the men—apparently your father took a knife belonging to someone—the owner saw it and hit him pretty badly,

and he had to be taken to hospital." I was shocked and bewildered at
the thought that Dad had a knife with him—what ideas could be running in his mind? This is the second time Dad has been in a sort of
disgrace—is he responsible for his own actions? I've noticed lately that
he rambles a lot about the past—not making much sense really. He
seems such a child in his manner, and I am worried about his mental
state. . . .

Dear Dad, to think the war has done this to you. Please God, take
care of him—he doesn't deserve this—help him please.

June 9, 1945

I HAD just finished my shower when Maureen came with the words—
"Get ready at once and go over to the Men's Camp. Your father has
had a seizure." I needed no explanation. I hurried over to Mom's
hut—she was crying. Dr. Winchester and "Goran-pa" [a sentry] were
waiting to take us over. Arrived in the ward—screens around the bed,
and I saw Father Cosgrove come out from behind the screens. He
came forward and spoke to Mom—could not catch what he said, but
when Mom let out a scream and turned sobbing to me, I knew—Dad
had gone—too late for us to say good-bye. . . .

Tried to remember Dad as he was, but tears kept clouding my
eyes. How I wished I was there before he died and even after his death.
I would have liked to have been able to touch his face and hold him
close to me and to say that I love him and wish him good-bye. Oh,
Dad—sorry we were too late to see you. Are you at peace and looking
down at us poor mortals? I'm going to miss you, oh so much—and
there is so much I wanted to say but most of all I want to say, "I love
you, Dad. Good-bye—rest in peace, Dad."

He is gone—no more will I see his face, hear his boyish laughter,
see his many tricks of expression—his jokes, his loving arms around
me. It is so hard to realize that I won't be meeting him again in the
Orchard—bringing him extra food—he was always very hungry and
always enjoyed the food such as it was. But now—he will no longer be
hungry, no longer be plagued with sickness. Dear God, thy Will be
done.

So, Dad dearest, Mom and I say, "Sleep now and be at rest for always."

The funeral service is set for 11 a.m. tomorrow.

JUNE 10, 1945

TODAY I awoke, heavy-eyed—everybody most kind. Went to Mass and Communion and prayed for Dad. After Mass was over, felt a tap on my shoulder and a voice whispered in my ear—"My deepest sympathy, Sheila. Come and see me when you feel like it and if talking will help." . . . There were flowers from all those who have gardens. . . .

The coffin was taken out to the cemetery—I don't know where. Too confused and too upset to ask—in fact, I can't remember much about what happened afterward—all I know is that I haven't been able to say good-bye to Dad in the proper way—"Oh, God, how could you do this to me—what am I going to do without his helping hand. Please help me to understand and to humbly say Thy Will be done and to thank you for those precious years we've had together. Maybe, Lord, you know best."

Mrs. Cummings and Harrison took charge of Mom. I went over to Jean's and Mary's hut for comfort and quiet. Tears flowed at last! Finally I went to see Mom, who was lying down. Her tear-stained face pulled me together—she needed comforting and so I held her close to me and together we let our tears flow freely—it helped to share our grief.

Later parcels were given out—how sad I felt as I opened them and almost choked at the sight of food, thinking how Dad loved food, always talking about the parcels and so thankful at any extras given. It doesn't matter now as he won't be needing them again— ever again!

AUGUST 16, 1945

THE LATEST—great excitement. POWs spoke to Hut 1—"War over on the fifteenth." Everything is over. Our military is taking over on the twentieth. . . . Felt ill—malaria and dysentery, also sore throat.

AUGUST 19, 1945

CONFIRMED AT last—all over! *Deo Gratias!* Cannot write more. Rain. Meeting.

AUGUST 31, 1945

GREAT EXCITEMENT—young uniformed RMC [Royal Marine Corps] came in.

M said "A visitor from Ceylon"—very young and shy and fairly mobbed by us—with several others from place—paratroopers came to report on suitable airfield—horrified at the state of Men's Hospital and Changi Prison—12,000 in there, 9,000 inside. . . . Radio in camp— heard news last night. A thrill hearing "Big Ben" chiming and in familiar words—"This is London calling"—what joy—gathered very little from news—as heard only end of it—something said about the leaders going to be tried by military tribunal for major war crimes— from USA heard about the POWs in Japan—was worse than Hell! Starved and brutally treated. Food and more food—today drawing in the Australian Red Cross parcels were wool, knitting needles, powder puff, face cream, lipstick, toilet paper and sanitary towels, writing pads, dark glasses, etc. Had powder and puff. Today had iced drinks— was delicious—smokes came in—more individual parcels from outside. Afternoon came with a man taking down where we wanted to go. M said Australia for me and nationality Australian. 3 others joining Nursing. . . .

Now wondering whether best to train in Australia or stay here. . . . Mom reconciled to idea of my going away. . . . Feeling rather sad in midst of laughter because of thinking of M—soon, very soon we will part, perhaps never more to meet.

SEPTEMBER 12, 1945

THIS MORNING, most of the camp turned out to witness the victory parade—it was the formal surrender by the Japanese officers to Lord Mountbatten on the steps of the Municipal Offices. The Padang was packed with (looked like the whole population of Singapore was there) people. Planes, flying boats, transport planes, fighter planes, and bombers (you name it, anything that flies) flew low and zoomed here, there. The army, navy were assembled on the Padang together with the band—the marines did look smart in their "whites." What a lovely sight—we cheered and clapped and we hugged each other and cried and laughed and then cried again! The atmosphere was unreal! . . .

The Flag (our beloved flag) was hoisted while the band gloriously and thrillingly played "God Save the King" followed by French, Dutch, Chinese, and American anthems. Heard speeches—had photos taken. We cheered and danced and cheered ourselves hoarse. There was dancing in the streets—we were mad, gloriously madly happy—Time stood still as we let our hair down—for a moment we forgot those 3½ years as we went into a frenzy of dancing, singing—we are FREE, FREE, FREE! AT LAST!

Finally exhaustion took over—physically and emotionally. How we got back to camp I don't know—I think we got a lift back—was too tired to think! And collapsed on my bed and knew no more! This evening had pictures showing in the Orchard but we (the Gang) decided to go to the Dutch Club in town—we had been invited by the R.A.F. boys. Unfortunately, I missed out due to having woke up too late to be ready in time when the boys came to pick the girls up in the gharry. So went to see the pictures instead—enjoyable but a bit long—maybe still suffering from the excitement of this morning! I was standing up when someone offered me a seat—we got talking—Arthur is his name, and he had nursed Dad. After the show we walked back toward the huts—it was a pleasant night as we ambled along. Talked of many things. He is also Scots—I sure can pick them. . . .

NOVEMBER 24, 1945

AUSTRALIA

I HAVE a very nice little room to myself, and I do all my writing in here. Here I am—6 stone 3 lbs [87 lbs]! but Aunty Grace is feeding me so much that I feel more than that, and to think I was nearly 10 stone [140 lbs] before the war—what a fat pig I must have been!

Have to be at least 8 stone [112 lbs] before I can start nursing—hopefully next year at the Queen Victoria Memorial Hospital.

Dear Diary, we have been on a long journey, you and I, and now we have come to a crossroad. You and I must take our leave here—sadly I must say good-bye, dear friend. Your journey is now ended and belongs to the past. Mine is the future—a road I must travel to begin a new life in Australia.

But you will not be forgotten, dear Diary. Your pages are my most precious memories of the past three and a half years of my life, and I will remember again those experiences shared with my family and fellow internees. In time bitterness and sadness will be replaced by sympathy, understanding, and love toward others.

"Memories live longer than dreams

They are much stronger than dreams."

So say words of a song. We've made our memories, you and I. Good-bye, dear, dear Diary, but I will remember through your pages.

AFTERWORD

It had been Sheila's late father's wish for her to go to Australia. She arrived in 1945 and became a triple-certificate nursing sister. She married in 1958 and has a son, who is a member of the RAAF, and a daughter. In 2002 she took part in a trip to London to find answers to some of the lingering questions about Changi Jail and the Sime Road camp. Finally, in 2004, she made an emotional trip to Singapore to say good-bye to Changi Jail, which was filmed as the documentary Sayonara Changi.

Sheila lectures extensively about her time in the camp and about the Changi quilts the women made, supposedly for the wounded in Changi hospitals but in reality to relieve the boredom of internment, to boost morale, and to pass information to other camps. Each woman was asked to put "something of herself" into the square, together with her signature. Sheila's work is represented in the quilt for Australia.

Sheila says that she "enjoys every moment being alive, thankful for having survived."

Inge Pollack
1939

Piete Kuhr

Children playing in the Changi camp, where Sheila Allan was incarcerated

*Sheila's father,
John Charles Allan,
in the years prior
to World War II*

1946

1940

Sheila Allan

EARLY
MORNING
--- HEART MOUNTAIN
NOV. 12, 1943

Stanley Hayami

Drawing from
Stanley Hayami's
diary, 1943

DEC. 8, 1942

Today, last year I went to school excited, scared (tho I had no reason to be) and sort of embarrassed. When I went to class everyone was talking about it and I felt a little conspicuous as if everyone was looking at me. The rest of the kids said hello to me as usual and all tried to keep off the topic of war. However I didn't feel much like talking about anything that day. All during English Class my English teacher had the news broadcasts on. One report was coming from Manila and was cut short as Jap. planes began flying over. After I got home I did little else except listening to news reports.

Today I took my physical exams.

HMM, MAYBE YOU'RE DEAD.

Stanley's diary, 1942

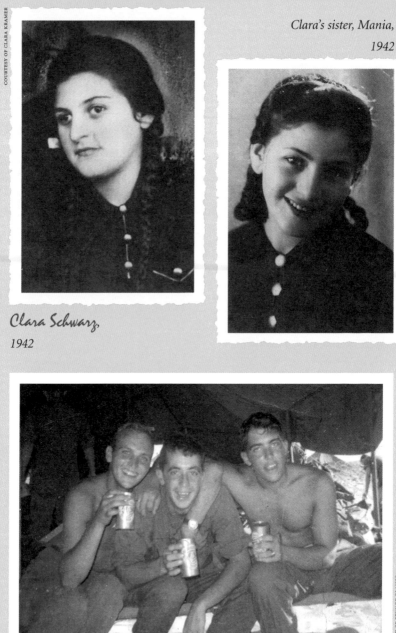

Clara's sister, Mania,
1942

Clara Schwarz,
1942

Ed Blanco
(right) in Vietnam, 1968

Ed in the field, 1968

Ed keeps track of the wounded and the dead

Zlata Filipović
in Sarajevo, 1993

Shiran Zelikovich
reads her diary, 2004

Mary Mazrieh Hazboun,
2004

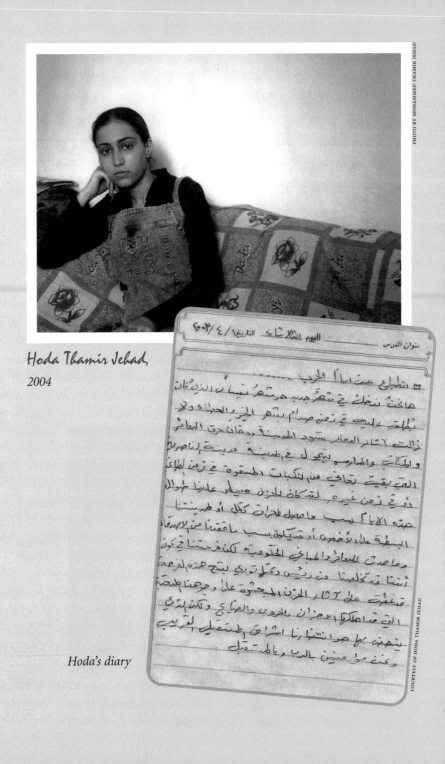

Hoda Thamir Jehad,
2004

Hoda's diary

Stanley Hayami

UNITED STATES
1942–44 (17–19 YEARS OLD)

I shall remember that day I was evacuated
for the rest of my life. . . .

One of the United States' significant national defense actions during
World War II was the mass evacuation of persons of Japanese ancestry
from California, the western regions of Oregon and Washington, and
southern Arizona. Persons of Japanese descent were also removed from
Alaska, and plans were laid down for the transfer of Japanese persons
from Hawaii to the mainland. This policy was a reaction to the aggressive bombing of Pearl Harbor by Japanese forces on December 7, 1941. It
was also in part a precaution taken by the government, because it feared
that the Japanese population living in America could prove a threat to
national security as the U.S. Army planned its retaliation. In an official
statement from the Department of Justice, Japanese immigrants were referred to as "dangerous persons." In some cases, individuals were given just
forty-eight hours to leave their homes. By 1943, all internees above the age
of seventeen were required to sign a loyalty pact that stated the following:

1. Are you willing to serve in the armed forces of the United
    States on combat duty wherever ordered?
2. Will you swear unqualified allegiance to the United States
    of America and faithfully defend the United States from
    any or all attacks by foreign or domestic forces and
    forswear any form of allegiance or obedience to the Japa-

nese emperor, to any other foreign government, power, or organization?

Born in 1925, Stanley Hayami, a Japanese-American teenager from California, was taken from his home and placed in the Heart Mountain internment camp. Heart Mountain opened on August 12, 1942, and closed on November 10, 1945. At its height, the camp's population was over 10,000—it is estimated that up to 120,000 Japanese Americans were interned during World War II across the United States. Most of the prisoners in Heart Mountain came from the Los Angeles area and central Washington. In July 1944, sixty-three prisoners who had resisted the draft were convicted and sentenced to three years in prison. The camp was made up of 468 buildings, divided into twenty blocks. Each block had two laundry-toilet buildings. Each building had six rooms, which were small and sparsely furnished. Military police were stationed in nine guard towers, equipped with searchlights; barbed-wire fencing surrounded the camp. It was not unheard of for individuals to die in the camps, especially those in the desert regions, due to inadequate medical attention. Many detention-center survivors admitted that their livelihoods had been destroyed to an extent that they could not fully recover after release.

Despite the devastating atomic bomb attacks by U.S. forces on Hiroshima and Nagasaki in 1945, Japanese insurgence was relatively minimal. Nevertheless, the paranoia was such that the Japanese earned the nickname "The Yellow Peril." It took nearly fifty years for Congress to pass the Civil Liberties Act of 1988, which finally acknowledged that "a grave injustice was done." Each victim of internment was to be paid $20,000 in reparations.

DECEMBER 8, 1942

TODAY, LAST year, I went to school excited, scared (tho' I had no reason to be), and sort of embarrassed. When I went to class everyone was talking about it, and I felt a little conspicuous, as if everyone was looking at me. The rest of the kids said hello to me as usual and all tried to stay off the topic of war. However, I didn't feel much like talking about anything that day. All during English class my English teacher had the news broadcast on. One report was from Manila and was cut short as Jap. planes began flying over. When I got home I did little else except listen to news reports.

TODAY I took my physical exam. *Oh no, I think he's dead* . . . [Stanley refers here to a drawing he makes of himself with the doctor.]

DECEMBER 14, 1942

LAST MONDAY the Kibei and Issei rioted at Manzanar. They were celebrating Pearl Harbor, and some loyal American soldiers tried to stop them and they killed one and injured several others. Among those who were injured and had to be taken away for their own safety was Tod Ujero. Tod lived over the road from us at San Gabriel and was our competitor. The internal police could do nothing, so the military police were summoned into camp. The rioters charged the nips with rocks, so they threw tear gas bombs. When this didn't work, they shot at the rioters and wounded a few. Now Manzanar is under martial law. During the riot, in which there was a mob of about 4,000, one group tried to haul down the "Stars and Stripes" but failed as fountain boy scouts stood guard with rocks and repulsed them.

I hope nothing like that ever happens around here. Now the politicians and such are starting again in trying to take the Jap. American's citizenship away and make things more strict in camp. Heck, those guys should remember that over half are loyal Americans and the rest are Kibei or Issei. I don't see why us innocent and good guys should have to pay for stuff that the Japanese do. Things like what happened at Manzanar make all of us look like bad saboteurs when just a minority are the ones causing trouble. Darn it, anyhow us loyal Jap. Americans have no chance. When we're outside people look at us suspiciously and think we're spies. Now that we're in camp the Japs look at us and say we're bad 'cause we still love America. And now the people outside want to take our citizenship away from us as if we're the bad ones, when it's really the Kibei and Issei. If they take our citizenship away from us, we'll be people without a country, 'cause, gee whiz! who in the hell wants a Japanese citizenship? I wouldn't go there for nothin'! I guess if they take away our citizenship, I'll just have to melt off to some island and start my own country.

P.S. Tonite we had a twenty-minute blackout.

JANUARY 1, 1943

WELL, TODAY is the first day of the year nineteen hundred and forty-three. I wonder what it has in store for me?

Wonder what it has in store for everybody?

Wonder where I'll be next year?

Wonder when the war will end?

Last year, today, I said I hoped that the war would end in a year. Well, it didn't, but this year I say again, "I hope the war ends this year, but definitely."

Another thing is I hope I'm out of here and a free man by '44.

Here are a few New Year's resolutions I hope I can live up to:

1. I resolve to be more tolerant,
   Not only with my family members but with everyone.
2. I resolve to be more understanding of others and more appreciative.
   This goes hand in hand with no. 1. Great men are great because they understand people better. They are great because they are not narrow-minded. One of the things a person wants most is appreciation—so I want to give people as much appreciation as possible.
3. I resolve to study as hard as I can and learn as much as I can
   So that when I am a man I won't be a dumbbell.
4. I resolve to help Ma and Pa more.
5. I resolve not to abandon any high ambitions.

. . .

PREDICTION: WAR will end between 1943–44, about one and a half years more.

TODAY IN the morning I played cards, and then in the afternoon I listened to football games. Well, the Rose Bowl game came out as I expected but not as I hoped. Most people said Georgia would smother UCLA, but I said it would be pretty close. UCLA held Georgia scoreless for three quarters, but Georgia piled it on in the last and won 9–0. I hoped UCLA would win, which they didn't however.

Last year at this time I was at home in San Gabriel, Calif. and now I am here in an evacuation camp in Heart Mountain, Wyo. Gosh a lot happened last year. In the spring we had to work hard to sell out our stock. In Easter we quit, handed over the nursery to Mr. Dailey. We moved to Los Angeles for a month until evacuation to Pomono A. Center. After Pomono we boarded a train, and after about three and a half days of traveling through Nevada, Utah, and Colorado, we reached this camp in Wyoming. And here I am today, hoping that next year at this time I'll be home or somewhere else outside of camp.

MAY 14, 1943

TODAY MARKS the end of one year in camp for me. I shall remember that day I was evacuated for the rest of my life. I shall remember how I stood on the corner of Garvey and Atlantic with a thousand others—then the buses came and whisked us off to camp. I shall remember the lump that came into my throat as the bus went down the street, and when some of the people on the sidewalks and Mexicans in the fields waved at us.

I shall remember the barbed wire, the armed guards, the towers, the dust, the visitors, the food lines, the typhoid shots, my busboy job, my messenger job, the crowded barracks, the nightly talent shows, the friends I made, my judo lessons, bed count, and finally my leaving on the train to here.

I shall remember the train ride, the sleepless nights, the deserts, the mountains, the beautiful scenery.

Now that I am here, I think of the cold weather I have been thru, the dust storms and the rest of my hardships. But I will also remember all the friends I made here, the tough school I went to, and I feel no bitterness to the government for the evacuation—though I still feel that it wasn't right.

JANUARY 31, 1944

NEW LEASE on life!

Man do I feel swell! 'Member I thought I had TB or something, well I don't. Dr. Robbins looked my X-rays over and told me there's nothing wrong with my lungs. So I guess I'll go on to college! or the army.

And I made up my mind on something else, too—I'm going into the artist-writer field. And I'm going to be the best artist in the world (even if my IQ is low), and another thing, after I graduate from college I'm going to bum my way around the world. So the world better watch out. Hayami is going to the top!

I'd better start building up my body, though. I want it to come with me.

Just a little while ago, I walked up to the hospital—I was jittery and nervous as hell. By the time I got to the hospital, though, I didn't feel as bad—I tried not to think about it—I felt that this might be the most unhappiest day or the happiest of my life—it turned out to be the most happiest! Dr. Robbins, smoking a long black cigar, said, "Nothing there, my boy," as he read my X-ray. "You can sing for joy." He extended his hand, but I was so stupefied and so sure that I had TB that I forgot to shake it. In fact I walked about a block back home before it sank in. Then I looked around—beautiful day isn't it!—sun shining down on the bright white snow, children yelling and playing— all happiness—no worries!—the future ahead of me!

God has smiled down on me. I thought maybe I'm not worth it. I'm *determined* to make myself worth it.

MARCH 24, 1944, 10:05 P.M.

Hawaiian guitars playing
Ukuleles humming

Warm summer nights
Crickets
Creak of the screen door
Cars in the street not far
Green plants and shrubbery
Eucalyptus trees sighing
and rustling in a cooling breeze
Brothers, sisters and ma and pa's
laughter, scolding, and just plain nothing
These are the thoughts I have tonight.

MARCH 26, 1944

LAST NIGHT I finished reading about the life of a great Negro, George Washington Carver. The story of his life is bound to influence greatly my own.

For one thing I no longer felt satisfied with my choice of becoming a book illustrator and taking art and literature in college. No, after I read that book I regained my former love for nature and science and felt my life would be wasted, so far as being of service to mankind.

My own feelings and interests and loves fell in remarkably close with Carver's. For one thing, we both love nature; secondly, he and I both love, could and can do creative artwork; third, we both like science; fourth, he too was handicapped by racial prejudice only more so than I; fifth, neither of us wanted to make a fortune. (I don't base success on how much money a person has. I want to use money as a means but not an end in itself.) Sixth, he and I in the most part have no desire for fame. I believe fame comes to those worthy of it. Not to those who go in search of it. The only difference between Carver and me is that Carver had brains. Carver was also excellent in music, and Carver believed firmly in God, heart, mind, and soul. (I want to believe in God, I hold him dear in my heart, but doggone it, my mind won't. I pray to God that he will make my mind believe in God also.)

Finally, Carver had to make a decision over his love for art and his love for nature and science. He chose nature and science because he said, "I can help my race better through agriculture."

I too have felt that I should serve God and mankind (had something of that sort in my mind on January 31 of 1944—last sentence). I too feel that life should have a lofty purpose, and reading that book convinced me of this. Wasn't it Edward Bok's mother who said, "Edward, leave this earth a little more pleasant, a little more beautiful because you have been in it"? And that's just what I'm thinking when I say I want to leave the earth a little more richer than the fertilizer in my body will return it. Come to think of it, my body is only returning what it took out, in other words, I should leave some pay for the interest too.

I want my life to be constructive, not destructive.

AUGUST 20, 1944

TODAY IS a beautiful morning. Up and down our barracks, I can hear kids playing, doors opening and closing. Radios speaking in the barracks across from me. Japanese records playing at the back of me. Pop's over at the shogi room, I guess—he's supposed to work out this morning with the dumbbells he received two weeks ago from York. Walt's still in bed sleeping, he went to our block social last night.

Gee, I sure wish I could dance . . .

I guess it's like everything else—you've got to drive yourself and learn—no use sitting and wishing. Mom is probably washing clothes. I wonder how Grace is over in New York—haven't seen her now for a year, she's taking psychology and math at Hunter College. Her birthday is next week—good thing I sent her a present already.

I guess Frank's over at that picnic at Shelby today.

Well, the reason I'm writing again after such a long lapse is because around next Tuesday I'm going to go to active duty. Probably this shall be the last time I will write in this book in a long time. Perhaps I should also go over some of the news that has happened to me over the past three months. Well, France has been invaded and the Allies are now close to Paris. Saipan Island in the South Pacific has been taken with the result that Premier Tojo and his entire staff were forced to quit. Hitler has been almost killed. In Italy the Japanese Americans are doing a wonderful job. The Hundredth is the most decorated out-fit in the army. Willie wrote from some place in Italy. Hasn't seen action yet. Volunteers from our camp have already met their death.

Heart Mountain has been a dead place—a wonderfully live place too. Dust has blown through it and snowstorms too. Someday, from a foreign battlefield, I shall remember it with homesickness. Mother, father, brother, sister, friends, mess halls, movie theaters, ice skating, swimming, school, weightlifting—all shall try to well up in my throat at once.

Aloha.

STANLEY HAYAMI

AFTERWORD

Stanley left Heart Mountain in June 1944 to join the U.S. Army. He never lost his faith in America and remained defiantly patriotic to the last. He wrote the final extract of his diary while awaiting his first assignment in his U.S. barracks. He was killed in combat in northern Italy on April 23, 1945, while trying to help a fellow soldier. He was nineteen years old.

HOLOCAUST

1939—45

Voices

Yitskhok Rudashevski

LITHUANIA
1940–42 (13–15 YEARS OLD)

I have been cut off from all that is dear and precious to me.

Clara Schwarz

POLAND
1942–44 (15–17 YEARS OLD)

Who knows if all this suffering is for nothing?
Will we survive?

The Holocaust is a term used to describe the organized persecution and murder of the Jewish people of Europe by the Nazis during World War II. Two thirds of the 9 million Jews living in Europe before 1933 were killed during the Holocaust, which lasted up until Germany was defeated in 1945.

The Nazis were the National Socialist German Workers Party, a political organization that came to power under Adolf Hitler in 1933. Once in power, the Nazis brought democracy to an end in Germany, restricting the life of its people through control of the press and the social structures of *the country. Hitler established an atmosphere of fear and suspicion in Germany, which enabled his party to perpetrate increasingly aggressive policies. Jews were scapegoated by the Nazis, who blamed them for Germany's defeat in World War I and for its economic hardships. The Nazis also believed that Germans were "racially superior" and that the so-called inferior races polluted Europe. Jews, Gypsies, and the handicapped were seen as a genuine biological threat to the "purity" of the German people, also called "Aryan." A policy of systematic murder developed out of such paranoia.*

In the late 1930s the Nazis killed thousands of handicapped Germans by lethal injection and poisonous gas. After the German invasion of the Soviet Union in June 1941, mobile killing units began shooting massive numbers of Jews and Gypsies in open fields and ravines on the outskirts of conquered cities and towns. Eventually, the Nazis realized that they needed a more efficient way of exterminating such large numbers of people. In 1942, the Wannsee Conference laid out the Final Solution of the Jewish Question. The Nazis created a segregated and organized method of killing by establishing six extermination centers in occupied Poland, where large-scale murder by gas (and body disposal through cremation) was brutally performed. Victims were taken from their hometowns and cities and transported to these centers to await their deaths. Many victims of the Holocaust also perished in the organized ghettos and concentration camps as a result of forced hard work, deliberate starvation, and neglect, and from diseases that were rife in the appalling conditions of the ghettos and camps.

Yitskhok Rudashevski was a young Jewish man, the only child of Rose and Elihu Rudashevski, who lived in the Lithuanian capital of Vilnius. In July 1941, the Germans massacred 35,000 Jewish men, women, and children in the Ponary forest outside Vilnius. In September, the remaining Jewish inhabitants were forced to live in a sectioned part of the city, designated as the Jewish ghetto. This law came with the German occupation of Lithuania between 1941 and 1944. Conditions in the ghetto were horrific, with little food available and the constant threat of violence from the Nazis. Despite these surroundings, Yitskhok continued to write in his diary.

Clara Schwarz went into hiding when her hometown of Zolkiew in

Poland was taken by the Nazis. Together with seventeen other Jews, Clara was forced to remain underground in the extremely cramped conditions of a bunker for two years, while Nazi soldiers lived above them and discussed their plans to exterminate the Jews, unaware of the people beneath their feet. For their survival, Clara and those hiding with her depended upon the continued existence and goodwill of the non-Jewish couple that also lived in the building. A trapdoor to their hiding place was hidden beneath the bed of this married couple.

YITSKHOK RUDASHEVSKI, LITHUANIA, 1940–42

JUNE 21, 1940

THE HITLERITES have attacked our land. They have forced a war upon us. And so we shall retaliate, and strike until we shall smash the aggressor on his own soil. I keep looking at the calm Red Army soldier who is standing on guard in our yard. I feel that I can be sure of him, I see he will not perish. He will perhaps be killed, but the star attached to his hat will remain forever.

JUNE 1941

OUR HEARTS are crushed witnessing the shameful scene where women and older people are beaten and kicked in the middle of the street by small bandits. . . . I stand at the window and feel a sense of rage, tears come to my eyes: All our helplessness, all our loneliness, lies in the streets, there is no one to take our part. And we ourselves are so helpless, so helpless! . . . It rains incessantly. We are so sad, so lonely. We are exposed to mockery and humiliation.

JULY 4, 1941

I AM looking through the window and see before me the first Vilna Jews with badges. It was painful to see how people were staring at them. The large piece of yellow material on their shoulders seemed to be burning me, and for a long time I could not put on the badges. I felt a hump, as though I had two frogs on me. I was ashamed to appear in them on the street, not because it would be noticed that I am a Jew, but because I was ashamed of what [they were] doing to us. I was ashamed of our helplessness. We will be hung from head to foot with badges, and we cannot help each other in any way. It hurt me that I saw absolutely no way out.

SEPTEMBER 6, 1941

I GO around with bleary eyes among the bundles, see how we are being uprooted overnight from our home. Soon we have our first view of the move to the ghetto, a picture of the Middle Ages—a gray-black mass of people harnessed to large bundles. We understand that soon our turn will come. I look at the house in disarray, I see things scattered that were dear to me, that I was accustomed to using. We carry the bundles to the courtyard. On our street a new mass of Jews streams continually to the ghetto. The small number of Jews in our courtyard begin to drag the bundles to the gate. . . . We, too, are carried along with the mass of Jews with their bundles. . . . People fall, bundles scatter. Before me a woman bends under her bundle. From the bundle a thin stream of rice keeps pouring over the street. . . .

I walk burdened and irritated. The Lithuanians drive us on, do not let us rest. I think of nothing: not what I am losing, not what I have just lost, not what is in store for me. I do not see the streets before me, the people passing by. I only feel that I am terribly weary, I feel that an insult, a hurt, is burning inside me. Here is the ghetto gate. I feel that I have been robbed, my freedom is being robbed from me, my home, and the familiar Vilna streets I love so much. I have been cut off from all that is dear and precious to me.

OCTOBER 1, 1941

MANY PEOPLE have gathered in the two stories of the hideout. They sneak along like shadows by candlelight around the cold, dank cellar walls. The whole hideout is filled with restless murmuring. An imprisoned mass of people. Everyone begins to settle down in the corners, on the stairs. Pillows and bundles are spread out on the hard bricks and boards, and people fall asleep. . . . From time to time, someone lights a match. By the light I see people lying on bricks like rags in the dirt. I think: Into what kind of helpless, broken creature can man be transformed? I am at my wit's end. I begin to feel very nauseated. . . .

We are like animals surrounded by the hunter. The hunter on all sides: beneath us, above us, from the sides. Broken locks snap, doors creak, axes, saws. I feel the enemy under the boards on which I am standing. The light of an electric bulb seeps through the cracks. They pound, tear, break. Soon the attack is heard from another side. Suddenly, somewhere upstairs a child bursts into tears. A desperate groan breaks forth from everyone's lips. We are lost. A desperate attempt to shove sugar into the child's mouth is to no avail. They stop up the child's mouth with pillows. The mother of the child is weeping. People shout in wild terror that the child should be strangled. The child is shouting more loudly, the Lithuanians are pounding more strongly against the walls. However, slowly everything calms down of itself. We understand that they have left. Later, we heard a voice from the other side of the hideout. You are liberated. My heart beat with such joy! I have remained alive!

SEPTEMBER 27, 1942

THE NEWS struck me like a clap of thunder: Teacher Gershteyn has died. How beloved and precious he was to me in his proud, pure appearance. . . .

The teacher Gershteyn suffered a great deal in the ghetto. He became grayer and grayer, his face darkened. He lived in a classroom of our school. He could hardly go up the steps, which he used to ascend so cheerfully. He had to stop on every step in his wrinkled coat, which probably served as a pillow for him. . . . Slowly, an old man before his time, he used to walk through the streets of the ghetto, but his head was erect as usual. That is how the best among us suffered in the ghetto. . . . The ghetto was too difficult for Gershteyn, and he did not survive it. He stands before my eyes. He appears so beautifully, so freshly before me from the midst of our dreary life. Forever and ever will we remember you as our dear friend, the image of your proud figure will remind us of something that is precious and dear. What you have given us of yourself will always flourish among us.

DECEMBER 10, 1942

I MADE up my mind not to trifle my time away in the ghetto on nothing, and I feel somehow happy that I can study, read, develop myself, and see that time does not stand still as long as I progress normally with it. In my daily ghetto life, it seems to me that I live normally, but often I have deep qualms. Surely I could have lived better. Must I day in, day out see the walled-up ghetto gate, must I in the best years see only one little street, the few stuffy courtyards? . . . I wish to shout to time to linger, not to run. I wish to recapture my past year and keep it for later, for the new life. My second feeling today is that of strength and hope. I do not feel the slightest despair. Today I became fifteen years of age, and I live confident in the future, I am not worried about it, but see before me sun and sun and sun.

AFTERWORD

Yitskhok's final diary entry is dated April 7, 1943. In August 1943, the Germans resolved to empty the ghetto, sending some of the Jews to Estonia and murdering the remaining. Yitskhok and his parents fled to a hideout in his uncle's home. They survived for two weeks along with five others but were found out by the Germans in October. Yitskhok and his family were taken to the forest and murdered. One of Yitskhok's cousins escaped the massacre and joined the partisans in the surrounding forests. After the war, he returned to Vilnius, whose population of 80,000 Jews had left or been killed, and found Yitskhok's diary.

CLARA SCHWARZ, POLAND, 1942–44

SUMMER OF 1942

THERE IS terror and panic in our city. The Jews are building bunkers (hiding places) of all kinds: underground, double-walled, or anywhere they can find a spot to hide. Others are looking for help from the gentiles. Others are crying in despair at the loss of their loved ones.

The cause of this is the trains crammed with Jews that pass our city on their way to Belzec.

The Jews are loaded in sealed cattle cars, 100–150 in each car. Belzec is located in a forest area, and that is where they are killed. What kind of death it is, we don't know. There are rumors that they are poisoned with gas, others say they are electrocuted, burned, or killed with guns. One thing's for sure, there is no return from there.

And now, the jumpers, the so-called *skoczki,* are beginning to appear. These are people who jump from the wagons, once they have succeeded in breaking the bars on the little window high in the car. A jump like this is very dangerous, but they have nothing to lose; they are doomed anyway. It's better to die on the spot than ride in the train with the knowledge of certain death. Most of them are naked because the heat in the train is unbearable. They have to be clothed once they have been given medical help. It's very rare for them to remain unhurt after jumping from such a height and having Germans shooting at them.

The first one to help them is Pepcia Fish. She is a hunchback but the only Jewish nurse in Zolkiew. She has a heart of gold. Young girls help her in this work, and I join them. I go with her and help dress the wounded, collect clothing and food. We get a little money from the Judenrat [Jewish Committee]; the Jews of the city give as much as they can. Most of the time, the *skoczki* are put in the hospital or in Jewish homes.

There are terrible tragedies, unbelievable tragedies. Parents jump and leave their children on the train, children leave parents, sisters leave behind sisters, and jump to save their lives. It's even worse than the dread of the kind of death awaiting them. Nobody really knows how they are killed. In Pepi's house, where most of the *skoczki* come, they meet people from the same city or friends, and they find out who was on the train. I once witnessed such a meeting that would surely cause a stone to weep. But I'm sorry to say, the Gestapo is not touched by Jewish tears. They shoot indiscriminately at the people who jump, young or old.

Our house doesn't have a proper place to build a bunker. Daddy, together with his friends Melman and Patrontasch, built two bunkers. One is in our factory, the second in Melman's house.

NOVEMBER 22, 1942

FINALLY COMES the memorable day. We slept in Melman's house because Saturday was a panic. They said that the city was surrounded by Gestapo. It's 5 o'clock in the morning, we are still in bed. Mr. Patrontasch, as always, is outside watching what is going on. He runs inside and says, "Get ready"; two trucks with Gestapo and Jewish police (from Lwów) have passed on the way to the city center. He goes out again but returns in a minute: "Akcja!" [*Akcja* means the time when the Gestapo come and round up the Jews.] He saw people being herded from the outskirts of the city. We can hear gunshots and Gestapo running and yelling. We do not have time to run to the bunker in the factory.

Mr. Melman runs to the next-door neighbors (the family Britwitz) to warn them. They don't know anything, they are eating their breakfast. They hardly have time to open their bunker before the Gestapo knocks on the front door. Mr. Melman runs out the back door, and Mr. Britwitz holds the front door closed with his body until the family have time to enter their bunker, then he lets go and starts running to get the Gestapo away from the house so his family have time to hide. He sacrificed himself for his family. We found out about it from Mr. Britwitz, who was caught and jumped from the train and came back.

In the meantime, we, myself, my sister, Mania, my parents, the Melmans, with their son Igo, the Patrontasches, with their daughter

Klarunia, all of us crawled to our bunker beneath the floor. We sit in darkness (the candles we prepared don't burn for lack of oxygen). Whatever we need we must do inside.

TWO DAYS later, Mr. Melman and Mr. Patrontasch (my father has difficulty moving because of his height—he is too tall) crawl out to see what is happening. After a few minutes, which seemed to us an eternity, they came back. *Akcja* is still on. They killed Lockman (a neighbor of ours), who tried to escape. We sat another night in the bunker—Mr. Patrontasch near a lookout hole. At dawn Laibak Patrontasch passed by the house that he knew we were supposed to be in and said, "It's over." The train had already left. We sat another hour to be sure, and then we went out.

IN THE city there is desperate mourning. Carriages bring the dead bodies of those that were killed on the spot trying to run, or trying to get up when they were told to kneel in the center of the city. Also the people who were killed while jumping off the train and those who were betrayed by the gentiles. Mr. Patrontasch lost his youngest sister, Pepcha, and her child. She was running to a gentile friend's house, who had promised to hide her, but she wouldn't let her in when she needed help. Mr. Taube said he saw her lying in a puddle of blood. He wanted to help, but she didn't respond. The next day a peasant from Wola came to Patrontasch's, saying he had seen Pepcha. They went for her but didn't find her. Probably the peasants killed her or betrayed her to the Gestapo. They also took my best friend, Klara Letzer, and her family. She and her mother jumped off the train. Her father didn't make it. A week later there came a decree for all the Jews to go to the ghetto. They assigned certain streets in the center of town where most of the Jews lived.

MY FATHER decided not to go to the ghetto. He was looking for a gentile family to hide us. Mr. Melman found Mr. Beck, a *Volksdeutsche*. He got from the authorities the house that belonged to the Melmans.

As a privileged person (a *Volksdeutsche*), he can get any Jewish house he wants. We, the Melmans, and the Patrontasches went into hiding.

We enlarged a bunker under the floor of the bedroom. There we have the trapdoor in the parquet floor. We pull on an electric cord so we have light and two electric plates to cook on. We make straw mattresses and begin our life underground. There are eleven of us; Mr. Patrontasch brought his widowed sister, Klara. The days pass in monotony, one day the same as the other. The women cook upstairs; downstairs we make breakfast and supper. Everybody washes once a week in the kitchen (upstairs, because it's cold down there). The Becks are wonderful people. You don't find people like them today. They are a family of four. Mr. Beck and Mrs. Beck, their eighteen-year-old daughter, Ala, and Mrs. Beck's sister, Mania. Christmas Eve they closed all the doors and windows, and they invited us all for dinner. It was wonderful. We sang Christmas carols until we almost forgot all our troubles, but most enjoyable of all, we ate a lot! We had to run down and hide again because somebody knocked on the door.

APRIL 6, 1943

THERE IS again *Ackja*. This time they kill everybody. They leave only fifty men and ten women to clean the ghetto. They are forced to go to the forest and add soil, because the mass graves are sinking; they are forced to sing as they march. Imagine they have to sing over the graves of thousands of people, otherwise they are hit over the head. One of the people left to work is Rela's brother, Dudio. Mrs. Beck saw him. The Germans said after the *Ackja* that they need people to work; they crawled out of the bunkers, the Germans told them to stand in a row, they just cut off sixty and killed everyone else.

MANY OF the men saw their wives being led to be killed, but they were helpless. Finally, Auntie Giza came by, in front of Artek. The women marched on, but Artek, Giza, and the Gestapo stood in the middle. She hugged Artek, asked him to tell the family how she died, and that she doesn't want to live anyway because she saw her dead husband on the barbed-wire fence. She asked Artek to avenge the killings. Then the Gestapo yelled "Genug" [enough]. He told her to take off the coat because he liked it. The women were told to sing. They sang "Hatikva" [hope]. What kind of hope can one have being led to death?

FOR SOME time a romance has been developing between Klara Patrontasch and Mr. Beck. I can't understand how she can carry on a romance after losing so much of her family; parents, two sisters, and three brothers. To top it all off, he is married to the woman who is risking her life to hide us. How can she be so ungrateful! Mrs. Beck took Klara into hiding before we even thought of coming here. Mrs. Beck has affection for Klara, because her mother worked for Klara's family, and they had known each other since they were children. Mrs. Beck, of course, is jealous, and they had a big fight. Klara has apologized, and things have quieted down.

But in reality the romance is going on. Whenever Mrs. Beck leaves the house, Mr. Beck calls Klara upstairs. One day Mrs. Beck returned unexpectedly and caught them. There was a fight. Mr. Patrontasch and Father went upstairs to talk to him, but he is stubborn. Mrs. Beck declared that she was not going to hide a snake under her roof. We begged Klara to go and apologize, but she refused. Mr. Patrontasch spoke to Mrs. Beck and said to her he was not going to let Klara go upstairs. But it still didn't end; they started up a correspondence. Mr. Beck wrote notes and sent them down, and Klara would send notes up. Mrs. Beck discovered these, and a big fight ensued. This fight took a whole night. Ala and Mrs. Beck are threatening to betray us to the Germans. Who can blame them? No woman would stand for it; that her husband should carry on an affair under her own roof! Especially with a woman who owes her so much! Ala also cannot stand for it, that her parents should have these fights after being married for twenty years. She lives in constant fear because of us; she doesn't need additional heartache.

The following day, the two of them went to Lwów. Apparently they made up, because when they came back everything was quiet upstairs.

The fight was terrible; I can't forget it. They were screaming very loud; we are lucky we have no neighbors. The fire destroyed most of the houses on our street. Our house stands all alone.

SUNDAY, APRIL 18, 1943

EARLY IN the morning when we were lying still on our pallets, the little window open, I caught a smell in the air. Before I could think what it was, Mrs. Beck knocked at the trapdoor and yelled that there was a fire on the street. A minute later the factory on one side and a house next to ours on the other side were on fire. The wind was very strong. Some of us ran upstairs and poured water on the floor, but the doors started to burn, and on the other side of the house a woodpile started burning. We started to panic, we started getting dressed. Some of us wanted to run, others wanted to go to the bunker underground and choke to death rather than be caught by the Germans, because the minute we got outside, we would be caught and killed. How can seventeen people come out without being seen? There is probably a mob outside. I was for going to the bunker. We were taking children (Mama and me) because we were afraid that they would be trampled when everybody had to go through the narrow passage.

We were sitting in the dark; everybody envies the pharmacist and his wife because they have poison (in a little pouch they have round their necks).

In the meantime Mania, my younger sister, ran upstairs. Seeing the fire raging, smoke all around, she said to Father, "Daddy, I want to live. I am going to run out." Maybe Daddy would have stopped her from going, but this day was the fortieth anniversary of his mother's death. She died in a fire, and Mania was named after her. I don't know how or why—maybe it was the children's crying that was heard by the Almighty—at any rate, the fire was contained and the house stopped burning. At least twenty houses burned down on both sides of our home, but a miracle left our house. But God gave us a terrible price to pay: Mania was caught. They caught her near the convent; maybe she wanted to ask them to hide her, we will never know. Tilzer, who went to school with me, and someone called Schihtling caught her and took her to the Germans. Mania knew what was going to happen. Poor child. God only knows what she went through. I will never know. My parents despaired; my father cannot forgive himself that he let her go.

It seems the neighbors saw Mania running out of the house and notified the German police. In the evening Mr. Beck told us to leave. Where should we go, straight to the Germans? To top it all off, it was a terrible night. The winds were like a hurricane. You shouldn't send a dog out in such weather, and we had two small children. It was a tragedy. We couldn't blame the Becks, after all it's we who have the death sentence. He shouldn't have to die because of us. Without us he is a free man. He is privileged because he has German ancestry. But in the worst situation he proved what a kind heart he has. He looked out the window, the howling wind outside, and said, "Go down, go to sleep, whatever will be will be."

SEPTEMBER 2, 1943

MR. BECK called Mr. Patrontasch to listen to the news from London. It is in German, and Mr. Beck doesn't know German very well.

The news is good. The Germans are getting a licking, but it is not enough for us. We need liberation soon.

TODAY MR. Beck came down to us under the pretext of showing us something in the newspaper. He said that he had to talk to Klara. Instead of talking to him in our presence, she said she wanted to go to her apartment, and crawled with him into the "corridor" (it's a tunnel under the corridor upstairs leading to the other part of the bunker under the other room, where five people sleep). Nobody would care about what they are doing, if it wasn't for Mrs. Beck. She came to the trapdoor, looked down, didn't see Klara and Mr. Beck, and naturally there was a fight again when he went upstairs. I felt terrible. The "poison" is in our bunker. Why should Mrs. Beck suffer? She has enough worries risking her life for us. Afterward the men in the bunker discussed what to do. What can we do? We are between a rock and a hard place. We feel sorry for Mrs. Beck, but we cannot go against Mr. Beck.

WEDNESDAY, SEPTEMBER 15, 1943

PATRONTASCH HEARD the news last night. It's not bad, especially the Eastern Front, which is important to us. In Yugoslavia, the partisans fight the Germans. Patrontasch didn't hear all the news because somebody rang the bell. Who can it be at this hour (1:30 a.m.)? It was our night watchman, Mr. Beck. He listened to the news and went back to work. It's dangerous to do what he is doing, but if you say something to him he has one answer: "The hell with them, I'm not afraid!" I'm sitting now in the "corridor" waiting for the rest of the news. Really, you sit here with mice and all kinds of crawling creatures and you only want to live. What we have been through! What we have suffered up to now, wanting to live! And who knows if all this suffering is for nothing. Will we survive?

TUESDAY, SEPTEMBER 21, 1943

THE DAYS are terribly hot. We are really suffering. In spite of the fact that we are half naked, we are perspiring terribly. Everybody has a little rag to wipe the perspiration, and a piece of cardboard to use instead of a fan. The women wear dresses only, with nothing underneath, and we cut open the back of the dress as much as possible. The men wear only shorts; they look awful. Everybody suffers. Everybody has prickly heat. As soon as we turn off the light, everybody is naked. I hope the days will be cooler soon, and we will have a little relief.

THURSDAY, NOVEMBER 11, 1943

WE START the day now at 10 o'clock. It's cold. We can sleep longer. In the summertime we couldn't lie on the pallets because of the prickly heat, but there is a bad side to it. We wear underwear now, and we have to launder it. Laundry is very complicated. We wash in soap powder, but we have not enough water. We have to save the water we wash our bodies in. We wash in two cups of water, so we have to collect the water and keep the linen soaking for days. We cooked the soup in the same water we used to cook the potatoes. We have the water rationed.

FRIDAY, NOVEMBER 12, 1943

MR. BECK came home drunk today. He was "celebrating" with Kruger, who is in the secret police. He shouldn't drink with him because it is dangerous; but we have no say in the matter.

Mr. Beck claims that such company is good advertisement for him. He says, "Don't be afraid, you are under my good star." God bless him. He gives us encouragement. Ala has a boyfriend. He is coming every day. He is a pilot in the German air force. He was on the Russian front for two years. He hates Hitler. Today he even listened with Mr. Beck to the radio from London. The news is very good. The Russians are moving fast.

MONDAY, DECEMBER 6, 1943

NO ELECTRICITY again. It's very depressing to sit with candlelight (one candle only). Maybe Mr. Patrontasch will bring good news to pick up our mood. Lately we have lost all hope of surviving.

TUESDAY, DECEMBER 7, 1943

MAMA ISN'T feeling well. She has very bad headaches. I think it is because she worries. She is breaking down. She worries about money. I'm sure she doesn't stop thinking about Mania. What can I do? Maybe there will be some good news to pick her spirit up.

FRIDAY, DECEMBER 17, 1943

I'M MAKING Christmas tree ornaments with Ala. We sit until 1 a.m. and make all kinds of toys. Maybe there will be a miracle at Christmas, and we will be free. Last Christmas I didn't expect to spend a whole year in the bunker.

SATURDAY, DECEMBER 18, 1943

WE DISCOVERED a treasure. Daddy's coat is still good, and we can clean it and sell it! There will be another day or two of food.

WEDNESDAY, DECEMBER 22, 1943

MRS. BECK sold my dress today. She gave us 200 zlotys and 5 kg [11 pounds] of flour. It's my last dress, but who cares? Who needs it? If I survive I will find a dress, and if not . . . ?

FRIDAY, DECEMBER 24, 1943

TODAY IS a memorable day for all of us. Once more we saw how noble a character our saviors have. In the morning, I was with Lola cleaning upstairs. We helped with the cooking. At one point we were almost seen by a stranger (they forgot to close the back door). We succeeded in leaving through Ala's room. In the afternoon, we all gave the Becks our presents and wished them a happy holiday. Later Mr. Beck came down to the bunker with a tray of cakes and vodka. We asked Mrs. Beck to join us; she came down, and we ate and drank. We kissed each other and wished for one thing: a speedy liberation. An end to our suffering—everybody cried.

FRIDAY, JANUARY 7, 1944

TODAY LUCZYNSKI visited the Becks. He brought a rumor that the Russians are killing people in the territories that they have taken back from the Germans. Mr. Beck took it very badly. Right after Luczynski left, he came down to us. He said he would like to run away, but he is not going to abandon us, even if it costs him his life. We tried to tell him that he would surely be rewarded. We probably succeeded, because later we heard him singing upstairs. If he sings, we feel better too. Mr. Beck asked us to write down on paper what we promised him: 25 percent of all our possessions (every one of us owns homes and factories). We will do it gladly, but that is hardly anything in view of what he is doing for us. After all, it's more than a year that they have been risking their life for us. Just him saying, "We will stay together till the bitter end, no matter what it takes."

WE HAVE a big problem. The Germans came and ordered him to vacate one room. They will probably put some German soldier or officer there to live upstairs. All right. We will sit quiet. But what are we going to do with the pails? How will we get water? What can we do? Whatever will be, will be!

WEDNESDAY, JANUARY 12, 1944
PEOPLE HAVE lived to a hundred and never been through what we are going through in one day. The most sensational novel doesn't have so many adventures—so many things have happened to us in the past year.

Take today. Everything was normal, quiet. We didn't have electricity until 4 o'clock. We didn't cook, we slept. Mrs. Beck wasn't at home. But it was enough to make our teeth chatter with fear.

In the evening, Adolf (Ala's boyfriend) came and invited himself to stay the night. The pails were full, so Mr. Beck left Ala with Adolf in the other room, and knocked on the trapdoor and said to go and empty the pails. Mr. Beck stood watch. Mr. Patrontasch went upstairs, barefoot, but anyway we took a big chance. We breathed a sigh of relief when we finally saw Mr. Patrontasch downstairs. I imagined what he went through upstairs, knowing that a German officer was in the next room.

THURSDAY, JANUARY 13, 1944
FOR SEVERAL days there has been bad blood between the Becks. Mrs. Beck is morose. Mr. Beck doesn't sing like he usually does. The Becks are our only link with reality. We mirror their moods. I hope they make up soon. Mr. Beck doesn't stay mad for long.

FRIDAY, JANUARY 14, 1944
LATELY THESE days seem to be very, very long. I don't know why. Maybe because we are always in a state of expectation. Maybe because we sit all day long looking at each other. I don't know. I only know that we have all had enough. I don't think there is anything worse than sitting and doing nothing. We have become animals. Everybody has lost their entire family (we are better off, I have my grandfather,

uncle, aunt, and three cousins in Russia) and yet we want to live, we eat. A slice of bread and coffee in the morning, potato or soup (made out of potato) for lunch, and potato for supper. Later to sleep on the pallet, then get up in the morning, and do the same again!

Thank God they made the upstairs. This lifts our spirits.

SUNDAY, FEBRUARY 6, 1944

THINGS ARE turning around for us. Maybe we will be the lucky ones in the end? The weather changed suddenly. It's freezing and it's snowing. Even here in the bunker we can feel the cold. We are glad, because it helps the Russians. The news was also good. They took two more towns; they are fighting again at Szepetowka, which is important for us because it's on the way to Lwów. There is another piece of good news. Mrs. Beck says the workers of the glass factory are on the run. I'm glad because they are the worst people, all collaborators. They were looking for bunkers, and they were also luring the poor Jews who jumped off the trains and robbing them of their money (if they had any) and then selling them out to the Germans. Well, let them run, but I will not rest until I find every person who betrayed Mania to the Germans. Right now I feel as if I could cut every German henchman to pieces. There isn't enough punishment in the world for Von Papen, the *stormführer* of Zolkiew, who grabbed children by the legs and smashed their heads on the walls. Mrs. Beck told me that when they left twenty Jews to clean the ghetto after "action," Von Papen took [a man] to the hospital to dress [his] cut and then took him to the cemetery and shot him. Why? The man worked for him, lost his finger, and that was the reason to kill him? Once people couldn't kill a dog when it grew old, today a human being is nothing.

SUNDAY, FEBRUARY 27, 1944

OUR SITUATION is very critical now. I don't know how long we can last this way. Anyway, one way or another, it can't be for long. Either we will be liberated or we will die. Already today we had a taste of it. In the evening the Germans came, and Mr. Beck went to work. Ala also had night duty at the post office. Mrs. Beck was all alone. It was very quiet upstairs. I don't know how or why, but suddenly Zosia started crying. They covered her with a pillow immediately. We thought nobody had heard it because it only lasted a second, but Mrs. Beck heard it. She knocked on the trapdoor and told us she heard a child crying; she told us to be quiet because the Germans were not sleeping but reading the newspaper. If that short cry was heard upstairs, then it's really bad. It's lucky that they are in the room with the radio because that room is on the opposite side of the house, so maybe they didn't hear anything. Of course now there is not one person in the bunker saying we will survive. Even I, the big optimist in the bunker, am losing hope. But what can we do? Go out of here? Outside is sure death; there is no place we can go.

WEDNESDAY, MARCH 1, 1944

IT'S ALREADY March; the winter is over, but the winter didn't help us much. It's raining, it's thawing, it's impossible for the military to move. Nothing is happening on the front. Our situation is terrible. Our nerves are frazzled from these constant alarms. Any little sound made by somebody in the bunker seems to us like thunder. We get heart palpitations when we have to dish out the food on the table, and to top it all, there is the fear of hunger. Almost nobody has money for March. If we had more money, we wouldn't have to cook the potatoes; we could eat bread.

A year ago, there was still a ghetto where we had relatives. Today, we are the "lucky" ones. We lost our family, and yet we live. This is supposed to be "luck."

TUESDAY, MARCH 7, 1944

WE HAVE company again. Six soldiers from the SS have invited themselves to sleep over. They are going to sleep on the floor with the others—not directly above us.

The more of them the better; there is more commotion upstairs!

SATURDAY, MARCH 11, 1944

THEY SAY that angels are in heaven and not on earth. But today's events proved to the contrary: they are on earth in the person of Mr. Beck! In the afternoon, he came down to us and said we shouldn't take to heart what we hear from upstairs. He doesn't want to be a part of people dying. He says all kinds of people are coming to visit. They are afraid of the Russians; they are afraid of Jews taking revenge. (I myself heard Kruger saying, "For their mothers, for their wives, for their children they will take revenge.") These people are talking, and they don't know that Jews can hear them. Mr. Beck is afraid that we will be doing it, and because he was hiding Jews, he would be helping in harassing friends. We of course promised Mr. Beck that if we survive, we will not harm anybody.

MONDAY, MARCH 13, 1944

DOOMSDAY!! ONE of the men saw Patrontasch. He went to the toilet while Patrontasch stood in the room and waited for somebody to hand him the pail, and saw him because the door to the bedroom was open. He came in the morning to the kitchen and told Mrs. Beck that he saw somebody in the bedroom. Mrs. Beck got excited and instead of saying she had a visitor, she said it was probably thieves; she went to the bedroom, opened the closet, and said she was missing things. He started searching because, since Luczynski's visit, they are suspicious. We could hear him looking in the room above us. He looked under the bed; luckily for us he covered the trapdoor with his body and looked under the bed. Patrontasch knew he had been seen; he should have warned Mrs. Beck, so she would know what to say.

FIFTEEN MONTHS suffering in this hole! To die now, when the Russians are in Tarnopol!

THEY CAME back, and then they went for lunch. We emptied the pails, we shut off the electricity; we are not going to cook. Mrs. Beck said that they secured a rifle. Maybe they think that they saw a partisan;

the Germans are afraid of partisans. That's a good sign! Maybe they are not thinking about Jews after all. They will probably be listening now. We will be as quiet as we can. There is a commotion upstairs! I think it's the police. God help us! I don't want to die now. There is hope, they are not talking about Jews; they are talking about thieves. They are joking about it. I have only one wish. If something happens, I hope the Becks can escape. They deserve better than a German bullet.

MONDAY, MARCH 27, 1944

WE HAD excitement today. Mr. Beck brought his nephew, Wladek, to the trapdoor. Actually, except for Melman, Patrontasch, and the pharmacist who went near the trapdoor, nobody has seen us. To tell the truth, I am not used to seeing new faces. I didn't even try to go near the trapdoor. Mr. Beck had a reason to show him the bunker, because in a few days he could be the new member of the bunker. He was called up for the army, and he doesn't want to go. If they look for him, he will hide with us. The people who talked to him say he is very nice. Of course he is nice; he has known about us for fifteen months and hasn't betrayed us. He also knows where Dudio is hiding, and he hasn't betrayed him either. (Dudio is my uncle Josek's brother-in-law; he was left in the ghetto with sixty, but they were caught and killed when they tried to bring food to Zosia and Zygo, who were hidden in an attic. They were shot instantly, Dudio later escaped.)

TONIGHT THE Becks are sleeping in the bedroom above us. They had to give up their room to some soldiers. I think there are three of them; it seems to us there are three of them.

SATURDAY, APRIL 8, 1944

TODAY IS Passover. The holidays bring sad thoughts and memories. Last year Passover came after the fire. Mania was no longer with us. I just can't comprehend that she is not here anymore. I see her in front of my eyes. I think I will see her when we leave this place. It is unbelievable that this lively soul who wanted so much to live is buried somewhere in a grave. How many like her are buried in the forest! But time doesn't stand still. A year has gone by, and a new holiday has come. We scrounged what we could to give presents to the Becks. The presents were very poor, but we are in the habit of giving presents to the Becks for the holidays. Maybe, God willing, we will survive and be able to give them real presents.

WEDNESDAY, APRIL 26, 1944

MR. BECK wants to leave. He is afraid. The Ukrainians are threatening to kill all of the Polacks. Even Prof. Lang, who was always saying he is not afraid, wants to leave as well. Mr. Beck wants to leave, but his conscience does not allow it. There is another reason for his despondence. How to feed us. The potatoes are finished. Nobody wants to buy dollars. But there is nothing we can do. If Mr. Beck was able to buy food for us, one weight would be lifted from his mind: he is afraid we will starve. Only one thing can save us. A speedy advance by the Russians. I hope it will come.

WEDNESDAY, MAY 3, 1944

THE DARKNESS is terrible. Each day is an eternity. When the light is on, I can read, do something, and the day goes faster. But mostly I lie on the pallet and look into the ray of light coming from the air opening, and feel I am going crazy. There is only one plus. Since we are not using the electric plates, it is cooler in the bunker, and we do not suffer as much as we did last year. But it is dank and humid—a real cellar atmosphere—if we stay here much longer we will probably all get rheumatism!

TUESDAY, MAY 16, 1944

HALF OF May is over, and nothing significant has happened. No offensive, no movement of the front—nothing. I am losing hope. Will we survive? Outside is May—spring—but we are not happy about it because the warmer it is outside, the worse the heat inside the bunker.

That heat weakens us. We cook less, there is less food to cook, yet it is hot and sticky in here. The trapdoor is closed most of the day because of the soldiers. The most air we get is through the trapdoor. Why, why have we to suffer? Why can others walk free in the streets? Sometimes, when I hear any company having a good time, I'm happy for the Becks, but at the same time my heart aches! Are they better than I? Hans, a murderer of thousands of helpless people, he has a right to live. Me, I never harmed anyone, and I have to hide like a criminal.

MONDAY, JUNE 19, 1944

EVERY DAY is an eternity, waiting and waiting, not knowing if and when we will be liberated. No matter how late we get up, the day is still long. I got up at noon because our day starts when the soldiers leave and Mrs. Beck knocks on the door. At nine in the evening, we were already on the pallets, yet the day had not reached its end. But the weeks and months glide by. There have been times we've thought we will be free any day and times when we've lost all hope, but never did I imagine we would be here such a long time. We see now that the war isn't going to be over so soon; it's like a death sentence for us, yet nobody has the courage to end it all.

THURSDAY, JUNE 22, 1944

FINALLY THERE is something going on at the front. Maybe it's the start of an offensive. If not, maybe it is enough to make the soldiers leave; then our chances of surviving will be better. We didn't have a chance to hear the news; we can always hear if we crawl under the soldier's room. The German radio mentions movement near Tarnopol and Kowel.

WEDNESDAY, JULY 19, 1944

LAST NIGHT we heard artillery fire. I can hear it now too. They have probably advanced. All day long, tanks, cannons, the military are passing in the direction of Lwów. Maybe they are attacking Lwów? Four soldiers invited themselves to sleep over. We are used to it. We can hear distant artillery fire. They come more often now. Perhaps the soldiers will leave in the middle of the night. Each of us has prepared some clothing to wear just in case something happens (here we go around half naked). We cannot leave here except to go to the cellar, because the field police have no qualms about killing Jews if they find them. The cellar has concrete walls; it can protect us from artillery fire. We have a good bunker in our factory next door, but we might find some soldiers already hiding there.

ALA IS probably worried about us. Who knows how long she will be cut off from us? There is no communication whatsoever; there is no administration in Zolkiew anymore. It will be soon now.

FRIDAY, JULY 21, 1944
WE HAD no idea what a big shot was living upstairs. He is the main officer of the general's staff in defense of Zolkiew. Through the night soldiers came on motorcycles, reporting from the front. Upstairs there are the "general staff," and under the floor are the Jews! That's not all—the Becks and Wladek had to stay in the cellar because the soldiers took the whole house. They came up in the morning and gave us water and some bread. Throughout this time, the soldiers kept coming with reports from the battle. We, of course, could hear everything. Around 11 o'clock we heard that Lwów was surrounded. There was only one road open through Janow. A minute later, the colonel said good-bye to the Becks and told them if they intended to run, they should do it immediately because the Russians would arrive tonight or no later than the morning. How long we had waited for this moment!

HOW LONG we have waited for this moment! I can't believe that I'm going to leave this hole! Now the danger is only the artillery, but we can't help that. It has to be. The cellar is safe; the Becks are there. If the fire is very strong, we will make a hole in the wall and crawl down to the cellar. We can't go through the house because the trapdoor to the cellar is covered with sand. The Becks are going through a small window, but we are afraid to go outside. They are communicating with us through a little hole in the wall.

AFTERWORD

Clara's sister, Mania, was killed during the liquidation of the ghetto. All remaining occupants of the Zolkiew bunker survived, thanks to the bravery and generosity of the Beck family. The Becks were sentenced to death as Nazi collaborators in the years after the war but were saved by the testimony offered by Clara's diary.

Clara met and married her husband in a displaced-persons camp in Austria in 1949. Since 1957, she has lived and worked in America, where she is president of the Holocaust Research Center at Kean University in Union, New Jersey. She has two sons and five grandchildren.

Stolen

VIETNAM WAR

1964–73

Voices

Ed Blanco

UNITED STATES
1967–68 (19–20 YEARS OLD)

This sure will be something.

The origin of America's war in Vietnam is rooted in the French attempt to reestablish colonial control of that country at the end of World War II. During World War I, Vietnam was occupied by Japan and came under Japanese military administrative control. Vietnamese nationals throughout these years hoped that once Vietnam shook free of Japanese control, independence would follow. Nationalists looked to the United States for support in their future bid for independence, and Ho Chi Minh held up the U.S. Declaration of Independence as a primary source of inspiration.

The Cold War put an end to these nationalists' hopes. Because Ho Chi Minh was a Communist, the American government moved away from the nationalist movement and instead supported France's attempts to regain colonial control of the country. This led to the First Indochina War (1946–54).

After the Vietnamese Communist forces, or Viet Minh, defeated the French colonial army at the battle of Dien Bien Phu in 1954, the colony was granted independence. According to the ensuing Geneva Conference settlement, Vietnam was divided into a Communist North and a non-Communist South. Ho Chi Minh ruled in the North, while the South would be under the control of Emperor Bao Dai. In 1955 the South Vietnamese monarchy was abolished, and Prime Minister

Ngo Dinh Diem became president of a new South Vietnamese republic.

The signers of the Geneva Accords had hoped for elections that would unify the two republics, but such elections were never held. President Diem, with the support of the United States, had no interest in holding elections that could threaten his control of the South. But the Communists in the North also refused to have free elections. Neither the United States nor the two Vietnams had signed the election clause in the accord, and therefore they were not bound by it. At the time, it appeared that a divided Vietnam would become the norm, similar in nature to the recently partitioned Korea.

In the North, the Communists formed the National Liberation Front (NLF) as a guerrilla movement in opposition to the South Vietnamese government. The United States referred to the NLF as Viet Cong, short for Viet Nam Cong San, or "Vietnamese Communist." The United States was keen to prevent a Communist takeover of the country by Ho Chi Minh. In response to the guerrilla war, the United States began sending military advisers in support of the government in the South. North Vietnam and the USSR supported the NLF with arms and supplies, advisers, and regular units of the North Vietnamese Army.

Under these circumstances, the United States entered the arena by sending in the marines in 1965, and ultimately building up troop strength until it peaked around 530,000 in 1968.

Americans back home became increasingly disillusioned with the war, especially after the Tet Offensive of 1968. Although the offensive had been lost by the Viet Cong, the American public became aware that the victory in Vietnam would be slow and painful, if possible at all. Up until then, American troop morale had been high, but after 1968, the majority of Americans turned against the war. When it also became clear the United States was planning a gradual troop withdrawal, troop morale dropped, and drug use increased. The United States finally withdrew its ground combat troops from Vietnam in 1973. North Vietnam ultimately succeeded in securing the South in 1975, uniting the two regions under a single Communist state in July of the following year.

Edward Blanco was born in New York in 1948 to Puerto Rican parents who had migrated to New York after World War II. In the winter of 1967 he volunteered for the draft and was inducted into the U.S. Army that spring. Like most of his friends who had already volunteered, he was looking for adventure and new experiences. After five months of training, he was sent to Vietnam with the 101st Airborne Division. American soldiers faced a wholly alien environment in Vietnam. It was a guerrilla war without clear boundaries, fought mostly in jungles and rice paddies, and inside and around hamlets. An attitude developed that the enemy was everywhere, and the strain of jungle-based conflict began to take its toll on the men.

NOVEMBER 4, 1967 (CAM RANH BAY)

AROUND 8 P.M. this evening, after eighteen hours of traveling via Anchorage and Tokyo, we landed in Cam Ranh Bay. It was hot, like we expected, and hotter in the buses that took us to the processing building where we filled out mucho papers. They let us go after that and we came to these barracks, which are surrounded by sandbags. We heard a firefight across the bay. They fired machine guns, flares, the works. First time I've heard them firing at men instead of paper targets.

We'll stay in Cam Ranh Bay two days, they said. We've been told it's the safest place in Vietnam. Too bad we got to leave so soon.

NOV 8, 67 (PHAN RANG)

I'VE BEEN in Phan Rang since the sixth. I was a little nervous when they told us we were traveling here by truck because you hear so much about ambushes. We did have one M-16 rifle on the truck, but we didn't need it. The road was busy and secure. Along the road, kids waved at us and asked for cigarettes or just held their hand out. They would keep looking at us until we disappeared around a corner.

Phan Rang is the home of the 101st Airborne, but most of the division is up North. The 506th (newest battalion in the division, just here from the States) is having a beach party today before they leave for the boonies.

Nov 9, 1967

Yesterday I heard General Westmoreland speak to the assembled 506th Battalion. He said if a combat jump is necessary he would consider the 506th for the job—that brought cheers. The 506th left for the boonies this morning.

November 10, 1967

It's 7 a.m. and it's raining outside. This is a week of orientation classes and exercises. Today's the first day I put on my jungle fatigues with the airborne patches—it feels good.

[Later] It's 10 p.m. and I just came back from the water tank where I tried to wash myself. Like usual the shower tanks ran out of water. We were issued most of our equipment today and after I put it away I went to the beer hall where I had a few beers and took a picture which I'm going to send home with a letter I'm going to write next.

I fixed up all my financial and insurance records today, and they told me I'm going to the 506th. That's terrible. They're green, like me, man. I was hoping to go to the 17th Cav or the 502nd. Very few fellows wanted to be assigned to the 506th. To be reassigned to another unit, one guy even reenlisted for four years when they told him he was going to the 506th.

November 12, 1967

Today I got the GIs [gastro-intestinals]. I've been going to the latrine mucho times. Other guys have it too. It's the food and weather. I've got to get used to it.

I've noticed another thing many of us have in common. As we start getting assigned to regular units, everybody starts talking about

"I'm going to make it." One of the guys said he's going home even if he's missing a leg or something just as long as he has his jewels and can get laid.

In the showers, I heard a fellow say if he spent twelve months in the front he'd be OK because Charlie doesn't have a bullet with his name on it. Some guy answered, "It's those to-whom-it-may-concern bullets you gotta watch out for."

They issued me my weapon today. I'm going to take good care of it. That rifle is going to be with me for a year.

NOVEMBER 20, 1967

THE LAST three days I've been doing work details. I went to the PX and bought Christmas cards to send home. I haven't received any letters yet, but I should soon. I'm writing this in my tent. Nobody's here. I'm going to the Red Cross and see a movie after I shower. I'm getting more homesick as we approach Christmas.

Nov 22, 1967

TODAY RODNEY and I waited until 2:30 p.m. with all our equipment ready; rifle, rucksack, ammunition. Then they told us we weren't going to the field. I didn't care but they put us on work details again. Tonight I went down to the Red Cross but didn't stay long. The movie was crummy. When I got back here to the tent the sergeant told me I got K.P. tomorrow. Tomorrow's Thanksgiving. The sergeant also said we're leaving the following afternoon for the bush, for sure. Like today was for sure.

Nov 23, 1967

THANKSGIVING. TODAY I was on K.P. all day. Worked hard. They served a big dinner. They had turkey, potatoes, cakes, shrimp cocktails. They put white tablecloths on the tables—they needed ironing but they were clean. When we finished K.P. the mess sergeant offered us privates some vodka and then rum. I went to the Red Cross after that and wrote letters home to Mom and Betsy, and I wrote Joe because the other day I saw his name on the KIA list but it can't be him because the name was listed under Marines Killed and Joe's in the Cav.

Nov 24, 1967

RODNEY AND I waited three hours on the helicopter pad this morning but didn't go to the field. We're back in our tent. Rodney is a brother from Philly. He's 23 and has a wife and kid.

NOVEMBER 25, 1967

LAST NIGHT there was a fight in the beer hall. It seems the 502nd and the 327th have something against the brand-new 506th. They don't like our motto, "We stand alone." I'm new to the 506th and don't feel involved, but I better be careful, those other battalions have been in the bush a long time. Anyway they greased two of our cooks.

A Mexican sergeant is in my tent now. He's a young guy. He got a three-day pass for killing the 506th's first gook. He said they spotted 12 VC and fired on them. The one they got turned out to be a pregnant nurse. He said the other bodies were dragged away by the VC as they retreated, but I don't believe that. I'm writing all this while he's here in the tent.

Everybody smokes pot in Nam. Well not everybody, but mucho people. There's one tall skinny fellow from Iowa who never saw the stuff until he came here. He likes to smoke now. His name is Paulson.

Then there's "D." He's a Texan. "D" smoked here in the tent for the first time a few nights ago and went a little crazy and took a bayonet and stabbed himself in the belly. Nothing serious. I was in the tent sleeping and found out about it the next day. Yesterday, he extended in Nam for an extra year.

[LATER] A little while ago Rodney and I were painting metal cones and the supply sgt. came and told us to get ready to leave for the bush. Well, history repeated itself. We waited. The helicopter came and left and here I am in the tent again. They told us again that tomorrow we leave.

November 26, 1967

It's late in the evening but it's still light. The skies are gray with clouds and it's getting dark quickly. I'm sitting behind the tent on sandbags writing this. The other fellows are on the other side of the tent, hitting a softball. I heard them call my name a few minutes ago, but I didn't answer because I was reading then. I like softball but I like reading, too. Especially this book by Hemingway I got. Then suddenly I felt like writing.

As I look around, it looks like something out of a movie. A war camp scene. Yet I'm still in Phan Rang, imagine how it will be in the field. I look forward to it.

If somebody saw me right now they'd see a young man sitting on sandbags writing in a notebook. He doesn't have a shirt and on his face, chest, and arms you can see a light film of sand dust, and his baggy pants are filthy.

Today I received my first letter. It was from Betsy, and she said Mom worries a lot.

Today Rodney and I got assigned to a Second Platoon by "The Bull," our first sergeant. The Bull promised us that we'd leave for the field tomorrow—we'll see.

November 29, 1967

I'm on top of a hill near the China Sea, and I'm very tired. Yesterday they finally brought me out to the field. . . . The China Sea is in front of us and to our right another hill. I'm finally in the boonies.

December 5, 1967

I haven't had much time to write in this journal. We made a helicopter assault (my first) on a paddy about seven miles from here. Since then I've been humping like a mule. We've heard a lot of firing but my platoon hasn't been in a firefight yet. A fellow from B company was killed the other day. There are VC in the area because we came across a VC camp and burned the hooches and destroyed the rice. I'm writing this in a hurry because we're moving out in a little while and I'm supposed to be watching the woods.

When I was on guard last night (about 4 a.m.) it was so black all I could do was listen. Up on this hill the wind sounds like a subway train when it's coming. The wind then shakes all the trees around you, then leaves quiet behind—last night the wind grabbed a branch and hit me with it. Man, I couldn't see what hit me and almost screamed out.

While on guard I'm often thinking about home and what time it is there and what I'm going to do when I get back, then this branch hits me. Wow.

December 10, 1967

Today we got ready to move out but all we're doing now is waiting around. It's very hot and Gunner just brought back some Cokes. They're hot but good. I received a letter from Betsy yesterday, she says Victor got wounded and is going home. It has always occurred to me that one of my friends would be wounded.

We think we're moving to the Cambodian border. It's a little hotter over there. All the guys are itching for a firefight because all we've done so far is hump.

Every day makes me more homesick. It's hard to believe I have to stay here eleven more months. In Mom's letters, she keeps telling me to have faith. Betsy's letters are funny. She writes them up like newspapers.

December 17, 1967

We got resupplied yesterday and with it came lots of mail. I read these letters bookoo times before burning them.

I'm making some hot cocoa now with cookies. I'm getting pretty good with these C-rations. I'm learning to fix them up like regular meals.

December 21, 1967

It's early in the morning and it's cold and damp. I'm under my poncho liner writing this. Soon we'll leave this hill and start down the valley. The grass is high and thick around here, and I've seen my first leeches in the water. Last night while I was just going to sleep I heard music. I thought I was dreaming but when I opened my eyes I still heard it. It was faint but distinguishable, and it WAS music. Gunner and Craig heard it too. We asked Sgt. Bunn about it, he said it came from a village nearby.

DECEMBER 25, 1967

LAST NIGHT we all slept on guard because the hill was packed with troops. It was Xmas Eve. Besides, a ceasefire was in effect, but that really doesn't mean anything. The RTOs spirited things up on the radios. They talked about Santa crossing the perimeter after midnight "so don't fire up." And another was singing "Jingle Bells" with different words

> Jingle Bells, shots and shells, VC in the grass
> Take this Merry Xmas and shove it up your ass.

This morning everybody was in good spirits. A fellow walked around the hill wearing shaving cream as a beard and a poncho liner under his shirt for a belly. He strode around saying "Ho, ho, ho," but Santa doesn't wear a steel pot and an M-16 rifle.

LATER THE choppers came in and we ate hot chow and went to mass. There was a Red Cross girl in a Santa uniform serving food—that was something really out of place. We sang carols near the choppers while we ate. Trying to sing "Silent Night" with turkey in your mouth. I didn't go to mass because I had to stand guard, but I sneaked over when the priest started giving communion and received, then went back on watch.

We brought beers, Cokes, C-rations, and other supplies back to our positions. I got two packages beside the letters. One was from Mom with bookoo stuff and the other was Spanish candy from *abuelo* [Grandfather] in Puerto Rico. I ate like a starving dog and traded all my ginger ales for beers. Lots of guys received packages and were giving food away. I have the cookies and canned fruit Mom sent me stuffed in my rucksack.

In Mom's letter she said they didn't put up a Xmas tree this year. I hope they had a nice Xmas at home. Hopefully next year I'll be home and we'll definitely have one gigantic Xmas tree.

JANUARY 8, 1967

MY SQUAD is pulling guard around some engineers who are blowing up trees to make a landing zone. You know why? Because we're going back to Phan Rang. As I write this, artillery is shelling a hill to my front. So far I count about ten rounds—two more—three more. We got resupplied with six meals yesterday and I thought they'd keep us out here, but we're going in. I tried to eat all my rations this morning. (Wow, Arty hitting hard.) I had two hot whole breads with pineapple jam. I stuffed them with hot cocoa, fried ham with hot sauce, cookies, pecan cake roll, fruit cocktail, and lemon-lime Kool-Aid. I was going to open my can of pound cake but I was too bloated.

Since we ran into that VC battalion base camp we haven't humped very much except yesterday when we humped down a bamboo cluttered mountain to get to where we are now. Up on the mountaintop we'd leave our rucksacks in a secure perimeter and go out on patrols. We destroyed everything we found. The attached engineers used C-4 explosives to demolish the enemy bunkers.

I saw VC bodies. They were piled on each other with thousands of flies and insects crawling all over them. I couldn't stand the smell. They looked like slimy stiff plastic dummies. We also found a foot blown off by the shelling. My company found seven VC bodies. I hope we killed more but we can't find more bodies. Our battalion had seven dead and twenty wounded.

Two guys were killed from C company and others wounded when a grenade went off accidentally in their command post. The company commander was wounded. I was nearby when it happened and could hear the yells and moans after the explosion.

January 10, 1968

Yesterday we had a seven-hour truck ride back to Phan Rang. Today they gave us passes after we cleaned our rifles. Most of the guys went to the Strip or Phan Rang, but I'm leaving it for tomorrow. Instead, I just took a shower (cold shower, but good), came into this empty tent (only Big Henry the Soul Sergeant is here) and reread my letters, smoked a cigar, and napped. The wind was flapping the sides of the tent and I was getting a nice breeze (the sides are up). Tonight I'll write letters at the Red Cross and get high drinking beer like I did yesterday. Today, I'm eating at snack bars. I'll eat French fries and steak or chicken, and ice cream or milkshakes. Man, I'm going to be piggish. I hope we stay here awhile. In any case, I'm going to see the doc about my eyes and see what I can do about getting off the line.

January 13, 1968

Yesterday, I went to the Strip with my new Yashica camera and got so drunk I forgot to take pictures. I blew about $30. I played cards with this baby-san (about 16 years old) for drinks. She was beating me until I changed the game to blackjack, and with me dealing and cheating it was easy to win five straight games and get drunk.

January 14, 1968

We're going to make a combat jump. We were told reporters will be there to cover it. We've been restricted to the area. They have barbed wire and guards surrounding the battalion. This will really be something.

January 15, 1968

This morning I dropped and broke my mirror in the showers. Everybody turned and looked. We're not usually superstitious, but it's close to jump day and we don't want to take any chances.

JANUARY 18, 1968 (LZ BETTY, PHAN THIET)

I'M AT LZ Betty, near Phan Thiet City. We didn't jump. The jump was canceled and we were trucked here instead. We're taking over the 1st Cav's section. Right now we're staying in tents or in sandbag bunkers.

JANUARY 26, 1968

ALL DAY was spent in the bunkers. Sgt. Pully just went to see what we're doing tomorrow. I'm in the bunker now having a difficult time seeing this since Gunner is covering the candlelight, but it's his candle.

Yesterday we went out on a patrol. Our squad was following some trail prints when the first three men saw some gooks. VC? Farmers? Whatever they were they took off running and we opened up. We didn't kill anybody because they ran so fast.

Gunner had just given me the machine gun to carry for a while because he was tired. (M-60 is heavy.) I gave him my M-16. It was then I heard gooks were spotted. I ran up to fire and got off two rounds when the mg jammed. I turned around looking for Gunner but he had gone off with my rifle. I always told him that whenever we get into action for him to take back the machine gun but instead he ran off firing my M-16. I took the belt out of the gun and reloaded. I fired and it jammed again. By the time I had fixed the gun the gooks were gone. I didn't get trained on the M-60 and when it jammed I was cursing him and we argued hotly later. Whenever we get into a firefight I want to have my M-16, not the M-60.

FEBRUARY 1, 1968

YESTERDAY WE killed fifteen VC and captured two. We also accidentally killed two civilians. We shot a Buddhist monk in the head and in the next house left a wounded old man with his daughter and grandchildren crying over their grandmother who was lying on the floor with a bullet through her face.

I was upset about that. Later, I put five bullets in a dying VC and shot another in the head just to make sure.

One VC came out of a bush with his hands up. He had a 45 pistol in his hand. When he started shaking it we opened up and he crumbled like a dummy. His arm and a finger was shot off and his guts and brains were on the ground.

One VC we captured was a political officer. He was wounded in the leg and stood up with hands way up. That saved his life. Earlier me and Gunner patched up an old man we wounded and left him babbling with fright. Agaro was hit in the arm.

That night we received fire from a pagoda. The First Platoon on the other side of the pagoda shot our way and accidentally killed two South Vietnamese soldiers and wounded two more. Earlier Gunner and I traded these little guys cigarettes for cake. Before the second soldier died, me and three other guys carried his litter over a graveyard back to LZ Betty. All the time he was moaning and drowning from blood in his throat. Craig was frustrated at our pace and later carried the soldier to a jeep that took off for the aid station. But the little man died soon after that.

That was yesterday. Today we went out on patrol for about four hours and came back.

FEBRUARY 5, 1968
ON FEB 2, we made an air assault into a VC area. As we combed the area we came upon a man and his family in a hooch. As we were checking them out we received fire from the next house. Schultz and Daniels were hit by the initial fire. Schultz in the chest, Daniels in the leg. A tiny shell fragment stung my foot, but hardly penetrated the boot.

During a short lull in the fighting, Gressett told me with his eyes wide open that there were gooks inside this house in a tunnel. We ran up to the house and Gunner put half a belt into the hole. When we looked, we had killed four people. Two kids, the father and a mother, plus shot the hand off an old lady. Another blind old lady and a small boy weren't hurt. What can I say?

Schultz was carried inside the house as we fired and received fire from other houses. Later, air strikes were called. We watched jets destroy the houses while Schultz moaned and the lady with her hand shot off moaned.

Daniels was left on the porch of the next house because we couldn't get to him. He bled to death.

Finally, they got men to carry Schultz back for a medevac. Schultz is a heavy guy. As they passed over open ground they were hit by automatic weapons fire. Gressett was hit on the hip. Rincon in the knee, Sgt. Henry in the arm, and another fellow also in the arm.

While I was in the house, I heard somebody say Sgt. Bunn was hit. His body was retrieved that night. The First Sgt. was killed, too.

In the house we received fire sporadically. I covered the dead kids with a bamboo mat and tried to console the old woman without a hand. But how can you do that? She stayed in that hole with the dead and stink and the flies. I bandaged her hand and gave her water. The kid too. One of the guys found a radio and turned it on and it played music.

Yesterday morning while it was still dark, they extracted us. It was good to be on the chopper riding back.

FEBRUARY 15, 1968

I HAVEN'T written in here for a while. I should keep this journal more diligently. Many things have happened since I last wrote in it. I'm too tired to write about everything but I'll write some. Jackie Walker, D'way, Georgia, and Owens were all wounded by a rocket attack. The first three were badly mauled. We now have eighteen men in the platoon and they're going to switch squad members around.

FEBRUARY 20, 1968

IT'S VERY early in the morning and the skies are red in the east where the sun will show itself in a small while. All night there was firing from that direction with bullets whizzing over our heads. I'm behind a dike and there's an open field in front of me, then a wide shallow river, then houses and palm trees. The gooks and South Vietnamese Army on the other side of the river have been at it all night.

Yesterday on this side (three bullets more now just whizzed over my head) we were badly mauled. Luckily my platoon was trail so the first and third platoons got all the casualties, which totaled eight dead and ten wounded. Rate was killed and D.J. wounded. How serious I don't know because of the confusion, but I'll find out today.

FEBRUARY 21, 1968
LAST NIGHT we shot up the perimeter and this morning found a dead gook, AK-47, rucksack, chicom grenade, and a few other things.

(LATER) WHEN I return home I'm going to learn how to play an instrument, take up radio as a hobby, and write. It'll be good for me.

Last night flares and artillery were fired all night, pieces of shrapnel kept flying over my head, buzzing. Some fell near me. We're going to move out now.

FEB 25, 68
WE MADE combat assault yesterday and again today. I'm writing from an LZ. We made an uneventful sweep of the area yesterday. Today we'll do the same.

Gunner came back from R&R pale and clean. The fool's leaving us. He reenlisted for three years so he could get door gunner on a chopper. The career counselor ate his mind up in Phan Rang. Well, I didn't want to stay with the mg so I traded Craig the mg for the M-79. Now I'm a grenadier and he's the machine gunner. Sgt. Days is my new squad leader and that's bad 'cause we don't like each other.

It's 12:15 now and everybody but me is eating C's. We're strung out along rice paddy dike and from here we can clearly see LZ Betty with its high antenna tower. I got the runs again and all the kinds of disturbances in my stomach. But I just went behind a burned house and relieved myself and feel a little better.

(SAME DAY.) It's nighttime and I'm writing this by the light of a flare. We're back at the LZ Betty and being mortared. The airstrip near the tower is in flames and a tremendous explosion that threw a cloud of fire into the sky must have been a gas tank. I'm in a little hole and around it I have duffel bags. The flare is dying.

FEBRUARY 27, 1968 (LZ BARTLEY)

I'M ON top of a mountain in a bunker. We got here this morning, pulled a patrol and came back here tonight. Everybody is outside bullshitting while I'm inside the bunker writing by the light—believe it or not—of an electric bulb. The bunker ports are draped with ponchos so light can't be seen outside.

Away from the group and behind the bunker on a slope, I can hear two PRs talking in Spanish. I'm sure they are from Puerto Rico and not from New York. They're from another unit. One is spending the night with us. He's a colored Puerto Rican with a mustache. They both have mustaches. Too bad 101st don't let me grow one.

I just heard one of our guys outside the bunker say the two PRs think they're better because they don't want to talk English. That gets me pissed. I often wish my name was Rivera or Gonzales so people would know right away that I was Puerto Rican.

MARCH 1, 1968

YESTERDAY WE went to Phan Thiet to get our A-bags and rucksacks. Somebody stole my rucksack with my camera, film, prepaid envelopes, and letters from Queens College. I had about $100 worth of stuff. Today, they're letting us relax on the bunkers. I just finished a book I started this morning and I'm starting another one now. We might go out to the field tomorrow.

MARCH 3, 68

YESTERDAY WE made another combat assault and walked a lot. It's morning now and we'll probably walk a lot like yesterday. At least there are no hooches around here to be fired from.

MARCH 4, 68

WE WOKE this morning at a quarter to six and soon after AK-47s opened up on us. The shots came right over my head. Right now we're using Arty to shell some tree lines where the firing came from.

MARCH 6, 1968

WE'VE BEEN back on the mountain, LZ Bartley, since the fourth. On that day, the third platoon took our place in the boonies, but their platoon leader sprained his ankle jumping off the chopper and our Lt. Harrison had to stay out with them. He was understandably pissed. We got a new guy in the squad from Massachusetts. He has a French name so we just call him Shortround. The day he joined us, me and Patterson started talking about the fighting we've seen. I think subconsciously we wanted to impress the new guy and let him know we're old hands, veterans. I guess soldiers have always been doing that.

There are rats in our bunkers. I just now saw one in front of our bunker. He was as large as a cat.

Our squad now consists of six men. Sgt. Days is the squad leader. I've never got along with him until recently. He goes home in about twenty days. He doesn't drink or smoke. He says he plans to be a priest when he returns. But that's bullshit. He probably made that promise before coming to Nam, but I doubt he'll become a priest when he returns.

Sgt. Patterson has five years of college. He is 24 years old. He's a careful soldier when he's awake. His biggest fault—he snores and sleeps on guard. Craig is 18 years old. He quit high school so he could fight for his country. He's from North Carolina. The other three in the squad are Hass, Shortround, and me. There's more to say about it, but I'm tired.

MARCH 7, 1968

WHETHER IT's my fault or not, this journal hasn't been what I wanted. But it's written mainly for me and as little as one sentence might rekindle a memory, filling my mind with things.

Tomorrow we'll be going out to the field again.

March 10, 1968

I'm TWENTY years old today. I always said I'd be a man when I reached this age and was no longer a teenager.

This morning a fellow called Nelson from another platoon was killed while his squad was on O.P. My squad was also on O.P. and when we heard all the shooting we dd'd the area.

Sgt. Patterson saw me writing in here just now and wanted me to mention that he saved this journal when we were running back from the O.P. He picked the journal up on the run after seeing it fall out of my pocket without my knowing it.

Man, am I funky. Me and my clothes stink. It's about ten days of soot and dried sweat that combines to perfume me with this odor.

March 11, 1968

YESTERDAY WE killed a VC for Nelson.

March 16, 1968

I DIDN'T know I had neglected this book since the 11th. Time disappears. The same thing happens with letters. I believed I wrote a letter just the other day, when in actuality, it'd been more than a week.

Last night they brought us back to the mountain bunkers at LZ Bartley. We got high and listened to music. There was a full moon out. It was a cool scene.

It just came to me, that the radio I'm listening to now is the same radio we found in that hooch the day Daniels, Bunn, and the others were killed.

March 19, 1968

I'm IN the rice paddies again. I've been here since the 17th when I made my 17th chopper assault. It hasn't been too eventful. We get shot at by snipers but that's a common everyday occurrence. We'll probably go back to LZ Bartley today or tomorrow, stay a few days, then come back out on patrol. They keep rotating the platoons.

Mar 22, 1968

We made another combat assault this afternoon after only two days at Bartley. I'm resting by a rice paddy dike and behind me some guys are digging up a bunker after throwing a grenade into it. They just pulled out three little girls and a boy, miraculously all alive, but in shock. Now they say somebody else is in there.

I just went over to see. It's gory. There's a dead woman with a dead baby on her stomach. There's another young woman, dying. I think they're digging up another body now.

March 24, 1968

Still in the field and will probably be here a few more days. We get shot at almost every day by snipers. Captured two detainees in a hooch after we saw another man running from it with a weapon. While we were searching the area we received automatic weapons fire. We called in Arty.

March 26, 1968

We're still in the boonies. I've been out of water since yesterday afternoon. There's a lake nearby and maybe we'll get water there.

March 27, 1968

Yesterday we moved to the lake like I thought. We got water and dug in. That night at 1:30 a.m., while I was on guard, AKs opened up to my front. I jumped into my position and quickly fired an M-79 round at a clump of bushes that I saw tracers coming from. After my round went off, he stopped firing. Maybe I got him, I thought. The firing was still going on and I reloaded to fire at the same spot. Then my face, head, and neck were slammed with shrapnel, a rocket went off in front of my position. I'm hit, I thought and got scared. Then I said I'd better keep firing but I only got off one more round. My head was aching and more rockets were coming in. I laid down in my position and searched for blood. There was a hole in my chin and another in my neck. Later I found another hole in the back of my head. All were bleeding. I was scared. I thought of bleeding to death but remained cool. When the firing stopped Pat called for a medic. Lopez was also hit, and we were both medevaced that night.

I'm in the Phan Thiet aid station now. My neck and chin are swollen, and I'm all bandaged up. I don't know what they'll do with me yet.

MARCH 30, 1968

MY FACE and neck are still swollen but that's my only discomfort. I sleep on a bed, female nurses, movies, good food, etc. For breakfast this morning I got two hard-boiled eggs and a slice of toast. We're not supposed to drink beer but I have three cans by me right now and it's only 7 in the morning. I have them in a green cloth bag so the female lieutenants won't see them.

APRIL 1, 1968

MY FACE is looking more like a face, but it's still swollen.

It came to me the other day that a few days before I was wounded the body of Christ fell off the little cross that I have hanging around my neck on a chain. The fellows had said—Oh-oh, He has abandoned you.

APRIL 2, 1968

THERE'S A lot of things happening in the news: Jonhson isn't going to run. Mao Tse-tung is dead. A de-escalation of war. Israel is fighting again. And Kennedy is having a good chance at the presidency.

In the local news—a 122 mm rocket hit here in Long Binh the other night. One rocket hit an officer's barracks, killing six.

And, the doc said he might wire my jaw today.

APRIL 7, 1968

TODAY I went down to the Red Cross to return some books. While there, I called home at $4.40 a minute. I thought Mom would come on the phone crying but she was calm. But soon she began to cry like I knew she would. I talked to Betsy too, who asked if they'll send me home. What I'd give to go home. Many guys are going to Japan and I envy them even though they're leaving with bad injuries. Because of what I've seen in this hospital, I'm more scared now of returning to the line. Earlier today, while I was reading something, I heard explosions and jumped. It was incoming enemy rockets like the one that got me. But I calmed down and laughed at myself.

I've been living on soup and ice-cream sodas since my jaw got wired. My weight is down to 157.

I was just visited by some old cowboy radio celebrity doing a goodwill tour.

APRIL 15, 1968

TODAY MY friend Pete came down from Danang to visit and to tell me our good friend Joe is dead. I was glad to see Pete and we started talking about home and our friends and I said to him that Joe must have about 30 days left in his tour, but that I hadn't heard from him. That's when he told me Joe had been killed on the 31st of December, almost four months ago. Nobody had told me. I believed Pete, but a part of me didn't. I don't know how I felt. I spoke of hatred for the VC that I didn't feel. I asked how everybody at home took it. Later the conversation changed to other things. In talking about the past, Joe's name would come up, as though he was still alive.

About 10 p.m. tonight the lights went out. Pete went to sleep in an empty hospital bed. I lay down in my bed but started thinking about Joe. I remember him playing softball and his marriage to Susie who he loved very much. We were close, like brothers. He probably thought he couldn't get killed, like I do. We were both wrong. I started saying a prayer for him but halfway through it I cried for the first time in years.

I can't sleep so I came out here in the hospital yard where there's light to write this.

APRIL 20, 1968

IT'S ABOUT 11:30 p.m. and I'm sitting outside my ward on blue benches facing the hospital yard where they show movies and give shows for the patients. The lights in the ward have been out since 10:30 p.m., but I wasn't sleepy so I came out here to read by the lights of the walkway. It's a comfortable clear night.

I had a dream a few nights ago. I saw Betsy and children who I knew were my brothers and sisters drowning in a muddy pond that they were trying to cross to reach me. I wanted to cry out to them but didn't and instead went to eat and tell Mom what happened. I saw Betsy, Mom, and Nereida eating at a table. I was glad to see Betsy was OK, but the other kids weren't there. I think the dream has something to do with Joe's death.

MAY 3, 1968

I'LL LEAVE the hospital in a day or two. The wires on my teeth were removed four days ago and they even cleaned my teeth, I'm starting to gain weight again.

I've been reading a little philosophy lately. I read every man should have a philosophy.

MAY 7, 1968

I SAW *Bonnie and Clyde* tonight in the hospital yard. I think it's one of the best pictures I ever saw. It's so good I have to say so in this journal. The part I like the most is the moment before they are both riddled with bullets. One minute they are happy and suddenly they knew something was wrong and the look they gave each other as Clyde tried to reach her—I thought, that's the way it would be at death.

MAY 15, 68

I'M NOW back in LZ Betty. Arrived yesterday. I was released from the hospital on the 10th of May, but I stayed in Long Binh for two days drinking. Then I went to Ben Hoa and stayed there two more days spending bookoo money in the tea houses there. One tea house was pretty expensive and when one of the girls tried to cheat Hernandez I straightened her out. She got mad and said she hoped the VC crocodiled me. That afternoon I left for Phan Thiet and LZ Betty.

This place has changed. Not all the fellows are here. I'll probably join the company in the mountains tomorrow.

Afterword

When his plane landed in California, eighteen hours after leaving Vietnam, Ed Blanco was refused service at an airport bar because he was considered a minor, despite being in uniform and a war veteran. That's when he realized he was back in the "real world, where they have rules about who can drink beer and who can't." He spent three months at Fort Bragg, North Carolina, before he was given an early discharge so he could continue his education. He majored in philosophy at Brooklyn College, graduating in 1973. He lives with his wife in Queens, New York. In 2005, his nephew did a tour of duty in Iraq with the U.S. Marines.

BALKANS WAR

1991–95

Voices

Zlata Filipović

BOSNIA AND HERZEGOVINA
1991–93 (11–13 YEARS OLD)

You can simply feel that something is coming,
something very bad . . .

The region of Bosnia and Herzegovina was taken over by Austria-Hungary in 1878 and finally annexed in 1908. It was the murder of Archduke Franz Ferdinand in Sarajevo that triggered World War I. By 1918 Bosnia-Herzegovina was incorporated in the Kingdom of Serbs, Croats, and Slovenes, which later became Yugoslavia. It came under Nazi German rule in 1941. During World War II around 10,000 of the 14,000 Bosnian Jews were killed, and some one million Yugoslavs died. Bosnia-Herzegovina— with its ethnic and religious mix of Serbs (Orthodox Christians), Croats (Catholic Christians), and Serbo-Croat-speaking Muslims—became a republic within the Socialist Federal Republic of Yugoslavia in November 1945, after the expulsion of the remaining German forces. Yugoslavia's founder and president was Josip Broz Tito.

The republic's Communist period was peaceful, but its authoritarianism led to the upsurge of various nationalisms. When Tito died in 1980, the economic situation was declining and ethnic tensions were growing; ethnic violence between Muslims, Serbs, and Croats increased in 1989–90. In the November 1990 elections, nationalist parties defeated the ruling Communists.

In 1991 the conflict in Croatia spread into Bosnia-Herzegovina. It was rumored that Serbia and Croatia intended to divide up Bosnia-

Herzegovina between them, with a reduced Muslim buffer state in between. In October 1991, the republic's "sovereignty" was declared by its parliament, which Bosnian Serbs rejected, establishing an alternative assembly. Violent ethnic clashes followed. In the spring of 1992 Bosnian Serb militia units, backed by Serbia, took control of border towns in eastern Bosnia and launched attacks on the capital, Sarajevo.

Born in Sarajevo on December 3, 1980, Zlata was the happy, sociable only child of Malik and Alica Filipović, a lawyer and a chemical engineer respectively. By her own admission, she was always busy, and delighted in the everyday activities of a schoolchild: piano lessons and singing in her local choir, tennis in the summer and skiing in the winter. Yet within one month of the arrival of war in April 1992, her life had narrowed to the family home and the solitary activities of reading and writing. From an early existence as a carefree, outgoing child, Zlata was suddenly housebound as sniper fire and shells rattled through the walls. Unlike numerous friends and relatives who left Sarajevo within the first month of war, Zlata and her parents made the decision to remain together. The situation escalated with such ferocity, however, that by May the city was under siege, and the Filipovićs found themselves trapped. The family was plunged into a primitive existence without water, electricity, or gas, and with limited supplies of food. In February 1992 the first United Nations troops had been drafted into Sarajevo. Their mandate later included the protection of the Sarajevo airport to ensure that humanitarian aid could get into the city.

Bosnian Serb forces established control over an area stretching from the northwest to the southeast, comprising almost two-thirds of the country, and declared it independent. Croats dominated large portions of the western part of the country and subsequently declared an independent Croatian state. There was increasing evidence of atrocities being perpetrated, particularly by Bosnian Serbs. Bosnian Muslims (also called Bosniaks) and Croats were forcibly expelled from occupied zones, or killed, as part of an "ethnic cleansing" process. There was also evidence of death camps and genocide.

Following the fall of the eastern Bosnian town Srebrenica and the *subsequent massacre of some 8,000 men and boys, NATO undertook air strikes against Bosnian Serb positions. In December 1995, after weeks of difficult negotiations, a peace agreement, brokered by the Americans, was signed in the U.S. military base in Dayton, Ohio. It ended the war and created two entities (one is a federation of Bosnian Muslims and Croats; the other, with a Bosnian Serb majority, is called Republika Srpska). An estimated half of Bosnia's prewar population of 4.3 million was displaced in the war, and at least 100,000 people were killed.*

SEPTEMBER 2, 1991

BEHIND ME—a long, hot summer and the happy days of summer holidays; ahead of me—a new school year. I'm starting fifth grade. I'm looking forward to seeing my friends at school, to being together again. Some of them I haven't seen since the day the school bell rang, marking the end of term. I'm glad we'll be together again and share all the worries and joys of going to school.

Mirna, Bojana, Marijana, Ivana, Masa, Azra, Minela, Nadza—we're all together again.

SEPTEMBER 19, 1991

CLASSES HAVE also started at music school now. I go twice a week for piano and solfège. I'm continuing my tennis lessons. Oh, yes, I've been moved up to the "older" group in tennis. Wednesdays I go to Auntie Mika for English lessons. Tuesdays I have choir practice. Those are my responsibilities. I have six lessons every day, except Fridays. I'll survive. . . .

OCTOBER 6, 1991

I'M WATCHING the American Top 20 on MTV. I don't remember a thing, who's in what place. I feel great because I've just eaten a "Four

Seasons" PIZZA with ham, cheese, ketchup, and mushrooms. It was yummy. Daddy bought it for me at Galija's (the pizzeria around the corner). Maybe that's why I didn't remember who took what place—I was too busy enjoying my pizza.

I've finished studying and tomorrow I can go to school BRAVELY, without being afraid of getting a bad grade. I deserve a good grade because I studied all weekend and I didn't even go out to play with my friends in the park. The weather is nice and we usually play "monkey in the middle," talk, and go for walks. Basically, we have fun.

OCTOBER 11, 1991

ANOTHER WEEKEND ahead of me. We're going to Crnotina (our place about fifteen kilometers [9 miles] away)—it has a big orchard with a house that's about 150 years old—a cultural monument under protection of the state. Mommy and Daddy restored it. Grandma and Grandad are still there. I miss them. I miss Vildana, her dog Ati; I miss the clean air and beautiful countryside.

OCTOBER 19, 1991

YESTERDAY WAS a really awful day. We were ready to go to Jahorina (the most beautiful mountain in the world) for the weekend. But when I got home from school, I found my mother in tears and my father in uniform. I had a lump in my throat when Daddy said he had been called up by the police reserve. I hugged him, crying, and started begging him not to go, to stay at home. He said he had to go. Daddy went, and Mommy and I were left alone. Mommy cried and phoned friends and relatives. Everyone came immediately (Slobo, Doda, Keka, Mommy's brother Braco, Aunt Melica, there were so many I can't remember them all). They all came to console us and to offer their help. Keka took me to spend the night with Martina and Matea. When I woke up in the morning, Keka told me everything was all right and that Daddy would be home in two days.

I'm home now, Melica is staying with us, and it looks as though everything will be all right. Daddy should be home the day after tomorrow. Thank God!

OCTOBER 23, 1991

THERE'S A real war going on in Dubrovnik. It's being badly shelled. People are in shelters, they have no water, no electricity, the phones aren't working. We see horrible pictures on TV. Mommy and Daddy are worried. Is it possible that such a beautiful town is being destroyed? Mummy and Daddy are especially fond of it. It was there, in the Ducal Palace, that they picked up the quill and wrote "YES" to spending the rest of their lives together. Mommy says it's the most beautiful town in the world and it mustn't be destroyed. We're worried about Srdjan (my parents' best friend who lives and works in Dubrovnik, but his family is still in Sarajevo) and his parents. How are they coping with everything that's happening over there? Are they alive? We're trying to talk to him with the help of a ham radio, but it's not working. Bokica (Srdjan's wife) is miserable. Every attempt to get some news ends in failure. Dubrovnik is cut off from the rest of the world.

DECEMBER 3, 1991

TODAY IS the big day—my birthday. Happy Birthday to Me!!! But, alas, I'm sick. My sinuses are inflamed and some kind of pus is trickling down my throat. Nothing hurts really, but I have to take an antibiotic, Penbritin, and some disgusting nose drops. They sting. Why did this have to happen on my birthday? Oh, I am unlucky! (Don't be such a pessimist, Zlata, things aren't so bad.) . . . Mommy and Daddy gave me a wonderful birthday present—HEAD skis, new Tyrolia bindings, and new poles! Super! Thank you Mommy! Thank you Daddy!

DECEMBER 19, 1991

SARAJEVO HAS launched an appeal (on TV) called "Sarajevo Helps the Children of Dubrovnik." In Srdjan's parcel we put a nice New Year's present for him to give to some child in Dubrovnik. We made up a package of sweets, chocolates, vitamins, a doll, some pencils, notebooks—whatever we could manage, hoping to bring happiness to some innocent child who has been stopped by the war from going to school, playing, eating what he wants, and enjoying his childhood. It's a nice little package. I hope it makes whoever gets it happy. That's the idea. I also wrote a New Year's card saying I hope the war in Dubrovnik would end soon.

DECEMBER 26, 1991

IT WAS Christmas yesterday. We went to M&M's (Martina's and Matea's). It was wonderful. A big Christmas tree, Christmas presents, and the proverbial Christmas table. And Bokica was there with Andrej. And there was a surprise. Srdjan phoned. Everyone was happy and sad at the same time. There we were all warm, surrounded by Christmas decorations and presents, with lots of wonderful food and drink in front of us. And there he was, like everyone else in Dubrovnik . . . in a war. This war will pass, Srdjan, we'll all be together again! You've got to hold on!!! I'm keeping my fingers crossed for you and for all the people and children of Dubrovnik.

It'll be New Year's Eve soon. The atmosphere seems different than before. Mommy, Daddy, and our friends and family aren't planning a New Year's Eve party this year. They don't talk about it much. Is it because of the war in Dubrovnik? Is it some kind of fear? I don't know or understand a thing. Mommy says we'll decorate the tree tomorrow.

Today was my last day at music school this year. And school?! I'm hoping for straight A's. YO, BABY, YO! As "The Fresh Prince of Bel Air" would say. That's one of my favorite programs on TV. PHEW! I certainly do talk a lot. Just look at all these words! PHEW!

JANUARY 14, 1992

I YAWNED, opened my pen, and started to write. I am listening to the music from *Top Gun* on Good Vibrations [on the radio]. . . .

I have something to tell you. Every night I dream that I'm asking Michael Jackson for his autograph, but either he won't give it to me or his secretary writes it, and then all the letters melt, because Michael Jackson didn't write them. Sad. Poor me. Ha, ha, ha, ha, I have to, ha, ha, ha, ha, laugh, ha, ha, ha, ha.

MARCH 5, 1992

OH, GOD! Things are heating up in Sarajevo. On Sunday (March 1), a small group of armed civilians (as they say on TV) killed a Serbian wedding guest and wounded the priest. On March 2 (Monday) the whole city was full of barricades. There were "1,000" barricades. We didn't even have bread; at 18:00 people got fed up and went out into the streets. The procession set out from the cathedral. It went past the parliament building and made its way through the entire city. Several people were wounded at the Marshal Tito army barracks. People sang and cried "Bosnia, Bosnia," "Sarajevo, Sarajevo," "We'll live together," and "Come and join us." Zdravko Grebo said on the radio that history was in the making. . . .

On March 4 (Wednesday) the barricades were removed, the "kids" [a popular term for politicians] had come to some agreement. Great?!

MARCH 30, 1992

HEY, DIARY! You know what I think? Since Anne Frank called her diary Kitty, maybe I could give you a name too. What about:

ASFALTINA	PIDZAMETA
SEFIKA	HIKMETA
SEVALA	MIMMY

Or something else???

I'm thinking, thinking . . .
I've decided! I'm going to call you
MIMMY
All right then, let's start.

APRIL 5, 1992

DEAR MIMMY,

I'm trying to concentrate so I can do my homework (reading)

but I simply can't. Something is going on in town. You can hear gunfire from the hills. Columns of people are spreading out from Dobrinja. They're trying to stop something, but they themselves don't know what. You can simply feel that something is coming, something very bad.

On TV I see people in front of the Bosnian-Herzegovinian parliament building. The radio keeps playing the same song: "Sarajevo, My Love." That's all very nice, but my stomach is still in knots and I can't concentrate on my homework any more.

Mimmy, I'm afraid of WAR!!!

APRIL 9, 1992
DEAR MIMMY,

I'm not going to school. All the schools in Sarajevo are closed. There's danger hiding in these hills above Sarajevo. But I think things are slowly calming down. The heavy shelling and explosions have stopped. There's occasional gunfire, but it quickly falls silent. Mommy and Daddy aren't going to work. They're buying food in huge quantities. Just in case, I guess. God forbid!

Still, it's very tense. Mommy is beside herself, Daddy tries to calm her down. Mommy has long conversations on the phone. She calls, other people call, the phone is in constant use.

APRIL 12, 1992
DEAR MIMMY,

The new sections of town—Dobrinja, Mojmilo, Vojnicko Polje—are being badly shelled. Everything is being destroyed, burned, the people are in shelters. Here in the middle of town, where we live, it's different. It's quiet. People go out. It was a nice warm spring day today. We went out too. Vaso Miskin Street was full of people, children. It looked like a peace march. People came out to be together, they don't want war. They want to live and enjoy themselves the way they used to. That's only natural, isn't it? Who likes or wants war, when it's the worst thing in the world?

I keep thinking about the march I joined today. It's bigger and stronger than war. That's why it will win. The people must be the ones to win, not the war, because war has nothing to do with humanity. War is something inhuman.

APRIL 18, 1992

DEAR MIMMY,

There's shooting; shells are falling. This really is WAR. Mommy and Daddy are worried, they sit up until late at night, talking. They're wondering what to do, but it's hard to know. Whether to leave and split up, or stay here together. Keka wants to take me to Ohrid. Mommy can't make up her mind—she's constantly in tears. She tries to hide it from me, but I see everything. I see that things aren't good here. There's no peace. War has suddenly entered our town, our homes, our thoughts, our lives. It's terrible.

APRIL 20, 1992

DEAR MIMMY,

War is no joke, it seems. It destroys, kills, burns, separates, brings unhappiness. Terrible shells fell today on Bascarsija, the old town center. Terrible explosions. We went down into the cellar, the cold, dark, revolting cellar. And ours isn't even all that safe. Mommy, Daddy, and I just stood there, holding on to each other in a corner that looked safe. Standing there in the dark, in the warmth of my parents' arms, I thought about leaving Sarajevo. Everybody is thinking about it, and so am I. I couldn't bear to go alone, to leave behind Mommy and Daddy, Grandma and Granddad. And going with just Mommy isn't any good either. The best would be for all three of us to go. But Daddy can't? So I've decided we should stay here together. Tomorrow I'll tell Keka that you have to be brave and stay with those you love and those who love you.

MAY 2, 1992

DEAR MIMMY,

Today was truly, absolutely the worst day ever in Sarajevo. The shooting started around noon. Mommy and I moved into the hall. Daddy was in his office, under our flat, at the time. We told him on the interphone to run quickly to the downstairs lobby where we'd meet him. We brought Cicko [Zlata's canary] with us. The gunfire was getting worse, and we couldn't get over the wall to the Bobars, so we ran down to our own cellar.

The cellar is ugly, dark, and smelly. Mommy, who's terrified of mice, had two fears to cope with. The three of us were in the same corner as the other day. We listened to the pounding shells, the shooting, the thundering noise overhead. We even heard planes. At one moment, I realized that this awful cellar was the only place that could save our lives. Suddenly, it started to look almost warm and nice. It was the only way we could defend ourselves against all this terrible shooting. We heard glass shattering in our street. Horrible. I put my fingers in my ears to block out the terrible sounds. I was worried about Cicko. We had left him behind in the lobby. Would he catch cold there? Would something hit him? I was terribly hungry and thirsty. We had left our half-cooked lunch in the kitchen.

When the shooting died down a bit, Daddy ran over to our flat and brought us back some sandwiches. He said he could smell something burning and that the phones weren't working. He brought our TV set down to the cellar. That's when we learned that the main post office (near us) was on fire and that they had kidnapped our president. . . . I saw the post office in flames. A terrible sight. The firefighters battled with the raging fire. Daddy took a few photos of the post office being devoured by the flames. . . . The whole flat smelled of the burning fire. God, and I used to pass by there every day. It has just been done up. It was huge and beautiful, and now it was being swallowed up by the flames. It was disappearing. . . . A terrible day. This has been the worst, most awful day in my eleven-year-old life. I hope it will be the only one.

MAY 5, 1992
DEAR MIMMY,

The shooting seems to be dying down. I guess they've caused enough misery, although I don't know why. It has something to do with politics. I just hope the "kids" come to some agreement. Oh, if only they would, so we could live and breathe as human beings again. . . . I want it to stop for ever. PEACE! PEACE!

I didn't tell you, Mimmy, that we've arranged things in the flat. My room and Mommy's and Daddy's are too dangerous to be in. They face the hills, which is where they're shooting from. If only you knew how scared I am to go near the windows and into those rooms. So, we turned a safe corner of the sitting room into a "bedroom." We sleep on mattresses on the floor. It's strange and awful. But it's safer that way. We've turned everything around for safety. We put Cicko in the kitchen. He's safe there, although once the shooting starts there's nowhere safe except the cellar. I suppose all this will stop and we'll all go back to our usual places. Ciao!

May 7, 1992
Dear Mimmy,

I was almost positive the war would stop, but today . . . Today a shell fell on the park in front of my house, the park where I used to play with my girlfriends. A lot of people were hurt. From what I hear Jaca, Jaca's mother, Selma, Nina, our neighbor Dado, and who knows how many other people who happened to be there were wounded. Dado, Jaca, and her mother have come home from the hospital; Selma lost a kidney, but I don't know how she is, because she's still in the hospital. AND NINA IS DEAD. A piece of shrapnel lodged in her brain and she died. She was such a sweet, nice girl. We went to kindergarten together, and we used to play together in the park. Is it possible I'll never see Nina again? Nina, an innocent eleven-year-old little girl—the victim of a stupid war. I feel sad. I cry and wonder why. She didn't do anything. A disgusting war has destroyed a young child's life. Nina, I'll always remember you as a wonderful little girl.

May 23, 1992
Dear Mimmy,

I'm not writing to you about me anymore. I'm writing to you about war, death, injuries, shells, sadness, and sorrow. Almost all my friends have left. Even if they were here, who knows whether we'd be able to see each other. The phones aren't working, we couldn't even talk to each other. Vanja and Andrej have gone to join Srdjan in Dubrovnik. The war has stopped over there. They're lucky. I was so unhappy because of that war in Dubrovnik. I never dreamed it would move to Sarajevo.

MAY 27, 1992
DEAR MIMMY,

SLAUGHTER! MASSACRE! HORROR! CRIME! BLOOD! SCREAMS! TEARS! DESPAIR!

That's what Vaso Miskin Street looks like today. Two shells exploded in the street and one in the market. Mommy was nearby at the time. She ran to Grandma's and Grandad's. Daddy and I were beside ourselves because she hadn't come home. I saw some of it on TV but I still can't believe what I actually saw. It's unbelievable. I've got a lump in my throat and a knot in my tummy. HORRIBLE. They're taking the wounded to the hospital. It's a madhouse. We kept going to the window hoping to see Mommy, but she wasn't back. They released a list of the dead and wounded. Daddy and I were tearing our hair out. We didn't know what had happened to her. Was she alive? At 16:00, Daddy decided to go and check the hospital. He got dressed, and I got ready to go to the Bobars', so as not to stay at home alone. I looked out the window one more time and . . . I SAW MOMMY RUNNING ACROSS THE BRIDGE. As she came into the house she started shaking and crying. Through her tears she told us how she had seen dismembered bodies. All the neighbors came because they had been afraid for her. Thank God, Mommy is with us. Thank God.

A HORRIBLE DAY. UNFORGETTABLE.

JUNE 5, 1992
DEAR MIMMY,

There's been no electricity for quite some time and we keep thinking about the food in the freezer. There's not much left as it is. It would be a pity for all of it to go bad. There's meat and vegetables and fruit. How can we save it?

Daddy found an old wood-burning stove in the attic. It's so old it looks funny. In the cellar we found some wood, put the stove outside in the yard, lit it, and are trying to save the food from the refrigerator. We cooked everything, and joining forces with the Bobars, enjoyed ourselves. There was veal and chicken, squid, cherry strudel, meat and potato pies. All sorts of things. It's a pity though, that we had to eat everything so quickly. . . . We washed down our refrigerators and freezers. Who knows when we'll be able to cook like this again. Food is becoming a big problem in Sarajevo. There's nothing to buy, and even cigarettes and coffee are becoming a problem for grown-ups. The last reserves are being used up. God, are we going to go hungry to boot???

JUNE 16, 1992
DEAR MIMMY,

Our windows are broken. All of them except the ones in my room. That's the result of the revolting shell that fell on Zoka's jewelry shop, across the way from us. I was alone in the house at the time. Mommy and Daddy were down in the yard, getting lunch ready, and I had gone upstairs to set the table. Suddenly I heard a terrible bang and glass breaking. I was terrified and ran toward the hall. The same moment, Mommy and Daddy were at the door. Out of breath, worried, sweating, and pale, they hugged me and we ran to the cellar, because the shells usually come one after the other. When I realized what had happened, I started to cry and shake. Everybody tried to calm me down, but I was very upset. I barely managed to pull myself together.

JUNE 18, 1992
DEAR MIMMY,

Today we heard some more sad, sad news. Our country house in Crnotina, a tower that's about 150 years old, has burned down. Like the post office, it disappeared in flames. I love it so much. We spent the last summer there. I had a wonderful time. I always looked forward to going there. We had redone it so nicely, bought new furniture, new rugs, put in new windows, given it all our love and warmth, and its beauty was our reward. It lived through so many wars, so many years, and now it's gone. It has burned down to the ground. Our neighbors, Ziga, Meho, and Becir, were killed. That's even sadder. . . .

I keep asking why? What for? Who's to blame? I ask, but there's no answer.

JUNE 29, 1992
DEAR MIMMY,

BOREDOM!!! SHOOTING!!! SHELLING!!! PEOPLE BEING KILLED!!! DESPAIR!!! HUNGER!!! MISERY!!! FEAR!!!

That's my life!! The life of an innocent eleven-year-old schoolgirl! A schoolgirl without a school, without the fun and excitement of school. A child without games, without friends, without the sun, without birds, without nature, without fruit, without chocolate or sweets, with just a little powdered milk. In short, a child without a childhood. A wartime child. I now realize that I am really living through a war; I am witnessing an ugly, disgusting war. I am one of thousands of other children in this town that is being destroyed, that is crying, weeping, seeking help, but getting none. God, will this ever stop, will I ever be a schoolgirl again, will I ever enjoy my childhood again? I once heard that childhood is the most wonderful time of your life. And it is. I loved it, and now an ugly war is taking it all away from me. Why? I feel sad, I feel like crying. I am crying.

JULY 2, 1992
DEAR MIMMY,

We gave ourselves a treat today. We picked the cherries off the tree in the yard and ate them all up. We had watched it blossom and its small green fruits slowly turn red, and so here we were eating them. Oh, you're a wonderful cherry tree! The plum tree hasn't got any fruit, so we won't even get to try it. I miss fruit a lot. In these days of war in

Sarajevo, there is no basic food or any of the other things a person needs, and there is no fruit. But now I can say that I ate myself silly on cherries.

JULY 5, 1992
DEAR MIMMY,

I spend my days in the house and in the cellar. That's my wartime childhood. And it's summer. Other children are holidaying at the seaside, in the mountains, swimming, sunbathing, enjoying themselves. God, what did I do to deserve being in a war, spending my days in a way that no child should. I feel caged. All I can see through the broken windows is the park in front of my house. Empty, deserted, no children, no joy. I hear the sound of shells, and everything around me smells of war. War is now my life. OOOHHH, I can't stand it anymore! I want to scream and cry. I wish I could play the piano at least, but I can't even do that because it's in "the dangerous room," where I'm not allowed. How long is this going to go on???

JULY 7, 1992
DEAR MIMMY,

There was no water yesterday, the day before or the day before that. It came on around 8:30 this morning and now, at 10:30, it is slowly disappearing again.

We filled whatever we could find with water and now have to conserve the precious liquid. You have to conserve everything in this war, including water and food.

JULY 11, 1992
DEAR MIMMY,

Nedo brought us a little visitor today. A kitten. It followed him and he couldn't just leave it in the street so he picked it up and brought it home. We'll call it Skinny, Lanky, Kitty, Mikana, Persa, Cici . . . ??? It's orange, has white socks and a white patch on its chest. It's cute, but a little wild.

JULY 14, 1992

DEAR MIMMY,

On July 8 we got a UN package. Humanitarian aid. Inside were 6 tins of beef, 5 tins of fish, 2 boxes of cheese, 3 kilos [7 pounds] of detergent, 5 bars of soap, 2 kilos [4 pounds] of sugar, and 5 liters of cooking oil. All in all, a super package. But Daddy had to stand in the line for four hours to get it.

JULY 17, 1992

DEAR MIMMY,

We named the kitten Cici. Nedo gave it a bath, we feed it milk and biscuits, even rice. She has to get used to wartime food like the rest of us! She's cute. She has a beautiful head. We've all fallen in love with her, and she is slowly getting used to us. Bojana and I hold her in our lap, stroke her, and she purrs. That means she likes it, she's happy. . . . So, now we have a new member in this family we call THE NEIGHBORHOOD.

JULY 20, 1992

DEAR MIMMY,

Since I'm in the house all the time, I watch the world through the window. Just a piece of the world.

There are lots of beautiful pedigreed dogs roaming the streets. Their owners probably had to let them go because they couldn't feed them anymore. Sad. Yesterday I watched a cocker spaniel cross the bridge, not knowing which way to go. He was lost. He wanted to go forward, but then he stopped, turned around, and looked back. He was probably looking for his master. Who knows whether his master is still alive? Even animals suffer here. Even they aren't spared by the war.

AUGUST 16, 1992

DEAR MIMMY,

Daddy has a hernia. He's lost a lot of weight, and carrying the water was too much for him. The doctor has told him that he mustn't lift anything heavy anymore. Musn't? But somebody has to bring the water! Mommy will have to do it alone now. How will she manage?

AUGUST 18, 1992
DEAR MIMMY,

Mommy is carrying home the water. It's hard on her, but she has to do it. The water hasn't come back on. Nor has electricity.

I didn't tell you, Mimmy, but I've forgotten what it's like to have water pouring out of a tap, what it's like to shower. We use a jug now. The jug has replaced the shower. We wash dishes and clothes like in the Middle Ages. This war is taking us back to olden times. And we take it, we suffer, but we don't know for how long.

SEPTEMBER 20, 1992
DEAR MIMMY,

YIPPEE! I crossed the bridge today. Finally I got to go out too! I can hardly believe it. The bridge hasn't changed. But it's sad, sad because of the post office, which looks even sadder. It's in the same place, but it's not the same old post office. The fire has left its mark. It stands there like a witness to brutal destruction.

The streets aren't the same, not many people are out, they're worried, sad, everybody rushing around with bowed heads. All the shop windows have been broken and looted. My school was hit by a shell and its top floor destroyed. . . .

I went to see Grandma and Granddad. Oh, how we hugged and kissed! They cried with joy. They've lost weight and aged since I last saw them four months ago. They told me I had grown, that I was now a big girl. That's nature at work. Children grow, the elderly age. At least those of us who are still alive.

And there are lots and lots of people and children in Sarajevo who are no longer among the living. The war has claimed them. And all of them were innocent. Innocent victims of this disgusting war . . .

Dear Mimmy, I have something to confess to you. I dressed up.

I put on that nice plaid outfit. My shoes were a bit tight, because my feet have grown, but I survived.

October 1, 1992
DEAR MIMMY,

Spring has been and gone, summer has been and gone, and now it's autumn. October has started. And the war is still on. The days are getting shorter and colder. Soon we'll move the stove upstairs to the flat. But how will we keep warm? God, is anyone thinking of us here in Sarajevo? Are we going to start winter without electricity, water, or gas, and with a war going on?

The "kids" are negotiating. Will they finally negotiate something? Are they thinking about us when they negotiate, or are they just trying to outwit each other and leave us to our fate?

October 16, 1992
DEAR MIMMY,

I sometimes go into the "dangerous room" now, where the piano is, and the notes keep me company. They take me back to the days before the war. Pictures flash through my mind of Jahorina, the sea, Crnotina, my friends. It makes me sad, it even makes me cry. God, they've taken everything away from me.

October 29, 1992
DEAR MIMMY,

Mommy and Auntie Ivanka (from her office) have received grants to specialize in Holland. They have letters of guarantee, and there's even one for me. But Mommy can't decide. If she accepts, she leaves behind Daddy, her parents, her brother. I think it's a hard decision to make. One minute I think—no, I'm against it. But then I remember the war, winter, hunger, my stolen childhood, and I feel like going. Then I think of Daddy, Grandma, and Grandad, and I don't want to go. It's hard to know what to do. I'm really on edge, Mimmy, I can't write anymore.

NOVEMBER 6, 1992
DEAR MIMMY,

Mommy and Auntie Ivanka are trying to get all their papers, because to get out of Sarajevo you need a heap of papers and signatures. It's now certain that Maja and Bojana will be going to Austria. They signed up for the Jewish convoy. Maybe we'll leave on that convoy too.

NOVEMBER 15, 1992
DEAR MIMMY,

An awful lot of people have left Sarajevo. All of them well known. Mommy said, "Sarajevo is leaving." Mommy and Daddy know a lot of them. They talked to them, and when they said good-bye, everyone kept saying: "We'll see each other again somewhere, sometime." It was sad. Sad and upsetting. November 14, 1992, is a day Sarajevo will remember. It reminded me of the movies I saw about the Jews in World War II.

NOVEMBER 19, 1992
DEAR MIMMY,

I keep wanting to explain these stupid politics to myself, because it seems to me that politics caused this war, making it our everyday reality. War has crossed out the day and replaced it with horror, and now horrors are unfolding instead of days. It looks to me as though these politics mean Serbs, Croats, and Muslims. But they are all people. They are all the same. They look like people, there's no difference. They all have arms, legs, and heads, they walk and talk, but now there's "something" that wants to make them different.

Among my girlfriends, among our friends, in our family, there are Serbs and Croats and Muslims. It's a mixed group, and I never knew who was a Serb, a Croat, or a Muslim. Now politics has started meddling around. It has put an "S" on Serbs, an "M" on Muslims, and a "C" on Croats; it wants to separate them. And to do so it has chosen the worst, blackest pencil of all—the pencil of war, which spells only misery and death.

Why is politics making us unhappy, separating us, when we ourselves know who is good and who isn't? We mix with the good, not with the bad. And among the good there are Serbs and Croats and Muslims, just as there are among the bad. I simply don't understand it. Of course, I'm "young" and politics are conducted by "grown-ups." But I think we "young" would do it better. We certainly wouldn't have chosen war. . . .

A bit of philosophizing on my part, but I was alone and felt I could write this to you, Mimmy. You understand me. Fortunately, I've got you to talk to.

NOVEMBER 25, 1992
DEAR MIMMY,

The shooting really has died down.

I can hear the whine of the electric saws. The winter and the power cuts have condemned the old trees, arbored walks, and parks that made Sarajevo so pretty.

I was sad today. I couldn't bear the thought of the trees disappearing from my park. They've been condemned. God, all the things my park has been through! The children have left it, Nina forever, and now the linden, birch, and plane trees are leaving it forever, too. Sad. I couldn't watch, and I can't write anymore.

NOVEMBER 29, 1992
DEAR MIMMY,

It's cold. We don't have enough wood, so we're conserving it.

There's wood at the market but, like everything else, only for deutschmarks, and that's very expensive. I keep thinking that my park's linden, birch, and plane trees are probably there with the other wood. They're selling for foreign money now.

Braco Lajtner comes by every day. We have lunch together and since he's alone, he stays until dark. Then he goes home. He goes back to a cold, empty house. That isn't easy either!

Mommy brings home the water, and when it rains we collect the rainwater, too; it comes in useful. The days are getting shorter and shorter. Mommy, Daddy, and I play cards by candlelight, or we read and talk, and around nine o'clock in the evening Boda, Zika, and Nedo come to listen to RFI, and that's how the day ends. It's the same almost every day.

DECEMBER 28, 1992
DEAR MIMMY,

I'm at home today. I had my first piano lesson. My teacher and I kissed and hugged, we hadn't seen each other since March. Then we moved on to Czerny, Bach, Mozart, and Chopin, to the etude, the invention, the sonata, and the "piece." It's not going to be easy. But I'm going to school now and I'll give it my all. It makes me happy. Mimmy, I'm now in my fifth year of music school.

You know, Mimmy, we've had no water or electricity for ages. When I go out and when there's no shooting it's as if the war were over, but this business with the electricity and water, this darkness, this winter, the shortage of wood and food, brings me back to earth, and then I realize that the war is still on. Why? Why on earth don't those "kids" come to some agreement? They really are playing games. And it's us they are playing with.

As I sit writing to you, my dear Mimmy, I look over at Mommy and Daddy. They are reading. They lift their eyes from the page and think about something. What are they thinking about? About the book they are reading, or are they trying to put together the scattered pieces of this war puzzle? I think it must be the latter. Somehow they look even sadder to me in the light of the oil lamp (we have no more wax candles, so we make our own oil lamps). I look at Daddy. He really has lost a lot of weight. The scales say twenty-five kilos, but looking at him I think it must be more. I think even his glasses are too big for him. Mommy has lost weight too. She's shrunk somehow; the war has given her wrinkles. God, what is this war doing to my parents? They don't look like my old Mommy and Daddy any more. Will this ever stop? Will our suffering stop so that my parents can be what they used to be—cheerful, smiling, nice-looking?

JANUARY 6, 1993
DEAR MIMMY,

It's freezing. Winter has definitely come to town. I used to love and enjoy it so much, but now it's a very disagreeable guest in Sarajevo.

Our flowers have frozen. They were in the rooms we didn't heat. We live in the kitchen now. That's the only room we heat, and we manage to get the temperature up to 17°C [63°F]. Cicko is with us. I'm afraid he might get sick, because birds are sensitive to winter.

We moved the mattresses into the kitchen, and now we sleep here. (Don't make me tell you how many sweaters and pullovers we wear over our pajamas.) The kitchen is now our kitchen and our sitting room and our bedroom and even our bathroom. We have an unusual way of bathing. We spread out the sheets of plastic and then—the basin becomes our bathtub, the jug our shower, and so on.

Daddy's got frostbite on his fingers from cutting the wood in the cold cellar. They look awful. His fingers are swollen, and now they're putting some cream on them, but they itch badly. Poor Daddy.

JANUARY 26, 1993
DEAR MIMMY,

I've noticed that I don't write to you anymore about the war or the shooting. That's probably because I've become used to it. All I care about is that the shells don't fall within 50 meters [160 feet] of my house, that we've got wood, water, and, of course, electricity. I can't believe I've become used to all this, but it seems I have. Whether it's being used to it, fighting for survival, or something else, I don't know.

MARCH 10, 1993
DEAR MIMMY,

There's a terrible problem. We've run out of bird food for Cicko. There's no bird food anywhere in town. What can we do?

We cook him rice, but he won't touch it. Auntie Ivanka brought unglazed rice, and he nibbled at it. He won't touch cooked peas. The only thing he seems willing to try is bread crumbs. We raised the alarm. We want to save our Cicko—we can't let him starve.

Today Mommy got bird food from Auntie Radmila and a colleague at work. They took it from the beaks of their own pets. Oh, you should see, Mimmy, how Cicko eats! But we mustn't give him too much, we have to save. We only have enough for a few days. . . .

There, even birds are sharing their food, helping each other out, like people. I'm so happy. Enjoy yourself, Cicko!

MARCH 15, 1993
DEAR MIMMY,

I'm sick again. My throat hurts, I'm sneezing and coughing. And spring is around the corner. The second spring of the war. I know from the calendar, but I don't see it. I can't see it because I can't feel it. All I can see are the poor people still lugging water, and even poorer casualties—young people without arms and legs. They're the ones who had the fortune or perhaps the misfortune to survive.

There are no trees to blossom and no birds, because the war has destroyed them as well. There is no sound of birds twittering in springtime. There aren't even pigeons—the symbol of Sarajevo. No noisy children, no games. Even the children no longer seem like children. They've had their childhoods taken away from them, and without that they can't be children. It's as if Sarajevo is slowly dying, disappearing. Life is disappearing. So how can I feel spring, when spring is something that awakens life, and here there is no life, here everything seems to have died?

I'm sad again, Mimmy. But you have to know that I'm getting sadder and sadder. I'm sad whenever I think, and I have to think.

APRIL 8, 1993
DEAR MIMMY,

More terrible, sad news today. Our dear, beloved Cicko has died. He just toppled over, and that was it. He wasn't sick. It happened suddenly.

He was singing. Now he's not cold anymore. The poor thing got through the winter; we found him food. And he left it all. Maybe he had had enough of this war. It was all too much for him—he had felt cold and hunger and now he's gone forever. I cried, but Mommy was worse than me. We're going to miss him dreadfully. We loved him so much, he was a member of the family. He lived with us for seven years. That's a long time. Daddy buried him in the yard. His cage is empty.

APRIL 19, 1993
DEAR MIMMY,

I've grown, Mimmy. I have nothing to wear. Everything's too small, too tight, too short for me.

I arranged with Braco to see if I could use some of Martina's things; Keka wrote to me and said to take what I need.

I went there today. I was in Martina and Matea's room. The room was empty, just their photographs, a few of their things, which they must be missing, broken windows, dust. The two of them aren't there. The room is sad, and so am I.

After that first encounter with the room, I remembered why I had come. Among Martina's things I found myself a black patchwork skirt, white tennis shoes, walking shoes, and a more feminine pair.

I remembered what Keka had said in her letter: "Take anything that can brighten up your day, Zlata, and enjoy it, because tomorrow will come. You can be sure of it."

JULY 10, 1993
DEAR MIMMY,

I'm sitting in my room. Cici is with me. She's enjoying herself on the armchair—sleeping. As for me, I'm reading through my letters. Letters are all I've got left of my friends. I read them, and they take me back to my friends.

> I have to tell you that I miss you, but I hope we'll see each other soon. I'm slowly getting used to this new life. Take care of yourself, Zlata, and be good to your parents.
> MUCH LOVE FROM YOUR MATEA

Dear Fipa, I think of you often and wonder what you're doing, how you're living. I miss you a lot, I miss the whole of Sarajevo—the most beautiful city in the world, with the biggest and warmest embrace in the world, the heart of the world. It's now in flames, but it will never burn down. I know it's hard for you. All I can say is that I love and miss you.

Many, many kisses from your Martina and all the other refugees who want to come home!

I heard two of Dr. Alban's songs: "It's My Life" and "Sing Hallelujah." I don't know if they've managed to come your way. Maja thought today of taping a cassette for you with hit songs by Mick Jagger, Michael Jackson, Bon Jovi. Nothing new in the fashion world. Oh, Fipa, how I wish I could talk to you.

MUCH LOVE FROM YOUR BOJANA

MY DEAR ZLATA,

You are and always will be my best friend. No one will ever be able to destroy our friendship, not even this war. Although you're in Sarajevo and I'm in Italy, although we haven't seen each other for more than a year now, you are still my best friend.

MUCH LOVE FROM YOUR OGA

MY DARLING LITTLE GIRL,

I'm sending you this flower from our garden and this butterfly from the woods. You can make a picture with them. If I could, I'd send you a basketful of flowers, the forest, trees, and lots of birds, but these people here won't let me. So I'm sending you my love with the gentle butterfly and the red flower.

Don't worry about the future. Remember that good and happy times come to all good people, and you and your parents are good people and you will be well, cheerful, and happy. I think of you often.

MUCH LOVE FROM YOUR KEKA

AND SO, Mimmy, in their letters they send me their love, their thoughts, pictures of a normal life, songs, fashion, best wishes for happiness and an end to this madness. I read them and sometimes I cry, because I want *them*, I want life, not just letters.

JULY 30, 1993
DEAR MIMMY,

I'm at the window. It's hot. I am watching the people lug water home.

You should see the different kinds of water carts they have. How inventive people are. Two-wheelers, three-wheelers, wheelbarrows, shopping carts, pushchairs, hospital tables, supermarket trolleys, and, topping them all—a sledge on roller skates. And you should hear the sounds! The various sounds and screeching of the wheels. That is what wakes us up every morning. It's all funny and sad at the same time. Sometimes I think about all the films that could be made in Sarajevo. There are loads of subjects for film here.

AUGUST 10, 1993
DEAR MIMMY,

I have more very, very sad news for you. OUR CAT IS NO MORE. Our Cici died. Awful. First Cicko [the canary], and now Cici.

I went to Auntie Boda's today and talked about all sorts of things. How I got a C in solfège, how I got a pair of trousers from Auntie Irena, how my piano exam was coming up. And I asked why they hadn't come over the night before.

Auntie Boda: "We had a problem."

Me (stupidly): "Whyyy?"

Auntie Boda: "We don't have our cat anymore."

Me (lost): "You, you mean it's d-d-dead??"

Me (a lump in my throat): "I have to go. I'm going home, I have to go home. Good-bye."

And when I got home: BOO-HOO! SOB! SOB! SOB! OOOOHHH!

Mommy and Daddy (in duet): "What's wrong??"

Me: "The cat, the cat. It died."

Mommy and Daddy (again in duet): "Aaaah!!"

And then an hour of tears. Can it be? Our cat, the most wonderful, most beautiful, most lovable, sweetest, best cat in the whole wide world—gone. My little cat. When I think of how lovable, sweet, and wonderful she was! I cry my eyes out. I know terrible things are happening, people are being killed, there's a war on, but still . . . I'm so sorry. She cheered us all up, made us smile, filled our hours. My yellow Cici. My friend.

Haris and Enes buried her in the yard next to Cicko. They made a little grave out of tiles. She deserved it.

I'm very, very sad.

September 17, 1993
Dear Mimmy,

The "kids" are negotiating something, signing something. Again giving us hope that this madness will end. There's supposed to be a ceasefire tomorrow, and on September 21 at the Sarajevo airport everybody is supposed to sign FOR PEACE. Will the war stop on the day that marks the change from one season to another???

With all the disappointments I've had with previous truces and signatures, I can't believe it.

I can't believe it because another horrible shell fell today, ending the life of a three-year-old little boy, wounding his sister and mother.

All I know is that the result of their little games is 15,000 dead in Sarajevo, 3,000 of them children, 50,000 permanent invalids, whom I already see in the streets on crutches, in wheelchairs, armless and legless. And I know that there's no room left in the cemeteries and parks to bury the latest victims.

Maybe that's why this madness should stop.

SEPTEMBER 25, 1993
DEAR MIMMY,

The electricity is back, but it's being rationed. And the rationing, like the life we're living, is stupid. We get four hours of electricity every fifty-six hours. You should see, Mimmy, what a madhouse this is when the electricity comes on! Piles of unwashed laundry waiting to go into the washing machine. Even bigger piles of laundry waiting for the iron. Dust waiting to be vacuumed. Cooking to be done, bread to be baked, and we'd all like to watch a bit of television. There's hair to be washed and dried with a hair dryer. It's incredible. You wouldn't believe it.

OCTOBER 7, 1993
DEAR MIMMY,

. . . Winter is approaching, but we have nothing to heat with.

I look at the calendar, and it seems as though this year of 1993 will again be marked by war. God, we've lost two years listening to gunfire, battling with electricity, water, food, and waiting for peace.

I look at Mommy and Daddy. In two years they've aged ten. And me? I haven't aged, but I've grown, although I honestly don't know how. I don't eat fruit or vegetables, I don't drink juices, I don't eat meat . . . I am a child of rice, peas, and spaghetti. There I am, talking about food again. I often catch myself dreaming about chicken, a good cutlet, pizza, lasagna . . . Oh, enough of that.

OCTOBER 17, 1993
DEAR MIMMY,

Yesterday our "friends in the hills" reminded us of their presence and that they are now in control and can kill, wound, destroy . . . yesterday was a truly horrible day.

Five hundred and ninety shells. From 4:30 in the morning on, throughout the day. Six dead and fifty-six wounded. That's yesterday's toll. Soukbunar [an area of Sarajevo] fared the worst. I don't know how Melica [Zlata's aunt] is. They say that half the houses up there are gone.

We went down into the cellar. Into the cold, dark, stupid cellar, which I hate. We were there for hours and hours. They kept pounding away. All the neighbors were with us.

AGAIN! Again and again they keep sinking all our boats, taking and dashing all our hopes. People said that they wouldn't do it anymore. That there would soon be an end to it, that everything would resolve itself. THAT THIS STUPID WAR WOULD END!

Oh, God, why do they spoil everything? Sometimes I think it would be better if they kept shooting, so that we wouldn't find it so hard when it starts again. This way, just as you relax, it starts up AGAIN. I am convinced now that it will never end. Because some people don't want it to, some evil people who hate children and ordinary folk.

I keep thinking that we are alone in this hell, that nobody is thinking of us, nobody is offering us a helping hand. But there are people who are thinking and worrying about us.

Yesterday the Canadian TV crew and Janine came to see how we had survived the mad shelling. That was nice of them. Really kind.

And when we saw that Janine was holding an armful of food, we got so sad we cried. Alexandra came too.

People worry about us, they think about us, but subhumans want to destroy us. Why? I keep asking myself, why?

We haven't done anything. We're innocent. But helpless!

DECEMBER 1993
DEAR MIMMY,

PARIS. There's electricity, there's water, there's gas. There's, there's . . . life, Mimmy. Yes, life, bright lights, traffic, people, food. . . . Don't think I've gone nuts, Mimmy. Hey, listen to me,

Paris!? No, I'm not crazy, I'm not kidding, it really is Paris, and (can you believe it?) I'm here. Me, my mom and my dad. At last . . . The darkness has played out its part. The darkness is behind us, now we're bathed in light lit by good people. Remember that—good people. Bulb by bulb, not candles, but bulb by bulb, and me bathing in the lights of Paris . . .

On December 6, three days after my thirteenth birthday (my second in the war), the publishers told us that on Wednesday, December 8, we were to be ready, that they would be coming for us—we were going to Paris for your promotion, Mimmy. It was a real shock. Although that's what I had wanted, I had wanted to leave that hell, to escape with my parents from death, hunger, the cold, because it really had become unbearable, but it was a shock all the same. . . . For me, the hardest part was to accept that I was going, that I was leaving behind people I loved, knowing the situation I was leaving them in. I was leaving them in war, in misery, without water, electricity, gas, or food. And who knew when or if I would ever see them again.

It's impossible to explain those mixed feelings of sorrow and joy. Joy at being able to leave the war and sorrow at having to leave EVERYTHING behind. ALL MY LOVED ones. Oh, Mimmy, all those tears! Saying good-bye in tears, packing in tears. I cried and my loved ones cried (but I most of all). When I packed my things I cried, and I think that all those things that were supposed to go with me, like those that remained behind maybe to wait for me one day in Sarajevo, cried too. I wanted to take everything, because I was equally fond of everything, but it wouldn't all fit into one suitcase. I had to choose. . . .

At about 5:00 p.m. we landed at the military airport in Paris. A wonderful reception, warm words of welcome. . . . You could see in everyone's eyes how happy they were to see us finally in Paris. And so the operation of leaving the hell of Sarajevo was a success. . . .

That's how Paris welcomed me. That's how I came out of the darkness and saw the lights. Are these lights my lights as well? I wonder. When even a glimmer of these lights illuminates the darkness of Sarajevo, then it will be my light as well. Until then . . . ???

AFTERWORD

In the summer of 1992, Zlata joined a makeshift school organized for the children of her neighborhood. At the time, UNICEF was appealing for children with war diaries to come forward. Through the channel of the newly established school, Zlata's diary was discovered and selected for publication in July 1993. Almost immediately, the diary garnered huge amounts of publicity, and Zlata was proclaimed the "Anne Frank of Sarajevo," a name that she has always been uncomfortable with because she was lucky enough to survive where Anne so tragically perished. Offers from publishers around the world flooded in, and the Filipović family finally struck an agreement with a Parisian publishing house, Robert Laffont. With the help of the publishers, and in conjunction with the French government and the UN presence in Bosnia, Zlata, Malik, and Alica managed to flee their native Sarajevo for Paris in the winter of 1993.

In more than a decade since that escape, Zlata has carved out a name for herself as an advocate of tolerance and peace throughout the world. Her diary has been translated into over thirty languages, and she has traveled through dozens of countries speaking of her experiences, which she calls the essence of experiences she shares with all the children and young people who stayed behind in Sarajevo. She has a bachelor's degree from Oxford University and a master's in international peace studies from Trinity College, Dublin.

SECOND INTIFADA

2000–

Shiran Zelikovich

ISRAEL

2002 (15 YEARS OLD)

Peace, love & rock 'n' roll . . .

Mary Masrieh Hazboun

PALESTINE

2002–4 (17–19 YEARS OLD)

Another day of death and destruction . . .

Israel and Palestine occupy a strip of land in the Middle East that has major historical and religious significance to both these entities, despite the differences between their faiths and cultures. Jerusalem, in particular, is of great importance to both the Israelis and the Palestinians (both Christian and Muslim). As a result of this shared but conflicting history and the competing claims to the land, the two entities have frequently clashed.

The majority of Jews left or were expelled from the Middle East in the Middle Ages. Since the end of the nineteenth century, discussions were held internationally about the possible resettlement of Jewish people in part of the Palestinian territory, and the purchasing of Palestinian land was in process in the years before World War II. The Palestinian territory had belonged to the Ottoman Empire for more than five hundred years. After the dissolution of the empire, the territory was placed under the British protectorate. In 1947 Britain decided to terminate its protectorate over Palestine and pass the responsibility for Palestine over to the United Nations. The UN's ensuing plan for partition—to divide the territory into Jewish and Arab states—never was implemented because Israel proclaimed independence before that happened. Following the events of World War II and the mass killings of an estimated 6 million European Jews during the Nazi-perpetrated Holocaust, one of the two states envisaged in the Partition Plan proclaimed its independence as Israel on May 14, 1948. Immediately, the nearby Arab countries of Egypt, Jordan, Syria, Iraq, Iran, as well as Palestine, which had demanded a halt on Jewish immigration in the previous years, launched military attacks on the fledgling state of Israel. The 1948 Arab-Israeli War was eventually won by Israel, but at the cost of immense resentment by their neighboring Arab countries. As a result of the 1948–49 war, around 711,000 Palestinians (UN estimate) fled or were expelled from territories that came under Israeli control, while immigration of Holocaust survivors and Jewish refugees from Arab lands increased Israel's population. Palestinian refugee camps still exist today, and the number of registered refugees has subsequently grown to more than 4 million in 2002 and continues to rise due to natural population growth.

The conflicts continued over the next decades, most notable being the 1967 "Six Day War," which lay the foundation for future discord in the region. Throughout this time, Israel sought greater control of the territory, which often led to occupation and the suppression of the Palestinians, while the Palestinians answered with attacks on Israeli-occupied areas. Mutual violence and deaths have been well documented on both the Israeli and Palestinian sides.

Shiran was born in Tel Aviv, Israel, in 1988, the second of two daughters. Her mother was a university professor, while her father worked for the Israeli ministry of education. She began writing her diary to chronicle life in Israel during the Intifada, and the effects of the conflict on her and her teenage friends.

Four years earlier, Mary was born in Bethlehem to Christian Palestinian parents. She was the first child and was followed by her two brothers. Her father owned a small grocery shop in Bethlehem, and her mother was a housewife. Throughout the Intifada, Mary excelled as a student and planned on becoming a journalist. She was also an accomplished Middle Eastern singer, having started singing when she was thirteen.

The Arabic term "Intifada" was used to describe the uprising for Palestinian independence. Intifada means "shivering free from" or "shaking off," as with an illness or a hardship. The first Intifada was begun by the Palestinians in 1987, and resulted in violent clashes between Israelis and Palestinians, particularly in the Gaza Strip. The Palestinian Liberation Organization (PLO), headed by Yasser Arafat, began peace talks in the early 1990s, resulting in a temporary peace agreement in 1993. At this time, the Palestinian Authority was created to recognize Palestinian control over certain areas of historical Palestine. However, the 1993 peace talks slowly unraveled and set the scene for the second Intifada. On September 29, 2000, Israel's prime minister, Ariel Sharon, and significant security visited the Al-Aqsa Mosque compound and declared that the complex would remain under perpetual Israeli control. This led to the outbreak of riots and what is considered the beginning of the second Intifada. Despite recent events, including the death of Yasser Arafat, Ariel Sharon's serious illness, and the building of the controversial West Bank barrier, the further development of this conflict and the possibility of a lasting peace remain very uncertain.

SHIRAN ZELIKOVICH, ISRAEL, 2002

APRIL 15, 2002

MY DEAR diary,

Here I'm starting to write to you; the first diary I have ever had. Maybe because I feel the need to talk to someone who will just listen.

A short introduction about me, dear diary.

My name is Shiran Zelikovich; I'm a 15-year-old girl (this week) from a country at war for its survival, Israel.

Almost everything I loved in this world is disappearing, all the fun, all the joy, all the values of life itself.

Happy Birthday!!! What do the two words connected together, "Happy Birthday," mean to you? You probably say it means to go out and to celebrate.

I agree with you, diary . . .

Nowadays, I can just kiss celebrating good-bye. It won't happen today, on my birthday. It won't happen soon. I wish I could be somewhere else, just for this special day, my birthday. All I am allowed to do is to invite friends and stay at home. The fear of life itself. My parents won't let me go anywhere.

Can I go to the mall? "No!"

Can I go to a club? "No!"

Can I go to the movies? "No!"

Oh, thanks! That's fun. . . .

Yesterday I heard about the suicide attack, in which six kids and old people were murdered and ninety were wounded. My wishes for celebration have already gone. My school's birthday "gift" was adding another three guards at the entrance. (At least they were good looking. . . .)

I love my country, and I feel sorry that we are at war. I can't say I feel safe, quite the opposite, but I try to. When I am bigger, I want to help my country, and fight those horrible terrorists.

Some of my friends want to live abroad, to feel free; I don't want to, because I want to be here when the war ends. To be with my friends and family, to live as a free person; and if the war doesn't end, then I will make it end, I haven't figured out how yet, but it will come. I'm just watching the news, they show people crying, dying, shouting.

To tell you the truth, diary, I am trying to ignore the fear of dying, but it's hard. The truth is, this was the saddest birthday I have ever had; it can only get better from now on.

I will write you soon.

Love,

SHIRAN

APRIL 22, 2002

HI DIARY,

I am writing you again because I really need to talk to somebody and just spit it out. I have so much to tell you.

So I will just start. . . .

Yesterday, I saw on TV that a 17-year-old girl named Samia Taktaka from Beit Fa'Gar was caught on her way to commit a suicide killing in Jerusalem. That is really alarming. How can a girl of my age kill herself? How can another 15-year-old girl succeed in committing [suicide], and take a six-year-old boy's legs, or leave him with no mom and dad?

I can't imagine myself being an orphan because my mom went to murder innocent people like last week in Jerusalem. This is not logical!

I see on TV how our soldiers are stopped from entering the Holy Church in Beit Le'hem [Bethlehem], while murderers are hiding there under "God's protection." And it makes me wonder how, during our holiest Passover, 28 people were murdered while praying to our God.

You know that today is a very special day. This is Remembrance Day for soldiers who were killed during wars and terror. This is also our fifty-fourth Independence Day of my country, Israel. Both days are following one another. We start the day with grief and end it with celebration.

Independence Day in Israel starts at the end of Memorial Day, exactly when the sun goes down. That's when Remembrance Day is officially over. This Memorial Day reminds me that for quite a long period, here, innocent people died for nothing because of terror. We have been killed for centuries, from the period of the Bible through to the Holocaust, nowadays and so on . . .

I don't understand why people want to kill me. Is it wrong to live? Or to be a Jew?

Today is the day that we should remember them.

Last night and today, I watched TV. I hate to see those innocent people smiling and laughing on TV, not knowing that within a few days they will be dead. I cannot believe they are really dead. They are so young, some of them are younger than I.

When I saw the body parts, I just began to cry, quietly, trying not to get noticed. Apparently I was not the only one who cried; my friends told me they were crying too. The next pictures were soldiers singing, happily telling jokes to the camera, and then later they were gone.

My dear diary, you don't know the feeling till you see it yourself. No one can react normally to such sights.

Now diary, let's turn quickly to Independence Day. Normally, Independence Day is a cause for celebrations and parties, with free live concerts. When we go out, I see flags hanging all over the place, and always, always when the concerts end, we get to see fireworks all around us.

Each city organizes a separate celebration . . . but diary. . . . I have some bad news. . . . Our city canceled the celebrations because of the bombing alerts and the unsafe situation.

I am not staying at home. No way! My friends are doing a barbeque, I will go there! I am not afraid! And neither are my friends!

Those terrorists won't stop our life!!!

Oh! Look at the time! I will talk to you soon. I have to get dressed. I will write you soon.

APRIL 29, 2002
HI DIARY,

It is quite a strange period. Here we start to act and behave normally, and it seems that the situation is more relaxed now. Is it? I am still waiting for the next explosion.

Many girls and boys, and also grown-ups, who planned a suicide attack are caught before they succeed in committing the next horror and killing. I remember my last vacation, not long ago, as a matter of fact, a month ago. It was in the middle of the huge terror attacks on our major cities.

We flew to Paris and Amsterdam for a few days only, in the middle of my school vacation. We were sitting in a café at Kalverstraat, watching the relaxed people sitting next to us and all those who were passing by, wondering how nice and easy life can be. No fear, no pressures, no security checks, no ambulances, no police . . . just moments for the soul, and relaxation.

Then I start thinking . . .

What if Amsterdam was like how it is in Jerusalem? . . .

Imagine myself walking in this street, Kalverstraat, now. Suddenly, the devil is walking toward me, with an evil smile on his scary face. He pushes a little button, and a boom!!!! Hands, fingers, legs, and lots of blood. People are screaming; others will remain silent forever. Those who survive will have nails stuck inside their bodies, because the bomb contained a huge number of big nails. The sight of a headless baby is a common picture.

Kids are looking for their parents, who will later be found at "the institute for legal medical research," which is the institute for after-death surgery but with a nicer name that doesn't help a bit. . . . People are in panic.

We watch the first stage of the horror when the injured people who are "less damaged" are trying to get on their feet and help the "more damaged" (those who don't stop bleeding . . .). The next terrible stage is when the people called "Zaka" arrive. Their "job" is to clean all the body parts and flesh from the street.

On TV they are showing the prime minister of the Netherlands, who will tell the Dutch people, "Stay strong and keep going out, the terror will not win, the Palestinians won't win, the terror cannot win, the world won't allow it."

But, this is illogical in Amsterdam.

This is another place, another country, and another world. What is so scary is that you never know who is a terrorist and who is not.

I don't understand the Palestinians. On one hand the say they want peace, and on the other hand they teach the kids to hate Jews.

Sometimes I wonder: can we have peace with these people?
Can we live with them side by side?

May 6, 2002
Hi diary,

I was so happy a week ago, all was quiet and I thought we were going to be like any other "normal" country. All looked terrific, and I thought that things are really getting better.

But it was too good and too early to be a truth.

I woke up in the morning, put on the TV as I do every day, and I found out that four people were murdered; some were injured while they were sleeping in their beds on Saturday morning, our resting and holy day, including a five-year-old girl with big blue eyes, light-colored skin, and a hole between her eyes. She was murdered in her small bed. I saw the pictures and it was horrible. A bed that was covered with blood, and the walls with small nice kid pictures were covered with blood too. Her silver laugh will not be heard anymore in her kindergarten because she was chosen to be the enemy of the Palestinian murderer.

I can't imagine it; it is worse than the horror movie with Freddy Krueger, *Nightmare on Elm Street*. In this movie, Freddy killed kids while they were sleeping . . . and here, this is not a movie, this is reality. I hope for them that they didn't feel pain as the bullets slashed their little heads.

Diary, do you want to hear something funny for a change? In Tel Aviv there is a place where my friends and I used to hang out a lot before this war. This place called Azriely Center. This is the highest building in Israel, and a huge mall with a shopping center, restaurants, and cinemas. A week ago, some terrorists were caught by the security force just a few hours before they were about to blow themselves up in this building. It could have ended like September 11 in New York. All my latest visits to the Azriely Center ran through my head. And I kept thinking and wondering about my life: what would have happened if the murderers had not been caught and I was there with all my friends?

And what would have happened if I had been murdered while I was sleeping? Or while I was shopping, or just drinking the hot chocolate that I so enjoy? What would I miss?

To die without knowing what true love is; to live real life and succeed on my own, developing a career and family life. And it made me think how precious life can be and how great it is to be alive. Thank you God for keeping me alive!!!! My friends are mad at me because I am going to Jerusalem on Sunday to meet an injured girl that I know. I said to them, "There will not be a blast."

This is not a funny thing, I know, but my way to face "the situation" is humor. It keeps me strong. My attitude to life is humor. It's the best way, diary, you should try this. . . .

Now, diary, if you will excuse me, I'm gonna watch the Euro League "Final Four," on which the team I like is participating for the Gold Cup. There is nothing like a good basketball game to make you forget what is happening outside, but what can I do when the teardrops are still wet because of the little girl with the hole between her eyes?

May 13, 2002
Dear diary,

I heard some bad news yesterday. A suicide bomber decided to blow himself up in order to kill; fifteen people were killed and many dozens were injured.

On Tuesday I was so sad all day, I knew something was going to happen, like a premonition. Somehow I knew. I can't even describe this awful feeling, I felt so helpless.

All day long I was so depressed, my friends at school asked me what was going on; they had noticed. And later in the evening I was about to enter the bed when I heard the terrible news.

My dad was yelling, "A suicide bomber killed himself in Rishon Le Zion," in a club where teenagers are playing with electronic games and machines.

I said to myself, "I told you so," but what can I do? I can't call 911 and tell them there is going to be a blast because I had the feeling.

Half of my family lives there; should I call them? But then I thought, It is too late, maybe they are asleep. But then I thought that they are probably awake from the terrible noise of the explosion. I decided to call them in spite of the late hour. Maybe one of my cousins went there with his friends? Or . . .

It was a relief when all were OK.

Still, I was so tired but I found it impossible to sleep. I was a "zombie" (out of order . . .) the next day at school.

In the news, the broadcaster says the Israelis and the Palestinian Authority have signed an agreement, and I am asking myself: What kind of an agreement can you have with people who have crossed every red line possible in humanity?

I'm talking about the merciless murdering that is crossing all possible lines, as many times as possible; in fact, those people do not consider it a red line . . . their real *red* line is the blood!

Another such red line was passed when those suicide murderers entered the most Holy Church for the Christian world in order to hide under God's protection. They knew that no one would touch them in a holy place, even though they are murderers.

It's unbelievable.

Are there any more red lines???

I truly hope there will be an agreement, which the Palestinians will honor. And I hope some day this stupid war will be over and the Israelis and the Palestinians will live peacefully side by side.

No bloodshed, no murdering children in their beds, no walking with explosive belts to places where many teenagers or old people are staying and having fun. No teaching young kids at Arab school to be a "Shahid" [saint] and to blow themselves up in order to become a "saint" and meet seventy virgins in paradise after they explode themselves. . . .

I wonder how life will be after the war ends. I think the first thing I will do is to go out to dance in the streets, so diary, if you see a crazy girl dancing in the streets, you know that the war is over, and that girl will be me.

MAY 30, 2002

HI DIARY,

I'm sorry I didn't write to you lately; the reason is that just now are the final examinations, and I don't have time even to breathe. Between my homework and the preparing for my examinations, it happened again! In Petah Tikva.

Now the following sentences keeping running in my head—as usual: One word, bombing; two words, suicide bombing.

In the background you can see the flames. So graphic, as the details are getting sharper, the map is getting brighter. Streets and events are appearing on the screen. And everything is drawn with such sharp lines; van Gogh would be proud of our television art.

And I keep watching and listening. It is like a routine. Isn't it a terrible way to think? Four are dead and dozens injured.

I don't want to, but my fingers don't press on any other channel; suddenly they freeze. As if it really matters if I see any more pictures or not. Not again, I keep telling myself.

Right now the news is not clear. We get only a global view of the situation, and this is enough to stop me from learning. Tomorrow is my math examination, and I can hardly see the numbers and solve the problems. If this goes on, I will not get a good mark.

The disinformation is still around and I hope that everything will be more clear on the eight o'clock news, but it still won't stop me from watching. The last bombing (so far) was at Petah Tikva. I am not familiar with anyone in this city; I am still worried that one of my relatives or friends will be there.

I keep saying to myself, What are the odds? But in fact it won't be the first time one of our relatives has been close to a suicide bombing. In fact, two car bombs were near my house; I felt the explosion. . . .

It was like an artificial earthquake.

I am out for the rest of the day. I will not do the math exam tomorrow as I am supposed to do.

I am sorry if you find me cold, diary, this is what happens after seeing so much of bodies and bloodshed.

JUNE 14, 2002

HI DIARY,

Nice talking to you again . . .

Finally, school is over!!!! I am free!!! (for now . . .)

It was a difficult year, there were moments I thought I wouldn't survive another minute in school because I got tired from all these stupid tests, but, as you can see, I made it! Despite all the complaining I will miss school, all my friends; with some of them I grew up, with some I have the greatest memories of my life. I am leaving next year for the school of the arts, here in Israel.

This week was so weird, diary; you can't imagine what was happening here.

A huge fire occurred near my house; it took hours for the firemen to put it out.

So much smoke! A friend of mine, her father is a policeman, told me that her dad said this fire was a result of a bomb left in a field. A suicide bomber would have taken it later. But something went wrong with the bomb, so it exploded.

At first I was telling myself, Nonsense, but then I realized it wouldn't be the first time a bomb exploded near my house. In fact, a year ago, two car bombs exploded close to my house, in front of the house of a friend of mine.

So then I thought, What would have happened if the bomber had succeeded with his mission, then what? But then I told myself that I won't bother my pretty little head about that stuff; I need to think about the positive side of life.

In Israel the soap operas are very successful, I think because people want to forget real life and move to a different reality. In this weekend, all the country talked about the last chapter of *The Life of Love*, an Israeli soap opera. People were so depressed that it was over. Even I, not a soap opera watcher (I don't have anything against it, I just don't like it . . .), watched *The Life of Love*; that's kind of weird, don't you think so?

Hey, I just remembered something very bad that happened this week; my parents and I went to a wedding. A normal wedding with

"Hopa" and all the regular Jewish ceremony, but in fact this wedding was anything but normal. At the entrance were two security guards; during the "Hopa" another two security officers were patrolling.

Is that a wedding or a military patrol? One of the security officers asked me, "How are you doing?" just like Joey from the TV series *Friends*. Do you think he was hitting on me?

Peace, love & rock 'n' roll.

AFTERWORD
Shiran and her family have remained in Israel. Shiran and her friends go out on the weekends, living by their motto: "If something is meant to be, then it will be." They try not to live in fear.

After Shiran's graduation, she will join the army, as is stipulated by the Israeli government. Shiran fears leaving the safe shelter of her school years to enter such a completely different way of life. She would like to work as a journalist or filmmaker when she leaves the army.

MARY MASRIEH HAZBOUN, PALESTINE, 2002–4

APRIL 8, 2002
HERE I am in the place where Jesus was born, now a most terrifying place. Monday last week we woke up at 1:00 a.m. I could hear bombing and shelling everywhere. At 4:00 I ran to my mother's room and hid under her bed because the bombing was very close. My father looked from the window and counted twenty tanks all around our house. They entered the old town of Bethlehem near the Nativity Church. My father has a shop there. Since last week no one is allowed to walk in the street or to look out from the windows. We don't see daylight; we have covered all windows with blankets. As if we are buried.

Our house has two floors, one for us, the other for my uncle with his three small children. We stay all the time in his place because it is safer there. I don't move, I just watch TV. Bethlehem is really a small town in which Muslims and Christians live together, and we know everyone. We knew Omar Salahat, who was killed near the church while he was checking his restaurant, which is near my father's shop. (They kill anything that moves, even a cat.) The Israelis went into so many shops. My uncle's friend has a jewelry shop; they stole 10 kg [22 pounds] of gold.

APRIL 11, 2002

TODAY WAS the worst day. Not because of what is happening in Bethlehem—we got used to that. Tanks all around; I can't sleep; I can't study. I just cried all day about what happened elsewhere, especially in Jenin. Hundreds of people killed. Many lie in the streets for three or four days; nobody can bury them. They don't allow TV to come in.

Now I can hear tanks near my room. It has become normal. I don't feel afraid. I wake up at the sound of bullets and I go to sleep at the sound of bullets. I was not afraid when, two days ago, I went out to buy some bread with my four-year-old cousin. The tanks in the street started to shoot and shell. Two days ago a man was killed on the street while he was bringing food to his children. He went out during the curfew because his family was in need.

The situation in the church is still the same. I called Father Rafael. He is one of the priests in the church. He told me that they had not eaten anything for six days.

I can't really write everything because I can't translate my feelings into normal words. In this world, the truth is buried. When you say a word of truth, you are smashed and killed under their tanks.

APRIL 12, 2002

Now I am sitting in the garden because we are allowed to go out for two hours. I can see the people rushing to the markets and stores to buy milk and bread. There are some children playing, and others are talking to each other. Five minutes ago the tank near our house started shooting in the air while we were all out. Thank God, nothing happened and none were injured. Then two tanks approached us. Everyone went inside, but I stayed outside.

Two days ago they buried a Muslim in the church. There was no place to bury him. I know so many people there, and now they have been without food for a week.

Everything has changed in my little town. The roads are damaged, cars are crashed. Even trees are damaged. Bethlehem is not Bethlehem anymore. It is now a desert with destruction everywhere. There is no hope for us to live peacefully. Now there is no difference between life and death. I prefer death so I don't see those evil crimes done to my people. Maybe it will be safer in the other world near God. My cousin asked: "Why can't we play and have fun like other children in this world? What did we do to suffer?" I laughed and told him that it is a crime to be Palestinian.

April 15, 2002

I woke up at 10:00 to prepare myself to buy some food with my uncle. The Israeli soldiers allowed the people to go out from 10:00 to 14:00. On our way to the market I saw my lovely Bethlehem ruined. The worst thing is the rubbish that is everywhere on the streets and which poisons the air and creates an unhealthy environment.

Today they entered a building in Doha, an area near the Dheisheh refugee camp, which is near our house. They ordered the women and children to go out and then took all the men, put them in armored vehicles, and drove them away. The women and children are now on the streets, the children sleep on the ground. The Israeli soldiers claim that there were some men with weapons hiding in the building. When they shelled it, a woman who could not run away was killed. Her baby of six months was injured.

It is now 12:00 p.m. I can't sleep because the soldiers are planning something terrible for the men in the Nativity Church. First a soldier speaking good Arabic started threatening them through a megaphone, "To those in the Nativity Church: know your destiny, go out and you will be without harm or loss, you will be safe." He kept repeating these words for an hour. Our house is far from the church, but we could hear it clearly. After that, they played a tape with terrible sounds that I can't describe. I still hear them: people screaming, sounds of machines, hammers, alarms, knocking, barking of dogs. I know we won't sleep tonight. I wonder how the people inside the church feel. I think they are getting crazy. No one can hear those sounds for long. The soldiers just want to make them crazy. They keep repeating the sounds for several hours.

I am going to pray the rosary with my family. We pray every night; we ask God to protect those who are in the church, Muslims and Christians, because they are innocent. I can't continue . . . I hear bombing, maybe they've started bombing the building. Now we are going to hide somewhere because it is really near our house and it is dangerous. . . .

I always say a prayer to God: Our case is clear as the sun but no one in the world wants to look at it and see the truth. So please, God, I am only asking not to let evil destroy us. I beg of You just to be with us and to assure that we will be safe and return to normal life like others in this world. Is this too much to ask? We just want to live.

April 16, 2002

Today was one of the worst days. I woke up to the sound of bullets from tanks crossing our street. The street was empty, but they just shoot to terrify people. I studied a little. Then I went to watch TV to see the latest news. I was very sad, hearing that they arrested Marwan Barghouti. He is a decent man who has faith in our case and always prefers peace and negotiations with the Israeli side. Now God knows what they will do to him. His only guilt is that he loves Palestine very much.

In the afternoon my uncle wanted to go out for a while and sit in the garden, which is behind the house away from the main street. He went out with his wife and three children, and my little brother went out too. My mother was praying in my room while I studied. I went downstairs so as to study outside and have some fun. The minute I wanted to go out, my uncle shouted at me not to move because there was a tank crossing the street. I could hear its sound clearly. Then my uncle's voice disappeared. I wanted to look out from the door to make sure it was safe. As soon as I opened the door, a rain of bullets came in my direction. I ran as fast as I could and hid behind a huge cupboard in my uncle's house. I heard my cousins and my brother screaming, but I could not do anything. I thought that they might die. After two minutes I could move, and my uncle came running, his face white. The children could not move from fear so he held them tight. My mother was hiding under the desk in my room. She could hear the bullets hitting the door of my balcony. After a while I went out to the balcony, and we found there a lot of bullets. That was the worst moment in my life. Death was very near. It is really terrifying. They know we are civilians, but they don't want to see anything moving.

At seven o'clock, the soldiers started shooting from all sides at the church. Two of the priests' rooms were burned. There was no shooting from inside the church. Windows were broken. Two men were injured. They continued shooting and shelling for forty minutes. I started to cry. Where are the Christians who have dignity and faith? My church has become a war zone. I wish that I can once again pray in it some day in the future. I will tell these words to all the people who live peacefully and happily in their independent countries: Just remember when you eat that there are hundreds of children who die from hunger because they are Palestinians. Remember when you drink water that there are hundreds of children who drink dirty water from the ground because they are Palestinians. Remember that when you go to sleep that there are hundreds of homeless children who sleep wearing nothing just because they are Palestinians.

April 17, 2002

TODAY WAS a bit calmer. New tanks entered Bethlehem with machines I had never seen before. The only hope that Palestinians had in

Powell's negotiations with Sharon and Arafat was that there would be an end to the massacres in Jenin and Nablus. I was really shocked when I heard Powell saying that Arafat disappointed him. What is this? He returned to America blaming Arafat. Is he blaming him because his people are killed by Israeli soldiers? Instead of blaming Sharon, he blames the man who is a prisoner in Ramallah. There are no words that can express my feelings toward this injustice. Are they blind, or are they making themselves blind?

There are people stuck under their destroyed houses, screaming and asking for help. The UNRWA was unable to rescue them because the Israeli soldiers prevented them from entering. They are left there; no one knows how many there are. Doctors say there is a strong smell in Jenin, a smell of dead bodies, some of which have not been found yet.

Today I called Father Amjad in the Nativity Church to know how the people are. He was desperate. They stay awake all night and sleep some time in the morning. There is no food. They only drink water and salt. The sounds from outside make them very nervous. Some of them start hitting the floor with their legs and scream.

I am desperate without hope. Our innocent children don't know the meaning of happiness. They just know death, war, tanks, fear, and suffering. How sorry I feel for my people, my lovely country.

Now after Powell has gone, there is no hope that somebody will move. We just hope that God will do a miracle and stop our suffering.

April 19, 2002

Here we are: Another day of death and destruction. More dead people, more suffering. It really has become part of our days and lives. Death is very near to us, and any minute anyone could be killed. Yesterday I was watching TV with my brothers at seven in the evening when suddenly a huge explosion shook our house. My mother told us to lie on the ground and be careful. The tanks were in front of our house and started shooting everywhere. Then another huge explosion. It was dark everywhere, and we could not see anything or move to hide in a safe place. After an hour of fear the tanks drove away, and we found out that the Israeli soldiers suspected a car in our street to be full of explosives, but the car belonged to our neighbors. The two huge explosions were from a plane that bombed the car, while the shooting was for nothing, just to make us and the other civilians here shake from fear and pain.

Today I woke up at nine, really desperate. I wish I could stay sleeping for a long time so as not to see innocent people getting killed each day. I asked my mother not to tell me anything if they enter the church and a massacre happens, because I don't want more pain, more tears, and more suffering.

I saw today on TV a baby injured from a bombing on Gaza. His body was full of wounds, and he was screaming from pain.

In the afternoon we went down to my uncle's home, and our neighbor told us to be careful. The soldiers reached our area, and they were going to enter the houses and arrest the men. My brother was very afraid. He is fifteen years old and very tall, so they would think he is old enough to take him away. They entered a big apartment building near our house, checked every apartment, and left without entering our house. They arrested many people from Bethlehem, but thank God, they haven't entered our house . . . yet.

NO MATTER WHAT

PALESTINE WON'T DIE

APRIL 20, 2002
NOTHING NEW: more killing, more suffering.

APRIL 21, 2002
I FEEL very sorry because each Sunday we go to church, but today we can't go as usual, and we just pray at home.

APRIL 22, 2002
I WOKE up at nine in the morning hearing my mother talking in a loud voice with the soldiers. I went to see her, and she told me that we have to go down. We went downstairs and I saw nearly twenty soldiers

at the door; one came in and told us that we have to stay in one room. They took my brother and my uncle so as to lead them to the rooms.

They searched everywhere; they took out everything in the cupboards, drawers, and everywhere. They made a mess in our house, turned everything upside down, nothing in its place. They stayed two hours. There was one outside and four were with my brother upstairs, four with my uncle in his house, and another four in my grandmother's house. A soldier came in the room where we stayed and told us, "Please, don't worry and stay here."

After a while they went, but they are still in our area. Thank God, they didn't take anyone. I thought that they would start ruining and destroying everything, but they were not really bad. I think it depends on who is living in the house. In some houses they destroyed a lot, sometimes didn't leave anything damaged. The important thing is that they didn't take anyone.

It is now 12:00. They gave the people permission to go out from two 'til six. So we are going to buy food.

MAY 2, 2002

As USUAL, I woke up at 12:00 because we stayed up watching TV late. I heard some sounds in the late afternoon, sounds of shooting. We were disappointed because the meeting between the Israeli and Palestinian side over the case of the church did not achieve anything. This will keep the situation as it is, or it may deteriorate. It is threatening to enter the church these days. One was killed in the church, and another injured. There is no first aid or medication that can save them.

Some of our relatives called my father, asking him for food. They are a big family, but they cannot go out and buy anything. They asked my father for help. I studied a little but not too much; the situation doesn't allow that.

MAY 3, 2002

As USUAL, tanks go around our house all day. The Israeli army gave permission to the civilians in Beit Jala and Beit Sahour to go out and buy food. My cousins and brothers were very happy and danced as they heard this news. This is the best news these days. One can see light and sunshine.

My father wants to check his shop, which is near the church. We will join him in the car. I hope that nothing will happen.

MAY 26, 2002

TODAY THE tanks that entered yesterday have gone out of Bethlehem. I don't understand what they did here; they did not achieve something real. I decided this month not to continue writing because there is no use in explaining the Palestinians' situation when no one cares about it. What really hurt me was when the fighters were transferred to several countries. My heart was going to split from the anger, the sadness, the injustice. These men who the whole world thinks are terrorists are the most faithful men in Palestine. When we suffered from Israel, they used to defend our lands and let Israel know that Palestine is not empty as they want it to be, but that it is filled with Palestinians who are not afraid of Israeli weapons. Every house in Palestine was sad. I felt something really bad the minute the bus went and disappeared from the Nativity.

I am a Christian, and I was anxious about all the lies and misleading stories the press started reporting about what had happened in the church. I went and saw it myself. There weren't any more blankets, cups, and plates. The relationship between the men and the priests had been very good. The priests used to give them from their own food. In Bethlehem we find this normal, because they were men from Bethlehem. Everyone knows them; we are living together; we see them when we go to school or the old town. They are not what the world or the press says.

If Israel thinks that the Intifada will end just like that, they are wrong. If the Israelis want to achieve this, they must kill every single Palestinian man, woman, boy, or girl, because not one of us will live happily without our freedom. You may ask yourself why the Intifada, after everything Sharon did, did not stop. The answer is that this

Intifada is a just revolution, and that we must continue and will continue. And I believe that the Palestinians who were transferred will return one day carrying the flag of Palestine. We will welcome them with singing and dancing and happiness, and hope will return to our soul.

Yesterday I went to the church to pray. Father Ibrahim expressed his feelings of anger and sadness, and he said: "Even we were in danger and anyone could be killed, but I was concerned for these men equally as for the other priests. Staying in the church with them was better than seeing them getting out of Bethlehem with no justice or mercy. When I got to know them, I found them really good, and they respected the church. I pray for them to be safe and secure and return some day to their own country."

SUMMER 2002

THIS SUMMER was so special and significant for me. After spending a whole year of massive studying for *Tawjihi*, I graduated with an honor degree and I got 97 percent out of 100 percent. I got several scholarships to study abroad, like Italy, Jordan. But I decided to go to Bethlehem University and study journalism. I was so proud of myself that I was able to get this high degree during war. I was honored by several organizations and educational institutes in Bethlehem for getting this high grade this year, especially because the *Tawjihi* tests are so hard, and the situation was not stable and secure for normal studying. Many students gave up and could not study in these terrifying conditions. As for me, honestly I did not study in those horrible circumstances just for getting high grades. As much as I felt desperate about everything I was going through in the Intifada, I always had a feeling of motivation to accomplish something for my land and my people. During the curfew I used to say to myself, "The Israeli soldiers are ending the life of many innocent Palestinians; they are taking my land and my rights. However, I am not going to surrender and let them win by being desperate and losing my purpose in life. . . . I should be the voice of my nation whose voice is being stolen. I want to study and study and get the highest grades. . . . They may prevent me from going out and buying food but they cannot stop me from studying. . . . I want to be a successful journalist, and I am going to work hard to accomplish my dream." So that was the reason why I used to study day and night, during bombing and shelling. Even when there was no electricity, I used to light a candle and study all night. The most difficult and dangerous part during that time was when the students had to go out to their schools and do the tests. It was known that when there was a curfew, no one was supposed to go out. So we used to stay day and night in front of the TV screen, waiting for news regarding the curfew. If they would announce that there was no curfew the next day for a couple of hours, the ministry of education would announce that the test would be held during those hours. The students would get ready and go and do the test during those hours. The most difficult part was when Israeli soldiers used to announce there was no curfew and then change their minds and keep the curfew. So after nights of not sleeping and studying for a very hard and long test, we would end up waiting for the next announcement, which could be the next day or the next week. God only knows . . .

NOVEMBER 1, 2004

I AM starting my diary again. . . . Since June 29, the day of my birthday, I stopped writing my diary. That is the same day that I arrived in the United States in order to start a new life here and forget about my whole life in my beloved country, Palestine. To the world it is still not a country, but to me it is a country that we have the right to live in. I am twenty years old, but I feel that I am much older from everything I have seen in my life. I lived all my life in Bethlehem—being a Christian was not a problem there. There are many Christians living there with Muslims, and we all live together as one family. I suffered from the occupation and seeing innocent people and children being killed without reason.

The last three years were the worst in the West Bank. We used to sleep every day with shooting and bombing going on everywhere.

There were always curfews. It is when Israeli soldiers are spread in the streets in tanks and no one is supposed to go outside the houses for any reason. We used to stay without food for two weeks . . . then they would give us an hour to go and buy food, and then there is a curfew again.

One day I went out to the garden to look for my little cousin, and by chance I saw a big tank coming toward our house, so I was so scared because if they see anything moving they would start shooting immediately. At that moment I heard the shooting and I felt I was going to die. Thanks to God that the bullet went through the door and not into me. On June 28, it was our day of departure, leaving Bethlehem and saying good-bye to my dear home, university, friends, earth, trees, love, and memories. . . . I started counting for that day, and I used to tell my friends: "After ninety days I will leave my dear Bethlehem." They would laugh and tell me that there is still a long time . . . for me it was a very short time. . . . I would go to sleep every night with tears and pain in my heart. It is weird . . . right? To live a difficult life and to love it . . . I want to make it easy for you to understand my feelings. . . . I feel that Palestine is my mother and she is sick, she is suffering and in real pain, but I would never think of leaving her; I would rather die than leave her. I have sad memories about the occupation but I also have very nice memories, with my friends, my university, and being a singer I have a lot of nice memories doing concerts in church, in my university, and in other cities in Palestine. No one can feel the pain of occupation unless you live it. I never stopped writing my diary until I arrived in the United States.

My heart was broken, and I felt that my life had ended. We did not want to come; my mother did not want to live here, nor my brothers, but my father insisted that here we will have a better future. I don't want a better future; I want a regular life with my people. . . . Today is the first day that I opened my diary and started writing again. Four months of stress, tears, and lack of hope that made me lose my purpose in life, coming from a forgotten land to the most powerful country in the whole world.

November 12, 2004

Day after day my life in the United States is getting more and more meaningless, lacking hope, and not being in my Palestine has made me feel that there is no purpose in life. I lost everything; I left my university without even graduating; I still have two years to finish. My singing career, which started a long time ago but became more professional since I started studying at Bethlehem University, stopped. What I sing is unique. I do not sing any regular songs, I sing national songs for my country, songs about freedom, justice, peace. . . . I remember when I used to stand onstage and all the students would be singing with me—it was the best feeling ever. I also participated in concerts in other cities like Jerusalem, Ramallah, and Hebron.

When I started singing, I always sang Marcel Khalife's songs. He is a Lebanese singer and composer who now lives in France, and he is so popular that he has done concerts in many countries in the world. The special thing about Marcel is that he is not just a singer. He uses his music and his amazing voice to speak for those whose voices are stolen.

I never thought I would be able to meet my hero until today when my uncle came to me and said: "Hey Mary, guess what . . . Marcel Khalife is coming to Chicago. . . . There is a concert for him on November 14."

Afterword

Mary is still in Chicago and graduated from Harper College, Northwestern University, Illinois, in 2006. She hopes to begin her postgraduate studies in journalism in order to pursue a career as a TV news reporter. Singing remains an important part of her life. She wants her writing to be dedicated to "my soul father, Marcel Khalife," a Lebanese singer.

IRAQ WAR

2003–

Hoda Thamir Jehad

IRAQ

2003–4 (18–19 YEARS OLD)

*The words teem inside me, demanding to be released into
the world to express truthfully what we are living today . . .*

Hoda is the youngest member of a moderate and cultured family of
lawyers, journalists, and teachers. Born on October 11, 1985, in
Nasiriyah, a town in the south of Iraq, she was largely raised by her older
brothers and sisters after the tragic death of her father in a car accident
when she was just two years old. Started in 2003, her diary recounts the
unfolding of the war in Iraq with the arrival of U.S. and British forces to
remove the dictator Saddam Hussein from power.

Following a series of military coups, Saddam Hussein became president of Iraq in 1979. By then the country, which spans the Tigris and
Euphrates rivers, was wealthy from its foreign exchange earnings from
oil, and a major seat of Arab nationalism. But the 1980–88 war with
Iran and the Gulf War in 1991 following Iraq's invasion of Kuwait, cou-
pled with successive international sanctions, devastated its former
wealth and status. Following the September 11, 2001, attacks on New
York, the American president George Bush described the regimes spon-
soring terror as the "axis of evil." This included Iraq, which was described as a threat to peace, particularly in relation to its alleged pursuit
of weapons of mass destruction.

American missiles hit targets in Baghdad in the early hours
of March 20, 2003, signaling the onset of a campaign to remove the
Iraqi leader. U.S. and British ground forces entered the country from

the south, while the leadership in Baghdad maintained its defiant posture. By April 9 U.S. forces had advanced into central Baghdad, and Saddam Hussein's grip on power had been markedly reduced. The regime collapsed in April 2003, three weeks into the U.S.-led campaign. Iraq's alleged possession of weapons of mass destruction formed the main justification for the military action. On the ground, the U.S.-led coalition forces faced armed rebellions and guerrilla-style attacks. Bombers targeted international agencies and civilians working for the coalition.

The transfer of sovereignty to the interim government took place on June 28, 2004, two days ahead of schedule. At the time of this writing (2006), the major challenges for postwar Iraq include the restoration of civil order, the creation of a stable political system, and reconstruction.

MARCH 20, 2003

AN IMPRESSION of the days of war . . .

In these difficult days we suffer, I want to express my feelings. What I am writing now is what I feel; but I do not know how others see this war, since today is the first day of war: today is Thursday, March 20, a difficult day for everyone to go through. The words teem inside me, demanding release into the world to express truthfully what I am living today. I want to mention that yesterday was a very beautiful and ordinary day, when the stars sparkled in the black sky. But this morning was not an ordinary day, because the twittering of the birds was mixed with the sound of gunfire. As for me, I want to speak about myself just a little in order to express the sorrow inside me. I am a pupil in the sixth grade, scientific section. This is the last stage of school where my destiny is to be decided; and you can't imagine the optimism I felt or the happiness I was wishing for.

MARCH 21, 2003

ONE SIDE of me is looking forward to the day when I will attain my certificate and go to the college of my choice, but I also feel intensely sad that we have lost peace completely in our country of Iraq. We have also lost the lovely life of studying, and communicating with friends, or the daily experience of discussing interesting and beautiful things with pupils and teachers. All this I miss today. I am distraught by the knowledge that when I wake in the morning, there will be nothing but the roaring of guns and enemy planes. Naturally, this forces me to do my daily work at home. This is how it was in the first three days, when there were terrible skirmishes.

MARCH 23, 2003

TODAY THE bombardment was unceasing and very violent, but it was worse in Baghdad and the other governing areas. We do not know what to do. Everyone is at home and no one goes out to work or to schools, universities, or anywhere in Nasiriyah except for the hospital, which constantly receives the dead and the wounded, where benevolent doctors are sacrificing themselves, giving their souls for the innocent; for them, it's a day like any previous day.

MARCH 24, 2003

WAR RAGED even more today, when the marine forces entered our modest residential areas, everywhere, and every corner, while clashes are on the increase from one day to the other. I wonder to myself if things will ever return to the simple life and the poverty that I was content with, and to the days of beautiful youth that are nothing but memory now, lost forever.

MARCH 25, 2003

I CANNOT convey the real picture of what happened this night, Tuesday, no matter how hard I try. I think it was worse than any night that I have witnessed, as the clashes started at 2 a.m., when I had just begun a nice sleep. And you know that there has been no power since the second day of the war, in addition to the fear, terror, and fright that we live in. So today I remained awake until the early morning; I cannot tell night from day. We are all holed up now in one room, under one roof. It is now 9 in the morning, and we have not opened the door of the room yet. The situation is so difficult for my family that we are unable to even prepare some breakfast. Now bombing has increased massively, and we do not know what is happening. There are very violent attacks and heavy bombing, and American armored vehicles are roaming the streets of Nasiriyah. What a state of anxiety I am in! Dear God, I pray to you for safety and protection, and from no one else. We are under your mercy, no one else's mercy, and I beseech you to protect all the good and the faithful of our family and relatives.

MARCH 26, 2003

WEDNESDAY WAS a night that was much worse than the night before. Clashes erupted again from around 2 or 3 at night, I do not know exactly, and lasted until midday on Thursday; meanwhile we were in the same room, not knowing what was happening outside. After the calmness that prevailed, and knowing how calmness is not a permanent state and always precedes the storm, we went out for some fresh air in the garden, and we discovered many things from the neighbors. That is, we discovered that the voice we had heard at around 5 or 6 at dawn was the voice of a woman from the neighborhood who was screaming after she was hit by the shooting of the American [snipers]. The moment that we heard it, my three brothers wanted to go out to ascertain the source of the voice, but the Lord was protecting them and they did not go out. We were told that the American army was at the end of our street, and our house is the last house in the street, and that they had killed one of the neighbors because he went out to help this woman and to find out what happened to us. But the Americans at that time had no mercy because they imagined that she was one of the Fidayeen who have started to disguise themselves, wearing black or women's clothes, and loitering in streets and alleys. We also heard that the reason this woman went out at that hour was to ask for help because her house had collapsed on her and her children, but the American shot her. Then another man from the neighborhood, who also lives in the house opposite us, went out to help her, to be showered with bullets like rain on a clear night. A bullet hit him in the back and came out the other side. At this, a large number of the young men in the area went out, and most of them were hurt, some were wounded and lost their lives. On that day the street became a very tragic place; it is hard to describe, reined in by sadness, screaming, and tragedies; even the sky was crying blood on this day. Is it possible after all this that I should have any hope of optimism, or even staying alive? It is not normal, this state of despair that I am in.

MARCH 27, 2003

ALL THAT I have said is little compared to the houses that have fallen, and the innocent who die, they are uncountable. I nearly forgot that this morning one of my best friends called. She told me that her nephew had died. He is young, no more than five years old. I loved him, and I used to buy things for him on my way back from school. He was very handsome; I was so sad to hear the news, and I cried. Is this all fair, I wonder? You expect that we will go back to the life we had before, or even to a better one; I think that our life has become a wreck that we cannot ever escape from.

MARCH 28, 2003

TODAY IS a sunny morning and a beautiful day, and the night that preceded it was almost quiet in terms of war. But it was a stormy night with lots of rain. However, when it was nearly five in the afternoon, and while my mother was preparing dinner for us, my younger brother was playing at the door, and I was in the garden, and while the rest were in the room that has functioned as our shelter during these days of the war, I heard a loud and horrible sound, and I rushed home screaming; the sound was so sharp it hurt my ears. At the same time, I heard my mother screaming and the sound of glass breaking. The glass in the kitchen windows was showering like rain, and Mother had fallen, for she was so frightened, and she was unable to get up. Shortly after, I heard the American army shouting in the streets with orders "to evacuate the area." I cannot describe the situation for you at that moment, as it was too awful. Everyone in the area, young ones crying, older people who would not be able to get up again if they fell, young men and women, and many others; such a big crowd, everyone running, some knew where they were heading, while some did not know in which direction they were going.

I am still standing while fear crawls in all parts of my body. We endure many humiliating situations, expecting death at any moment; everyone wants to escape the planes flying overhead, and the tanks surrounding them. We visited friends of ours in another area, and they received us very well, despite the fact they were hosting two other families at the same time, and a large number it was! But they spared no effort in hosting us and made a very luxurious and generous dinner. But it was a very worrying night, full of fear and lost sleep, as the place was very crowded, plus thoughts about what would happen the next day or what would await us tomorrow.

MARCH 29, 2003

WE ARE still staying at our friends', but we want to go home to see what has happened and to find out if there is any damage to the house, or if there was any loss of life, or any other event that we do not know. This morning, two of my brothers went out to have a look at the house and they found out that it was not damaged, thank God; only the glass of the reception room was broken. So they called us to tell us we can go back home, and we did. All that was at seven o'clock in the morning. When we arrived home, we saw American tanks in the area, and we heard that they have occupied nearly all Nasiriyah. All this happened today.

MARCH 30, 2003

I AM writing now while it is Sunday afternoon, and I do not know what will happen to us or what I will witness today. Is it calmness that awaits us, or more worry? But so far it seems quiet, and God willing,

He will protect us. We laughed a bit today, and tried to release our tension. Moreover, and more dangerous, the food and water that we have stored has started to run out, and we have no alternative. We cannot go out to buy anything as the situation is still very difficult, and what can be said but "Thanks to God"?*

MARCH 31, 2003

I MUST admit that today was the most beautiful morning that I have seen during the days of the war because we called my sister, who lives outside Iraq, and that was at 8:30 in the morning. We all talked to her, and we were all missing her. She was fearful for us because the things she hears about the war, about Iraq, and what is happening inside Iraq are untrue. But we reassured her.

But there is a water crisis and a shortage of food, and I passed the day feeling depressed; I am sick of this life. Is there any hope of getting out of this big crisis?

APRIL 1, 2003

TODAY IS the first day of the new month, but there is no hope and no calmness, as bullets still continue to fly. Sadness prevails. As for the night, oh how miserable the night is! After the calm that dominated the whole day, what is happening now during the night is very sad: the usual bombing, and all that just so that regiments of the U.S. Army can pass—the continuous and endless actions of guns, snipers, and explosives.

During the time of Saddam, April was called the month of plenty and giving, but now the marks of destruction prevail in the city, while the smoke billowing from burning government departments, offices, and schools wanders like a ghost in the city, the City of Nasiriyah, which still suffers whether in the time of the tyrant or in other times.

---

* In Arabic, and probably Islamic, cultures, this phrase has the double meaning of thanking God for whatever reason one feels compelled to thank God but also to show acceptance for God's actions when they are unfavorable! It shows submission to God's will and acceptance of His actions.

Sadness continues throughout these days because of what has happened in Iraq in general and what has happened to our simple city in particular. Perhaps such sadness is simply caused by the friends that we have lost and what has happened to all these governmental departments and buildings, but our joy in having got rid of an ugly dictatorial president has limits: this joy that has concealed the marks of sadness spread across our tired faces, faces that have been exhausted by grief and wars and loss. We can only wait for the sunrise of the near future.

APRIL 2, 2003

THE SUN is shining, and it is warm; the windows of hope are still open. But there are still some matters that spoil the moment for me. Around three o'clock in the afternoon I received a call from one of my close friends, and she said that my friend had died as a result of the war; her death was a shock, as she was simply in the garden of her house talking and laughing with her siblings, and suddenly a bullet came as if it intended to kill this innocent person. That was what got me so mad. I did not know what to do or what to say. I could not look into the faces of my family with such a bad piece of news, so I kept it to myself, and I do not know for how long I can conceal the sadness in my heart. By the evening I was collapsing with tears as I remembered her beautiful face, the innocence that shone from her features, and the smile that never left her lips. Thus ended everything yesterday; I lost my studies, my simple hopes, and the safety that every Iraqi child, young person, and elderly person hopes for. And today I lost my friend, and I do not know what awaits me tomorrow too.

I cannot lie and say it is a beautiful day, because after today Iraq does not know joy or happiness, nor do the Iraqis, whose hearts have been frozen by the period in which they lived with the dirty president for thirty-seven years. And as if that is not enough, it is followed by the storm of the Americans, and we do not know what awaits us in the future.

Today water problems were nearly solved, but not sufficiently; God willing, all our problems will be solved.

APRIL 3, 2003

HER DEATH was more than I could bear, and I do not know how to face it or face any of these difficulties and sorrows that I am going through. All I know is the feeling one gets when there is nobody to look after you, when you are defeated, when you are lost, and I am now in this situation. No one looks after me, and there is no one to gaze inside me while I am in this state of despair, so that I might rid myself of the feelings that drive me into the thick of depression. But now, I am trying to free myself from all this by spending my spare time in reading foreign books such as *Pushkin, Jonathan Livingstone,* and *The Holy Tree,* as well as plays such as *Condemned to Death, Elsmere,* and *Arms and the Man,* as well as other books such as *Life of Lenin.* I was reading all these books before, [and I continue them] so that I do not allow these circumstances to conquer me. Instead, I can overcome them through interest in daily life, through listening to the news, through following events, and through reading books to nourish my mind.

Today was truly a very special day, as my uncle came to visit us, and he is my most favorite and beloved uncle. He told me the story of his work in the Republican Guards before the war and how when he heard that the war had started, he came back running on his feet, facing many problems along the way. We thank the Lord for his safe return from the army.

APRIL 4, 2003

A DAY no different from other days; as usual, I woke up to the sound of rifles ringing like school bells in my ears. I had to listen to them, as there was no escape from the noise. Everyone wakes up after having been asleep on their modest mattresses, in a simple room packed with old furniture, a telephone to stay in touch with our friends, and a simple radio for listening to the news. And at night, around six in the evening, my brother makes his comical entry into the small and very sparse room, imagining that it will cover and protect us from the stormy bombing that must end one day. Meanwhile, we are sitting around the radio to hear the news, listening very attentively to the speech of the American president (George Bush). We were happy with what he said, but we are more proud of them when we hear them say that they have come to Iraq as liberators, not occupiers.

Today Iraq was occupied, but not completely—only a few cities of it including Nasiriyah, my city. More and more, I long to see my dear friends, sisters, the many people that I love, and the beautiful bygone days; I loved those days when peace prevailed. By God, I am a peaceful woman, and I hate wars, brutality, and killing.

Throughout all these days, some relatives, friends, and neighbors have visited us to make sure we are safe and to usher in a happier atmosphere.

APRIL 5, 2003

EARLY IN the morning, while I was standing in the garden of the house, I heard a noise outside and discovered that the disturbance was caused by the arrival of a large car that was carrying lots of onions. Suddenly, most of the sons of the neighborhood in which I live gathered around in delight at what had reached them; one of these young men was my brother, who is two years older than me, and he bought us a bunch of onions. Then a question came to my mind: Does the happiness of Iraqis depend on a bunch of onions? Or is it need that has driven them to this state? But deep inside I totally refuse to believe this, because the hopes and desires of Iraqis are much more than that. In addition, Iraqis have this blessing that many others do not have, and that is patience. We are used to hearing it about everything and in all the circumstances that we go through. We are also used to hearing it from our fathers, mothers, grandfathers, grandmothers, and our great-grandparents, and so despair can never have a hold on us as long as there is hope that we will live in a country reigned by democracy.

The day was a very clear day, but the night was very difficult, as by sunset a group of people came running away from their houses. They said a number of Fidayeen were nearby, and that tonight they wanted to perform some suicide missions against the Americans. I cannot describe the scene for you, where all the people started rushing out of their houses; only we stayed, while a small number of our neighbors remained in their houses. We spent the night in anxiety, more anxiety than we have experienced in all the days that passed, and we were uncertain whether to go or stay, but finally we resolved to stay.

And indeed, some violent bombing took place, and we spent this horrible night, as we have spent other nights, in darkness, bullets, and sadness.

APRIL 6, 2003

AND THE city wakes up to poverty and crisis, and people are divided into two sides, a side seeking refuge from fear and a side searching for a solution to their financial situation, which is close to insolvency. As for the evening in Nasiriyah, it has become as sad as yesterday, as almost our entire city is occupied and so are many of the provinces. I do not know how long we will live in this vicious circle that we cannot leave or escape, while all fingers point at us without attempting to save us or to get us out; so we will end up devouring each other, and the story ends. The sorrows still show on my face, and that is why I took to writing this diary not only as a means of entertainment but also because I like writing about events and matters that happen in my life. You may wonder what kind of tragedy a girl my age could be suffering from. Of course, these are trivial issues for a girl living in any country apart from Iraq, issues such as, for example, living in a country where peace, development, and continuous improvement prevail, as well as having access to good studies or to the college that I would like.

Today something very bad indeed happened: some saboteurs*
of the sons of Nasiriyah looted some government offices, schools, universities, hospitals, and even some banks. Is this an honest and a

---

* This is the most faithful translation for the Arabic word Hoda uses. However, the term generally means someone who acts against the good of society.

devout hand? No, he is a dirty person who has no mercy in his heart who has done such a deed, because this country is our country and we have to look after it. They did not stop at that, however, but they also burned them.* On this day, the sky turned pitch-black from the smoke of these buildings; even the sky was angry about what happened. My God! Is this fair, and just? Is this a happy event? I do not think so at all.

And I think that more is yet to come.

APRIL 7, 2003
Be like a bird
Rebellious in its flying
While it is standing on a weak shaky bough
Knowing the bough will fail
It remains though singing
As if it knew it has two wings

I love these words; they are the words of the great writer (Victor Hugo). I started my morning writing these words, but I do not know how I will end my evening. It could be with the words of the great writer (Albert Camus). Anyway, today's morning was very normal, and around ten o'clock in the morning I heard a piece of news regarding schooling. They said that schools will reopen to receive their children and pupils, and the news was confirmed later in the afternoon when an American car arrived, broadcasting in a very loud voice, encouraging pupils to go back to schools, and employees to go back to their work. At that moment I could not contain my happiness; I thought I would die or faint from joy. I started laughing and running and screaming with joy at the top of my voice, and I ran around the house saying, "I will go back to school," while scarcely believing the news. But the important thing is whether my family will allow me to go to school in such extremely disconcerting

---

* Hoda is referring to the buildings.

circumstances, I do not know! Nevertheless, I started calling all my friends to deliver the good news so they might share my happiness with me. But the happiness was soon over because my family refused me, which made me hate this situation in which I live and the miserable life to which I was born. But there is a glimmer of hope that life will go back to what it used to be in the past, perhaps even better.

It is a day that is no less miserable than all the days that preceded it. I am sorry if I said too many bad things, but what am I supposed to do? This is the new reality that I must get used to. But the worst thing was a call from one of my friends today in the afternoon, when she told me that my best friend had died and left us. She was beautiful, and faithful, and loved to study. I could not believe it and would not believe it! I will die of crying and of the sadness that I feel. Whom do I have left after her? Whom should I talk with and whom should I tell my secrets to? Whom should I read and laugh with? Who else? I have no one left but God!

However, my mother says this is something predetermined for us; as it is preordained for all humans to die, what can we do about it? And now I have started to write to relieve some of the suffering inside me.

HODA JEHAD THAMIR

APRIL 8, 2003

THESE DAYS great desires awake in me that urge me to absorb directly the matter of the world, its elements and character. It seems to me as if I am rediscovering feelings or maybe recovering them. At night, when I was lying in bed during these hours of horror, my brother (Ahmed) was sitting on the floor and in the light of a candle was holding in his hand one of those books that takes the reader on a journey to another world. At that moment I was stealing some glances at him from underneath my warm cover, but after few moments, and in that clear sky with its beautiful stars, an airplane stole all my brother's illusions and words, and shortly after that came the roaring of cannons.

At the time, I knew that my brother was reading this book, distracting himself from the bad situation and the bitter terror with its words, making this book a friend to which he can reveal his secrets and which will lessen his solitude, sadness, and fear of what awaits him in the near future. And I admire my brother because he always had imagination, and he always made us forget the tragic atmosphere we live in by narrating to us movies such as *The English Patient, The Matrix,* etc.

April 9, 2003

THIS IS the greatest day in the life of Iraqis; a historic day that this nation and the whole world is witnessing. It is a day in which the provinces are reborn. It is the day the Iraqi capital (Baghdad) fell. Today the empire of Saddam is finished. When this news was announced, I saw smiles on the faces of my family and neighbors that I have never seen before; smiles that express the happiness and joy that has been frozen for years, frozen by the former regime. Only today did I feel that I am eighteen years old, that I am in the beginning of my youth, and that I can rely on myself and express my opinion in a frank and serious manner. Today, every family that has suffered under the former regime has regained its happiness. But we are still waiting for the greater day, the day Saddam is arrested or killed. This man, who snatched the happiness of every child and closed the doors in front of every young man, took the life of every old man and planted sadness on the face of every woman. We spent our lives saying "yes" to every right and wrong deed—thirty-seven years of poverty, illness, hunger, and deprivation, of no freedom of expression. This empire has ended; with it ended all the dark history. Today, we turn all the bloodstained pages and open a new page full of roses, and our new motto is Democracy.

April 10, 2003

. . . THE CONTINUOUS drop affects the stone.

It has become difficult for me to obtain what I wish or desire. This is a time deprived of emotions and love and dominated by black history filled with sadness, but I see a bright spot hiding behind the stage of life, and one day we must reach it.

I felt I was choking while I was sitting on the ground in the garden of the house, looking at the sky. It could be that the feeling was the result of the situation we live in today—I do not know—and during this, a few words about our tragedy occurred to me, so I took a pen and some paper and jogged my memory. Then I wrote some words expressing the feelings inside me in the hope that it would help me breathe normally. Some of these words were:

> Inaudible whispers . . .
> Failed government . . .
> And a worse life,
> And the hours pass by,
> And an agonizing hunger . . .
> Children suffering,
> And truth does not rise up.
> Suppression is spreading,
> And no wise mind to deliberate,
> And no one listens to Right.
> The eyes of simple people look on . . .
> And no generous people in sight.
> But there is a voice in the distance . . .
> That starts to spread . . .
> It is the voice of Truth,
> Though not of fulfillment.

APRIL 18, 2003

MANY IMPORTANT things happened during the week, which is why I stopped writing in my diary, such as the fact that we have power again. And you cannot imagine the day when power was back; all Nasiriyah, every household, started shouting to express their joy. You cannot imagine how happy we were that water and electricity were back, and that life was nearly back to normal, though in a simple form. Also, some benevolent men in Nasiriyah have started a new TV station called "Nasiriyah Television." This will help to lessen our sadness and improve the situation we live in. Also, during this period, I went back to school, but the situation is very frightening as we cannot go alone, and someone in the family must take us there or we must go with a group of friends. Our family situation has not changed from previous days. As for my life, it is continuing in the words of the great writer, Albert Camus, which are: "Oh my soul, do not aspire to more of this eternal life, but exhaust the boundaries of the possible."

DECEMBER 15, 2003

THE GREATEST day in the history of Iraq, even in the history of the Arabs. No, it is the greatest day in the history of the whole Arabic nation! It is a day that I find hard to comprehend whenever I think of it. I still cannot believe that one particular moment of this day truly happened: It is the day of Saddam's arrest. It is truly a difficult feeling to express; the injustice that stems from his tyranny perplexes and saddens me; and what is more difficult is getting the truth to the ones who do not know it, those Arabs who wrong us in the way they talk about us and about what happened to us.

As to what the Americans did, it was an act witnessed by the whole nation. Today is truly the birth of the honest Iraqi. Congratulations to us all on this day.

DECEMBER 20, 2003

WE HAVE nothing left but disappointed hopes, which in my view are only hopeless expectations. Life for us has turned into blood splattered on every corner and every road, and hopes are limited to wishing that the day would end with no loss of life, while our goals and hopes have narrowed to wishing that Iraq would become a great country united by concord and democracy, and its people united by love and brotherhood. I can only find a few laughs and smiles, and sometimes they are fake or nonexistent.

We have reached a stage where we avoid each other in every

possible way in order to protect ourselves. Sometimes I think to myself that there will be days when Iraq will be much better than it used to be; while at other times I lose all hope in ever seeing tomorrow. Even the common laws that govern the whole world, such as dignity and respect for the young and the old, have changed today, when everyone is attacking everyone else. Will these disasters end? Will there be peace? Will our country develop? Will we have love again in our houses? Will the tears be wiped off our faces? This is all that we are asking for in the near future! And we have not found any answers.

DECEMBER 27, 2003

ALL I can say is that the situation is now semi-settled, despite having worsened over the past few days. There are basic construction efforts on some schools, government offices, hospitals, and other buildings. Of course, this progress is vital for us. Another important improvement is that we can go to the market to do shopping and go freely in and out, but this is only in the city. I mean, I am not saying there is no activity outside the city, but it is limited. Also, the day for starting school is getting closer, although the city is not at all ready for such things; for example, all the books were burned during the war, as well as school records for elementary and secondary schools. And the same goes for workers' buses. When you also consider the dangers of kidnapping and premeditated murder, pupils begin to doubt [that school will start again]. We only hope that the situation will be quieter.

JANUARY 4, 2004

HERE IS Iraq rising again after the bitterness of years that were pointlessly stolen from our lives. But how can Iraq rise after the theft of its archaeological remains? This has pained me since the beginning of the war, and I cannot forget it, as I feel a kind of shame. How could that thief steal those relics? He cannot be a person with human qualities; he must be deprived of emotions. What is left for Iraq after its monuments are stolen, after its civilization is stolen, and after its wealth is stolen? Iraq has nothing left but sighs and sad thoughts, and it has nothing left but the slogans on the walls.

JANUARY 10, 2004

OF COURSE, as I mentioned before, school has started, and I am now preparing for the first-semester examinations. You may wonder where I am studying. I was admitted to the Educational College (Pedagogical College) in Nasiriyah, and as you know, it was not really my dream, but [it is the best that I can manage] because of my personal circumstances, not to mention the frightening days of the war. But thank God in any case. Construction projects continue but at a very slow pace because of events that are still taking place in Iraq, be they explosions or assassinations or the many incidents of kidnapping. A state of anxiety clings to us, and [there are] many factors that prevent charitable hands from continuing their good deeds. There are also a number of different groups and militias headed by certain organizations acting on behalf of unknown parties, who bring about destruction with the deliberate aim of causing discomfort for people and the country as a whole. Every time we think Iraq has started to regain calmness and is heading toward development, new affairs arise that obstruct the working process. I do not know who is the cause of all these stupid things! Each day a new group emerges; yesterday it was the Mahdi Army, today we have Abu Musab Al-Zarqawi and the Al-Qaeda organization, and tomorrow there will be a new story. My dream now is to switch the TV on and not hear a painful news item about Iraq, but this is the most difficult thing to achieve, because every day millions of people of different ages die pointlessly and in the worst and ugliest circumstances of murder and kidnapping and robbery. All this has not been confined to innocent people, but it also affects school headmasters, company managers, heads of government offices, hospital managers, even members of the government. It has also reached universities, with the killings of teachers, college deans, and others; even students, men or women, the old, and the very young are not safe from those whose hands are covered with the blood of the innocent. Not to mention car bombs and explosive devices that leave behind only sorrow for those whose loved ones were lost and fear for our own lives.

Keep in your mind every child or young person who has lost his future, every beloved who has lost her lover, every mother who has lost her child, every child who lost all that he loved of his family and friends, and every poor family that has lost their home.

JANUARY 20, 2004

THE WORLD seems dark and bleak for me, and people look only like monsters wanting to devour their prey and run away. I am this prey, lost among the multitude, frightened and scared and not knowing how to escape. Do I stay here and remain silent like this until they devour me and cut me to pieces? Or do I run away from this alien world? Is this weak of me? But my escape would not be an indication of weakness; rather, it would be the song of my flight from injustice.

I also cannot find anyone who understands me and listens to my inner thoughts. All are busy with their own pain, worries, and sadness, and all they do is ask me why I am sad. I do not know! This is my answer. I really do not know the cause of my sadness, or perhaps I have been trying to forget about this bitter truth suppressed inside me for years. I have done all that I can to get myself out of this situation or to find someone to take me out and carry me to another world.

But what I am always thinking of is the events that have made me such a devastated human being, running away from time and truth.

But if I go back to reality and search carefully, I find that it [is not my fault]. It has been [caused by] the difficulties that I live through, the tragedy that does not want to leave, and the years in which Saddam destroyed all our dreams and sowed hatred inside us instead of love. Saddam, who destroyed our lives and planted mines in the paths of young people and children, created the situation in which we live today, our unusual way of life, life that is full of mines, explosive devices, and parties who had no role in the past and yet control us today. But we must believe in the people who entered our country to rid us of a tyrant and say they want to bring happiness to our hearts; we should put our hands in their hands and stand together until the end of the road.

AFTERWORD
Although her life remains troubled and difficult, Hoda is determined to complete her training at college and pursue a career. Her brother, Mohammed, who has worked tirelessly to send out extracts of the diary under extremely difficult circumstances, describes his situation in his own words: "My family suffered more from the last regime because this family has good principles and keeps them even in bad and difficult circumstances."

Glossary

PIETE KUHR

East Prussia: The northeasterly region of the kingdom of Prussia, which comprised most of what is contemporary north Germany. After World War I, the northernmost region was incorporated into the newly created independent Lithuania. The southernmost portion of East Prussia became part of Poland. In 1945, East Prussia was divided between Poland and Russia. German inhabitants of East Prussia either escaped in 1945 or were expelled afterward. Only a fraction of the Polish-speaking population from the southern districts remained.

The emperor: A title referring to the ruler of a vast territory where people of more than one nationality live. At the time of World War I, the ruler of Germany was Emperor Wilhelm II.

Hohenfriedberger March: A musical march, composed by Frederick II of Prussia, which was performed by bands of marching soldiers in Germany.

Luttich: A region in Belgium also known as Liège. During World War I, the Battle of Liège ran from August 5 to August 16, 1914. This was the first land battle of the war, as the German Second Army crossed the frontier into neutral Belgium in order to attack France from the north. The Belgian forces eventually surrendered.

Masuria: A region of northern Poland, covered by large lakes and forests. Masuria was part of East Prussia and comprised a largely German population. The Masurian Lakes region was the scene of heavy fighting early in World War I. Two Russian armies were defeated in the region—at Tannenburg in August 1914 and in the lake country in September. The advancing Russian troops were also driven back in Masuria in the so-called

Winter Battle in February 1915. Masuria passed to Poland in 1945, after World War II, and most of the German-speaking population was expelled and replaced by Poles.

Mohammedan: A term for believers or followers of Mohammed, the prophet of the Muslim faith.

Montenegro: Constituent republic, with the far larger Serbia, of Serbia and Montenegro. Montenegro participated in the Balkan Wars in 1912 and 1913. It was overrun by Austria in World War I, and in 1918, after the deposition of King Nicholas, voted to become part of the Kingdom of Serbs, Croats, and Slovenes under the Serbian Peter I. The kingdom was renamed Yugoslavia in 1929 and was restructured in 1946 as a federation of republics.

Pfennig: A German coin.

Serbia: Constituent republic, together with Montenegro. See *Montenegro.*

Zeppelin: A large airship designed like a rigid balloon, named after the German army officer and aeronaut who designed it, Count Ferdinand von Zeppelin. The German navy acquired the last zeppelin to have been built, which carried a machine gun. A passenger air service that used zeppelins also started in 1910.

NINA KOSTERINA

Baikal: A lake found on the border of Siberian Russia and Mongolia, and popularly known as the "Pearl of Siberia." It is the largest lake in Eurasia and the deepest lake in the world.

Batyi's Golden Horde: The original Mongol state (which comprised most of Russia), which was given to Genghis Khan's grandson in the thirteenth century. Batyi's Golden Horde ruled Russia for 250 years, after destroying the armies of Poland and Hungary.

Fascism: An authoritarian political movement founded in 1919 by the Italian leader Benito Mussolini. The Italian word for the movement, *fascismo,* is derived from *fascio,* "bundle, [political] group," but also refers to the movement's emblem, the *fasces,* a weapon in ancient Rome that symbolized authority and power.

The name was adopted for similar nationalistic movements in other countries that sought to gain power through violence and ruthlessness, such as the National Socialists (the Nazis) in Germany.

Gorky Park: A large park in Moscow, with gardens and an amusement park. Officially the "Park of Culture," named after the Russian intellectual and author Maxim Gorky.

Kaluzhskaya: A street in Moscow.

Khvalynsk: A Russian port town on the Volga River.

Komsomol: The Young Communist League.

Kremlin: The Russian parliament buildings in Moscow.

Messerschmitt: A German war plane. Messerschmitt was the manufacturer.

NKVD: Officially termed the "Commissariat of Internal Affairs," NKVD, the Communist secret police, was formed in 1934.

Pushkin: The famous author Alexander Pushkin (1799–1837) was considered Russia's greatest poet and the founder of modern Russian literature. He was celebrated for using everyday speech in his poetry.

Shashlyk: A style of cooking meat that originated in Russia. Cubes of meat are skewered onto wooden sticks and cooked with onions and seasoning.

TETs: Russia's energy company.

Transbaikal: The major railway line linking Moscow with the Baikal region (now part of the Trans-Siberian Railway).

Trotskyism: Followers or sympathizers of Leon Trotsky, a politician who was part of the original Bolshevik Party that set up communism in Russia during the early twentieth century. At the time Nina wrote the diary, this would have been a term of contempt.

Volga: Europe's longest river, running through Russia.

WILLIAM WILSON AND HANS STAUDER

Colombo: Major city and port of Sri Lanka, established as Ceylon's capital by the British.

Hurricane: The British fighter plane the Hawker Hurricane was developed by plane designer Sidney Camm in 1938.

Maadi: A suburb in Egypt, south of Cairo. Around 75,000 members of the Second New Zealand Expeditionary Force trained at a camp in Maadi.

Onehunga: A suburb of New Zealand's capital, Auckland.

R.A.P.: Stands for Regimental Aid Post, an acronym popular in the Australian forces.

Sidi Azeiz: A city in the Western Desert, on the borders of Libya and Egypt.

Sidi Rezegh: A city in Libya where a number of decisive battles were fought.

Stuka: A German warplane used by the Nazis. Known for its ability to arrive unheard until the release of its bombs. Nicknamed "Storm Trooper of the Skies."

Swastika: The emblem adopted as the symbol of the Nazi Party.

Tommies: A nickname for the British forces and soldiers, used by the Germans.

Trigh Capuzzo: A road in the Western Desert to the south of Tobruk.

SHEILA ALLAN

Kampar: A city in Malaysia, where a number of horrific battles were waged by the Japanese.

Padang: A major port in Sumatra, Indonesia. Predominantly trading in coffee, spices, and tobacco.

Renglet: A town in Singapore on the road to Pahang.

STANLEY HAYAMI

Issei: A term for the first generation of immigrants from Japan, who arrived before the Immigration Act of 1924. Between 1861 and 1940, over 250,000 Japanese emigrated to America and Hawaii.

Kibei: A person born in America of Japanese ancestry, who returns to Japan for their education.

Manzanar: An internment facility for Japanese Americans during

World War II, located in California. It was the focus of several major protests by Japanese Americans angry at the government policy of internment.

YITSKHOK RUDASHEVSKI AND CLARA SCHWARZ

Belzec: A complex of Nazi Germany concentration and death camps near the village of Belzec in the Lublin province of Poland.

Stormführer: A commander in Hitler's "storm troops." *Führer* means "leader" in German.

Szepetowka: A town on the borders of Poland and the former USSR. Often used as a point of registration and transportation for Jewish people captured by the Nazis.

Tarnopol: A city in western Ukraine (former USSR).

Volksdeutsche: An individual with German heritage—Nazi Germany offered privileges to individuals in occupied territories who could prove they were of German descent.

ED BLANCO

Arty: Slang for artillery.

Baby-san: Young Vietnamese girl.

Betsy: Ed Blanco's two-years-younger sister.

Bookoo: A lot; very good. Derived from the French *beaucoup*.

Boonies: Infantry term for the field; jungles or swampy areas far from the comforts of civilization.

C-rations: Commercially prepared meals issued to marines and the army in Vietnam, coming in individual packs designed to be eaten hot or cold. Each menu contains one canned meat item, one canned fruit, bread, or dessert item, and an accessory packet containing cigarettes, matches, chewing gum, toilet paper, coffee, cream, sugar, salt, and a spoon.

Cam Ranh Bay: A deepwater seaport of Vietnam that became a huge U.S. military complex during the Vietnam War.

Charlie: Slang used for Viet Cong.

DD the area (verb): Slang, meaning "to clear out the area."

Gook: Derogatory term for an Asian; derived from Korean slang for "person" and passed down by Korean War veterans.

Hump: March or hike carrying a rucksack; to perform any arduous task.

M-16: The standard U.S. military rifle used in Vietnam from 1966 on.

M-60: The standard lightweight machine gun used by U.S. forces in Vietnam.

Mg: Machine gun.

O.P. (verb): To send out a group of soldiers on a mission to investigate beyond the front line; derives from "observation post."

Perimeter: Outer limits of a military position. The area beyond the perimeter belongs to the enemy.

Phan Rang: Site of a U.S. Air Force and Army base.

Phan Thiet: A province capital and a coastal town in Vietnam that was a site of a U.S. military base called LZ (Landing Zone) Betty.

PX: Stands for "Post Exchange," retail stores on U.S. military bases.

RTO: Radio telephone operator.

VC: Viet Cong; the National Liberation Front, the Communist-led forces fighting the South Vietnamese government.

Zlata Filipović

Dubrovnik: An old city on the Adriatic coast in the extreme south of Croatia. Dubrovnik is a very popular tourist destination.

Ducal Palace: Built in the fifteenth century in Dubrovnik, the palace functioned as a museum. During shelling through the 1990s, it was hit and damaged several times; however, the building survived the war.

Jahorina: A large mountain near Sarajevo, the site of the 1984 Winter Olympics. It is commonly visited for winter sports activities.

NATO: North Atlantic Treaty Organization, an international organization whose chief aim is to facilitate defense collaborations for the benefit of security in North America and Europe. NATO was formed after World War II in support of the North Atlantic Treaty, which was signed on April 4, 1949. The underlying premise was that an attack upon one country in Europe or North America is an attack upon them all.

RFI: Radio France Internationale. RFI broadcasts news and other programs in various languages, including English, Russian, Chinese, Spanish, and the languages of southeastern Europe.

Sarajevo: The capital city of Bosnia-Herzegovina. A Bosnian, Gavrilo Princip, assassinated Archduke Franz Ferdinand here in 1914, thereby precipitating World War I. From April 1992 the city was the target of a siege by Bosnian Serb forces in their fight to carve up the newly independent republic. A United Nations ultimatum and the threat of NATO bombing led to a ceasefire in February 1994. Serbian heavy weaponry was withdrawn from the high points surrounding the city, but the Bosnian government did not officially declare the siege of Sarajevo to be over until February 29, 1996.

Solfège: A scale used in singing; doh-ra-mi-fa-so-la-ti-doh.

UN: The United Nations is an international organization formed after World War II; it had originally been a name used by the American president Franklin D. Roosevelt for the Allies. The UN now includes 191 member states that agree to abide by the guidelines set out by the UN charter for the furtherance of world peace.

Shiran Zelikovich and Mary Masrieh Hazboun

Arafat: Born in 1929, Yasser Arafat was the president of the Palestine National Authority from 1993 until his death in 2004. A controversial figure, he was the founder of the Palestine Liberation Organization and won the Nobel Peace Prize in 1994.

Beit Le'hem: Alternative spelling for Bethlehem, the town on the West Bank to the south of Jerusalem, which is traditionally considered the birthplace of Jesus.

Beit Jala: A town near Bethlehem.

Beit Sahour: A town near Bethlehem.

Gaza and Gaza Strip: A strip of land bordering the Mediterranean Sea between Egypt and Israel. Gaza is the major city and port.

Jenin: A small, mainly Palestinian town in the north part of the West Bank. The UN established a major refugee camp here in 1953 to house refugees from the 1948 Arab-Israeli War. Jenin has been the seat of extensive Israeli-Palestinian conflict and is allegedly the place where the second Intifada began.

Marwan Barghouti: A Palestinian leader who was controversially captured and put on trial by the Israeli government for mass murder.

Nablis: Also spelled Nablus; a major city in northern Palestine and the former center of the Intifada.

Petah Tikva: A major industrialized city in Israel, to the northeast of Tel Aviv.

Powell: Colin Powell, the U.S. secretary of state.

Sharon: Born in 1928, Ariel Sharon was elected prime minister of Israel in 2001. He served extensively in the Israeli Army and went on to hold positions in government as defense minister and foreign minister. He suffered a massive stroke in January 2006 and remains in a coma.

Tawjihi: Set of final-year exams for Palestinian high school students.

UNRWA: The United Nations Relief and Works Agency for Palestine Refugees in the Near East provides education, health care, social services, and emergency aid to over 4 million Palestinian refugees.

HODA THAMIR JEHAD

Abu Musab: Abu Musab Al-Zarqawi was a major leader within the Islamist militant group Al-Qaeda and one of the most wanted men in Iraq. He was born in Jordan in 1966 and is alleged to have masterminded multiple terrorist attacks. In June 2006, he was killed by U.S. forces in Baghdad.

Al-Qaeda: The name, meaning "The Foundation," of a worldwide alliance of Islamist militants, headed by Osama bin Laden. It has been recognized by most countries and international organizations as an international terrorist organization. Al-Qaeda claims that it is responding to the U.S. military presence in several Islamic countries (particularly Saudi Arabia), to the U.S. support for Israel in the Arab-Israeli conflict, and more recently to the 2003 invasion and occupation of Iraq.

Fidayeen: The term generally refers to "one who is ready to sacrifice his life," but it is also used as a proper name for a group that are pro-Saddam in postwar Iraq.

Mahdi Army: A militia group formed by Shiite insurgents in Iraq. The Shia people of Iraq were brutally suppressed by Saddam Hussein during his reign.

Nasiriyah: A city in Iraq that straddles the Euphrates River. As a crossroads city, it became strategically important during the Iraq War and witnessed significant military action.

Grateful acknowledgment is made to the proprietors of the following copyrighted works:

Piete Kuhr: *There We'll Meet Again: A Young German Girl's Diary of the First World War* by Piete Kuhr (later known as Jo Mihaly), translated by Walter Wright. Published by Walter Wright, 1998. Reprinted with permission.

Nina Kosterina: *The Diary of Nina Kosterina*, translated by Mirra Ginsburg, Vallentine-Mitchell Publishers, 1972. Reprinted by permission of the publisher.

Inge Pollak: *My Darling Diary: A Wartime Journal—Vienna 1937–39, Falmouth 1939–44* by Ingrid Jacoby (Inge Pollak) (United Writers Publications Ltd, UK, 1998). Reprinted by permission of the author.

William Wilson and Hans Stauder: By permission of Auckland War Memorial Museum Library. Reference: Wilson, William Geoffrey, war diary, 1941–1942, Auckland War Memorial Museum Library, MS 2005/29, Principal translator, Betty Lobl.

Sheila Allan: *Diary of a Girl in Changi: 1941–45* (third edition) by Sheila Allan (Simon & Schuster Australia, 2005). Reprinted by permission of the author.

Stanley Hayami: Estate of Frank Naoichi and Asano Hayami, parents of Stanley Kunio Hayami, Japanese American National Museum (95.226.1)

Yitskhok Rudashevski: *The Diary of the Vilna Ghetto: June 1941–April 1943* by Yitskhok Rudashevski, published by the Holocaust Library, 1993. Used with permission of the United States Holocaust Memorial Museum, Washington, D.C.

Clara Schwarz: Published by arrangement with author. Translated by the author.

Ed Blanco: © 2006 Ed Blanco. All rights reserved. Published by arrangement with the author.

Zlata Filipović: *Zlata's Diary* by Zlata Filipović, translated by Christina Pribichevich-Zoric. Translation copyright © Fixot et Editions Robert Laffont, 1994. Used by permission of Viking Penguin, a member of Penguin Group (USA) Inc.

Shiran Zelikovich: Published by arrangement with the author. Translated by the author.

Mary Masrieh Hazboun: Published by arrangement with the author. Translated by the author.

Hoda Thamir Jehad: Published by arrangement with the author. Translated by Musab Hayatli and Melanie Challenger.